DEFENSIVE REAL ESTATE INVESTING

DEFENSIVE REAL ESTATE INVESTING

10 Principles for Succeeding Whether Your Market is Up or Down

William Bronchick, Esq.
With Gary R. Licata

New York

Editorial Director: Jennifer Farthing
Development Editor: Joshua Martino
Production Editor: Julio Espin
Typesetting: Black Diamond Graphics
Cover Design: Rod Hernandez

Published by Kaplan Publishing
A Division of Kaplan Inc.

Printed in the United States of America

May 2007
07 08 09 10 9 8 7 6 5 4 3 2 1

ISBN 13: 978-1-4277-5463-9
ISBN 10: 1-4277-5463-2

Kaplan Publishing books are available at special quantity discounts to use for sales promotions, employee premiums, or educational purposes. Please email our Special Sales Department to order or for more information at kaplanpublishing@kaplan.com, or write to Kaplan Publishing, 888 7th Avenue, 22nd Floor, New York, NY 10106.

Contents

Preface

Instead of the Latest "Secret Formula," Learn Proven Steps to Success

The recent "real estate boom" has led to an equally great boom in the number of books published on the subject of how to make money in the real estate market. Everywhere you turn—whether it's print, television, or the Internet—people are talking about real estate. Is it going up or down? Do you get in now, later, or is it too late? There are many resources: some good, some bad, some original, and some just a rehash of old ideas. Occasionally, though, an author writes a special book that really sets him or her apart from the pack. That such writer is William "Bill" Bronchick.

Bill Bronchick is an accomplished author, speaker, commentator, and real estate investor. This book, *Defensive Real Estate Investing*, is a culmination of his years of practical experience and the experiences of other investors we know. For those of us who view real estate investing as a profession, Bill has produced a book that anyone can use, whether you're a novice or seasoned professional.

Defensive Real Estate Investing is an in-depth look at the challenges of succeeding in both the short term and long term as a real estate investor. Novice investors are often looking for a "magic bullet"—an idealistic, hopeful way to make a quick buck. These impetuous investors soon realize that their approaches to investing don't work consistently and they're off in search of the next "secret formula" that will make it all work.

At some point, novice investors (and even some experienced investors) come to the frustrating conclusion that real estate investing is harder than they thought. If this is the case, why do so many people believe you can get rich quickly by investing in real estate? Given this conundrum, is it possible that success in real estate investing is limited to the lucky or privileged few?

Bill says, "Success in real estate is for just about everyone." It doesn't matter whether you have an hourly job in a fast-food restaurant or you're the CEO of a large corporation. You must, however, follow certain steps to be successful. If you take shortcuts, you run the risk of failure. Instead of offering a magic bullet or secret formula, *Defensive Real Estate Investing* provides you with concrete steps to success.

Successful Investors Are Made, Not Born

To be a successful investor, you must acquire the correct real estate investor mindset, learn sound money management skills, and most important, develop a "can do" attitude with an appropriate plan of action.

Bill has developed several brilliant acronyms that make it easy to learn and remember these steps to success, like the "Buy the WOB in the MOB near the Blob" and the CLEAR method of analyzing a deal to determine if it is a great deal. (You'll learn about these concepts later in this book.)

Remember, to succeed, you must first learn to think like a successful real estate investor. After you read this book, you'll have gained the real estate investor's mindset and you will have a set of guidelines to use and review. Success in real estate investing looks easy and it can be—but only for those who know how.

This book is both for serious beginners who are studying real estate investing and for experienced investors who need to go back to the basics to polish their techniques and improve their profits.

I've known Bill Bronchick for more than ten years. Together, we offer more than 40 years of combined real estate experience. It's been a privilege collaborating on this book. In fact, through him, I've relearned real estate investing techniques that have helped me become a more profitable investor.

My recommendation therefore is to enjoy *Defensive Real Estate Investing* to develop the proper real estate success mindset, learn sound money management skills, and develop your "can do" attitude and plan of action. I invite you to read, enjoy, and learn from our experiences.

—Gary R. Licata

Introduction

The Key to Success is Using Ten Principles of Defensive Investing

Countless people are attempting to become real estate moguls in today's market. All of them, in one way or another, strive to be successful. Gary Licata and I know from our past 40 years of combined experience that, unfortunately, the vast majority of these people will fail. Despite their best efforts, many of them won't be able quit their day job or, if they do, they may not be able to sustain a steady income stream by being a real estate investor. Many of them will go to from one seminar to another, read book after book, and eventually quit the business altogether out of frustration, failure, or impatience. You may know someone like this or you may be that someone. Is there an answer to this dilemma? Yes, and you'll find the answer in this book, *Defensive Real Estate Investing*.

Real estate markets go up and down, and every investor, whether novice or experienced, must learn the principles of successful investing to survive. While the title *Defensive Real Estate Investing* suggests that this book is intended for those investing in falling housing markets, the principles apply to every market. This book conveys ten universal principles that have stood—and will continue to stand—the test of time. Regardless of where the market is heading, ten principles of defensive investing will work for you every time, in any market.

The Ten Principles—Proven and Reliable

These ten principles are not magic bullets; they're tried and tested concepts that are proven and reliable. We use these methods in our own real estate investing careers. In addition, we've met thousands of investors who have succeeded and failed. We've elicited a common thread from their successes and failures for this book.

Take one of our clients, Sharon. A few years ago, she and her husband wanted to make a move out of their stressful business. Doing fairly well, they had managed to save a few hundred thousand dollars.

However, they were nearing retirement age and didn't have enough money in their retirement savings to retire comfortably.

Sharon enrolled in one of our coaching programs. She learned the successful principles of the real estate investing business, and in less than three years, has purchased 17 properties with a net worth of over one million dollars! Her success was typical of someone who has a sound investing strategy, not just because she had a few hundred thousand dollars to invest. Many people start out with a decent nest egg and lose it because they don't have a plan or squander it in low-yield investments that take too many years to accumulate the sufficient funds for a healthy retirement.

You may be thinking, "I don't have several hundred thousand dollars. How can I get started and be assured of similar success?" You simply don't need a lot of money to get started. In fact, most people we meet have less than $20,000 when they start their real estate investing careers. In fact, the more cash you start out with, the more you have to lose, and thus the more "defensive" you have to be in your approach.

"Defensive," among other things, means being thoughtful, conservative, and not-too-risky in your approach. It means knowing where you are in the real estate cycle, whether you are in an up or down market; you don't want to sell too early or buy too late. It also means knowing how to preserve your cash flow, analyze a deal from all angles, and run your investments like a business.

If you use the techniques outlined in this book you can be independently wealthy in fewer than ten years. Keep in mind that real estate investing isn't a "get-rich-quick" scheme. It takes time, diligence, persistence, and good planning. Above all, it takes using intelligent investing principles.

If you apply what you read in this book, you can be a successful real estate investor, no matter where you're starting. When we speak at one of our seminars, it gives us great pleasure to look at the faces in the crowd and wonder who will be the next success story. This book shares the message of intelligent investing. We hope it will have an impact that will set you in the right direction. We've written this book as a resource you can use daily. Please don't read it only once and put it away.

Each chapter in this book directs you towards one of the ten principles of defensive investing.

In Chapter 1, you learn what it takes to be a real estate investor: the virtue of patience. We provide real-life examples that guide you through the investing process and help you develop the necessary skills to be a successful real estate investor. Getting rich is a matter of degree. How rich do you want to be, where do you start, and how do you reach your goals? We help you answer these questions in Chapter 1.

Chapter 2 discusses in detail the real estate market, how to determine the market you're in, and how can you use that information to profit. Discussions include median versus average prices and what this means to you. In addition, you learn whether market timing is a good or bad idea.

Chapter 3 is the essence of the investing world—that is, learning how to determine the true value a house and sell it for a profit. We detail what it takes to rehab a property, identify which repairs add value, and determine which improvements and repairs to avoid because they won't increase your return on investment. You'll also learn which real factors determine value and how they can help you buy a house at the right price.

Chapter 4 is probably the most important chapter in this book. You'll discover how to make your profit when you *buy* (versus making a profit when you *sell*). If you don't understand what we mean, be sure to read every word of this book more than once!

Chapter 5 provides insight into where to invest. Do you invest in your own backyard or in another part of the country? Is location more important than price or vice versa? We provide specific examples of the types of projects that are worth taking on and show you how to analyze a deal. You'll also recognize the certain types of properties that are more profitable than others—and which properties you should avoid at all costs.

Chapter 6 discusses the critical topic of cash flow versus cash reserves. We detail sources of cash and formulas for analyzing cash flow. Moreover, if you aren't starting with much cash, we teach you how to generate a cash reserve.

Chapter 7 prepares you for exit strategies. The reality is that not all deals work the way you anticipate so it's important to have multiple plans of action and a backup plan.

Chapter 8 gives you details about legal and tax aspects of real estate. You'll learn simple techniques to keep the profit you earn.

Chapter 9 reveals common real estate investment scams and traps you must avoid, the common myth about "nothing down," getting cash back at closing, and other "get-rich-quick" schemes. You'll identify these schemes and determine how to protect yourself from unscrupulous investors. We also show you what to look for when researching an investment club.

In Chapter 10, we provide specific examples of how to treat real estate investing as a business. That includes how to set up your company and your office, set goals, bring in partners, hire employees, and take the steps necessary to be a professional real estate investor. You'll assess your strengths and weaknesses and bring together the important members of your real estate success team.

The Real Secret to Successful Investing

The secret is there's no secret. Nevertheless, we can offer a solid piece of advice based on our years of experience: *Take investing one step at a time*.

That means plan carefully, don't overdo it, and build up slowly so you don't get off track. If you were planning to run a marathon, you wouldn't just show up for the race, would you? Of course not; you'd prepare and take it one step at a time. You'd consult with experts, plan your training schedule, work on your stamina, eat well, cross train, stretch before and after each run, and build up to the big race.

Writing this book has been a labor of love based on our personal experiences, failures, and successes. We enjoyed collaborating on the ideas for this book. We want to share our experience with you to prevent you from making mistakes. Most of all, we want to help make the investing process easier and more profitable for you.

After we speak in public, we often ask each other, "Who's going to be the next successful investor from this group?" Will it be you? If you apply the ten principles of defensive investing, you'll change your mindset about real estate investing forever.

Remember, success is a *process*, not a place. We hope you enjoy the process and can benefit from our help to get you to the top—wherever that is for you.

—Bill Bronchick and Gary Licata

CHAPTER

1

Don't Try to Get Rich Quick

"The things that will destroy America are... the love of soft living, and the get-rich-quick theory of life."

—Theodore Roosevelt

As we discussed in the introduction, investors should be defensive in their approach to real estate investing, whether the market is up or down, good or bad.

To build wealth quickly, the assumption is that one must accept more risk. This assumption is generally correct, but lowering risk means more than just doing things more slowly; it means thinking things through before you take action. The ten principles in this book determine exactly how you can do that in your real estate business.

Getting Rich in Real Estate Isn't Easy or Instant

Generally speaking, people want something for nothing. This statement may sound cynical, but ask yourself these questions and answer honestly:

- Would you rather work more time or less?
- Would you rather have more income or less?

- If we can show you how to make more and work less, would you be interested in hearing how?

Doesn't the last question sound like a typical late-night infomercial? This is why advertisers are so good at exploiting human nature!

If getting rich in real estate were easy, everyone would be doing it. It's not easy. Many aspiring investors are lured into the world of real estate investing because they see other people doing it and want to taste a better life. Unfortunately, it isn't realistic to expect instant wealth without first investing considerable time and effort. While many people have gotten rich quickly in real estate in recent years, more often than not, it was pure luck. Most investors who succeed in real estate do so in the long term—through hard work and patience. Those who try to "crack the code" and shortcut the system are often disappointed.

Another common mistake impatient investors often make: They learn a few tricks and think success will instantly follow. Another common mistake is seeing the instant success of someone else and believing you'll have the same results. In reality, this rarely (if ever) happens. These people may have had a good plan, but face failure because they didn't give the required effort necessary to achieve the goal. It takes a lot of work to achieve long-term success in real estate, which is why so few accomplish it on a grand scale.

Many people start out in real estate investing with great fervor, only to become discouraged after a few months when they don't attain instant fortune. They discover they can't get rich quickly and easily so they move on to the next investing scheme.

Surprising as this may sound, real estate has a lot in common with weight loss. In real estate, as in the weight loss industry, everyone talks about it and many try it, but few experience real long-term success! Both industries offer thousands of "get rich quick" and "get slim quick" gimmicks, making billions of dollars in sales in the "getting people to try."

If you've tried to lose weight, you know it isn't easy. In fact, it's a serious challenge. Yet the basic concept is simple: eat less, exercise more. Even with this approach, most people give up after a few weeks because they don't have the discipline or the patience to work consistently at a well-defined plan.

Does this mean that all the weight loss plans you see on television are a scam? No, most of them will work if you follow their plan. Likewise, most of the techniques advertised on real estate investing infomercials do work if you work. Admittedly, like weight loss commercials, the results take longer for some people than for others. The problem is that too many people are impatient and either give up or, worse, engage in risky or speculative real estate deals that end up bankrupting them.

The bottom line is that if you set realistic expectations, apply our principles, have a good plan, and work hard, you'll succeed.

Start with Realistic Goals and Expectations

Thinking big is great, but we cringe when we hear someone say, "I want to make a million dollars in real estate in my first year." Everyone loves a dreamer, but there's a fine line between dreams and delusions! Someone who earns $50,000 a year and has no prior experience in real estate probably wouldn't make that kind of money by next Christmas.

What kinds of expectations are realistic for a beginner? The best approach is to set short-term, intermediate, and long-term goals. Be sure your goals are realistic, specific, and attainable. For example, your goals may look like this:

- Fifteen-year goal: Retire with $10,000 in passive income per month, inflation-adjusted. This may require between $3 and $4 million in free-and-clear rental real estate.
- Five-year goal: Acquire between $3 and $4 million in real estate in steadily appreciating areas. Buy, fix, and flip five properties per year at an average profit of $20,000 to replace current income.
- One-year goal: Buy, fix, and flip two properties and acquire three rental properties to keep.
- Six-month goal: Buy one rental property and one fixer-upper.

Be as specific as possible and take time to do the math. For example, if your goal is to retire within 15 years, how much income will you need to attain that goal? If you need $10,000 per month, will that require owning and collecting rent on five houses? Ten houses? Will you be managing that property? If you pay a manager, how will that affect your bottom line? If you need $10,000 in today's money, what will that amount be worth adjusted for inflation? The more diligently you put the pen to paper—or the fingers to the keyboard—the better prepared you'll be.

To avoid setting yourself up for certain disappointment and possible financial disaster, you must forget the dream of becoming an overnight millionaire. Instead, focus on the slow-and-steady route, aiming to accumulate wealth one small step at a time, one deal at a time. (We'll discuss setting goals in more detail in Chapter 10.)

Most important, be *defensive* in your approach. Think things through. Be conservative and cautious while always considering the risks. Real estate generally goes up and down in natural market cycles about every seven to ten years from top to bottom to top (or from bottom to top to bottom, whichever way you view it). Could property values decline after you buy them instead of increase? Could you end up at the bottom of a cycle when you plan to retire, and how will this affect your decisions? Could inflation be more than you expect? Could your kids' college cost more than you anticipated?

When you develop your goals, spend plenty of time. Be sure to look at the positive and also anything that could negatively impact your goals. Imagine that you're preparing this plan for your boss—what would he or she think about it? What aspects would you need to clarify and present in more detail if you had to "sell" it to someone else?

A True Story: Focus on Quality, Not Quantity

Steve bought 140 investment properties in his first three years of investing. Each house he purchased had less than 10 percent in equity. He hoped that appreciating values would be his payoff. Unfortunately, the real estate market in his city leveled off and he ended up with multiple vacancies, negative cash flow, and financial distress. Steve would have been better buying one-third as many properties with more equity while focusing on quality deals rather than quantity.

Developing Skills Takes Time

When you invest in real estate, risk is directly proportional to education. Compare this to the stock market where even the most educated professionals still can't invest and achieve great returns with any degree of certainty.

On the other hand, real estate has a higher learning curve than the stock market, which means you must be willing to invest more time and resources to get results. Real estate is more like running a business than managing an investment, so it takes more time to learn. If you're hoping for success in real estate (or any challenging field), you must be prepared to invest time to develop the necessary skills and expertise. Too many aspiring investors assume they can jump into the fray and learn as they go. Certainly many people do this, but the stakes are high; there's plenty of money to be made in real estate, but there's plenty to be lost! More often than not, foolish investors jump into investing without knowing the rules and end up paying an expensive lesson.

At any given time, in virtually every major city across the nation, numerous real estate seminars are offered to guide you through the learning curve. Seminars run the gamut from affordable to expensive and from useless to very helpful (and everywhere in between). We recommend that you attend a few reasonably priced seminars; you'll likely learn at least a few helpful tips. In addition, this gives you the opportunity to meet other investors in your area.

How do you know if a real estate seminar is worthwhile? Here are a few facts to consider when determining whether to invest in a seminar.

- **Price**—Be cautious of seminars at either extreme of the price spectrum. If the seminar is free, it's usually because the promoter plans to make a profit by selling his products to the attendees. If you attend free seminars, be prepared for a sales pitch for books, CDs, coaching, or other seminars. By contrast, expensive seminars sometimes leave investors feeling as if they didn't receive sufficient material to justify the high cost.
- **Class size**—Free or low-priced seminars generally require large audiences to make the event cost-effective for the promoters. This means it'll be difficult to ask questions or receive individual instruction.

- **The expert's teaching ability**—Some experts are knowledgeable in their field, but they simply don't have the teaching skills necessary to convey information in an interesting and easy-to-understand manner. Unfortunately, it's difficult to judge a speaker's teaching ability beforehand unless you can get feedback from others who have previously attended one of the speaker's events.
- **Refund policy**—All legitimate seminars should offer some type of refund policy. Always ask about the refund policy before registering for any events.
- **Your commitment level**—Until you're completely certain that you wish to pursue the real estate business seriously, avoid spending an excessive amount of money on seminars or coaching programs. It's wiser to attend a few low-priced seminars first while you're deciding whether you're really committed to this field.

Many investors go to one extreme or the other—they jump into real estate investing without an education or they spend tens of thousands of dollars on education and don't ever buy a property! Neither outcome is desirable, but certainly there needs to be a balance. Our advice: Learn a little, take action, then learn more and apply it. Education is a lifelong process. *Chances are, the more you learn, the more you'll earn.*

Success Requires Education plus Action

Some people are critical of the real estate seminar business because it attracts so many people to real estate investing, yet few people make the grade in real estate, even with the right education. Success takes more than education; it takes massive action in the direction of your goals. If you don't plan to apply new information, then getting an education and spending money on seminars and books is a waste. Nevertheless, given the two extremes, you can lose a lot more money by making a mistake than by attending seminars and doing nothing. So invest in your education, or you'll learn an expensive lesson with the first mistake you make. We call that going to a "real-life seminar."

Mentoring and Coaching Programs

Ideally, finding an experienced mentor who can guide you through the process of real estate investing is infinitely important. However, few people offer mentoring for free and, even so, such a person may be a poor teacher or mentor. Currently popular are coaching and mentoring programs from "gurus" who charge as much as $25,000 or more. If you're willing to pay a high price for this type of program, ask the seminar leaders the following questions before you sign up:

1. Who will be teaching me—you (the guru) or someone else?
2. How quickly will you respond to questions?
3. Are you currently active in real estate investing?
4. How many students are in the program? Will you give me their names and contact information?

The Internet is a great place to find reviews from people who've participated in coaching programs, but keep in mind that most of the opinions you get from people about anything on the Internet are negative. It's human nature for people who are dissatisfied to voice their opinions, particularly those who don't succeed and want to find someone else to blame for their failures.

In today's information age, there's no excuse for making a mistake that someone else has made and can teach you to avoid.

The more you learn, the less daunting real estate investing will become for you. Being defensive means taking time to anticipate potential pitfalls and, most important, being aware many pitfalls exist that you didn't even think of. The only thing more dangerous than ignorance is the ignorance of what you are ignorant about! (Think about that last sentence for a moment.)

Key Points to Remember

The most important concepts addressed in this chapter are:

- There is no magic bullet or secret to overnight real estate success.
- You must have patience to accumulate wealth.
- Take the time to plot an action plan—and stick to it.
- Get an education before attempting your first deal.
- Learning isn't enough; you must take action to achieve results.

CHAPTER

2

You Can Profit in Any Market, but You Must Know Your Market

"Give me six hours to chop down a tree and I'll spend the first four sharpening the axe."

—Abraham Lincoln

The most common myth in real estate: You can only make profits when the real estate market is rising. While it's true that *more* people make money in rising markets than falling markets, the reason is often luck, not good market timing. Armed with the right knowledge, you can profit in any real estate market.

First, however, you need to apply the second principle—*know your market*—so you can plan your investing strategy to fit that market. The defensive investor cannot operate in the dark with improper assumptions about where the market has been and is going. Different strategies apply to different market conditions, so it's critical to first assess the investor's target market thoroughly.

What Determines the Market?

Most people think of the real estate market as something that's measured like the stock market—bearish or bullish. In real estate, the common expressions for a bull market are "up," "strong," "good," "hot," and "seller's." A bearish market is described as "soft," "bad," "down," or "buyer's." On a daily basis, you'll hear the media use these expressions to describe the real estate market based on facts and figures, most of which are confusing to the average investor. Let's discuss each of the categories for the numbers you may be hearing and see how they affect the market and, more importantly, your investing strategies.

Market Categories

New home sales. Sales of new-construction homes is an indicator used by many market economists to measure the strength or weakness of the housing market. This data comes from homebuilders in the form of scheduled permits for new home builds and orders for new homes from consumers. This data is somewhat relevant to your investing plan because it can show how strong the demand is for new homes. However, keep in mind that in some places—such as inner cities where there is no available land—developers aren't building new homes in mass quantities. Likewise, in suburban areas where land is plentiful, there is endless room and an oversupply results.

Note that most of the homebuilders in the United States are large companies that operate in many different markets. These companies work on large volumes and may continue building houses in markets where they are breaking even or possibly losing money, simply because they've committed to building permits and plans. Therefore, while large builders are still making new homes in a particular market, they're often looking at long-range plans, not short-term financial decisions. This can create a false sense of market strength, not to mention an oversupply problem that can affect the rest of the local housing market.

A good way to tell if a builder in your market is doing well is to look at its supply of housing. A typical supply for builders is about six months of homes, that is, if they stopped building, they'd run out of existing inventory in six months. Having more than six months on hand is a sign of oversupply. The reverse is also true. Plus, if builders are selling lots without homes on them, this generally means they own too much land, another sign of a soft market for new homes in that area.

Be sure to compare apples to apples. When you analyze home-building and sales data, it's important to compare single-family homes with single-family homes. Condominiums and multifamily homes have different buyers, so it's possible to have a strong demand for one and not the other. This is why data for single-family homes, condominiums, and multifamily homes is often broken down in sources that report on real estate.

Our Advice: Look for Investment Projects Near New Developments

One side effect of building new housing is having a place for new homeowners to shop. Massive new home developments are often built in places where there is no shopping, so inevitably a strong retail market will follow. We suggest that you look for opportunities to invest in projects that "feed" off new residential housing developments.

Home resales. The resale of existing homes is another indicator of your local real estate market, particularly in areas where there isn't a large supply of new homes. This data comes from the REALTORS® associations such as the National Association of REALTORS® (NAR). Note that the price of home resales is more important than simply the number of homes sold. Also, home resales may be stated as, "sales of homes down 15 percent." This simply means the number of homes sold has decreased, not the price. A decrease or increase of the number of homes sold is only part of the equation. Data for home resales can be found at **www.realtor.com**.

Mortgage applications. Applications for new mortgage loans show data that is ancillary to the sale of new and existing homes. Of course, some of this is refinancing, which is driven by the rising efficiency and falling cost of loan processing and in large part driven by low interest rates. Statistical data for mortgage loan applications can be found at the National Association of Mortgage Brokers' Web site at **www.namb.org**.

Rental vacancy rates. Rental vacancies are relevant to the values for multifamily housing, and they can be a good sign of what's happening in the single-family homebuying arena. When interest rates are low, homebuying goes up on the low-end of the price scale, simply because it's cheaper to make mortgage payments than rent payments. This trend leads to higher vacancy rates in an area and, thus, lower rents. Why? Because in this market, managers and owners lower their rents to make properties more attractive to the few renters that are available. Likewise, when interest rates and home prices rise, renting becomes a cheaper option. This causes a drop in the demand for single-family housing and an increase in the demand for rental units and homes. Daily interest rate data can be found at **www.bankrate.com**.

Cost of materials. The increase in the cost of certain building materials can affect housing prices. For example, a rise in the cost of timber can affect the cost of housing nationwide.

It's worth noting that often these statistics are based on nationwide facts and figures. The nationwide statistics aren't as important to you if you're only buying in your local market. (In most cases, this is your own backyard or a particular "emerging" market.) The stock market uses indexes to determine the market as a whole, but is this really important if you only own two stocks? Likewise, does it matter how many homes sold nationwide when you only buy homes in Cleveland? In short, you need to focus primarily on local trends rather than national trends. (The two exceptions to this rule are interest rates and income taxes, discussed next.)

Interest rates. Nationwide and even global factors such as the Federal Reserve rate, worldwide markets, and competing investments such as stocks and bonds control interest rates on mortgage loans. When interest rates fall, housing becomes cheaper across the nation because homeowners' monthly payments are lower. However, the flip side of the equation is that when interest rates rise (particularly for borrowers who are getting adjustable-rate loans), the mortgage default rate will increase, causing a boost in the number of properties available for sale as foreclosures. Foreclosures are generally sold cheaper than other houses, which can drive down prices. If lenders are dealing with too many defaulted loans, they may tighten their practices, making it harder for people to borrow money, particularly those with poor credit and low income as well as those who want very large mortgages (called "jumbo" loans in the business).

Income taxes. Federal income tax rates, particularly on investment properties, can have sweeping changes on the real estate market nationwide. A prime example was the Tax Reform Act of 1987, which changed depreciation rules on investment properties and was a major catalyst to the downfall of real estate in many parts of the country. A similar change to the tax laws in the future (e.g., a change in whether property owners can deduct interest payments) can significantly affect the profitability of real estate for investors. A drastic change could drive investors away from real estate, causing a drop in the number of buyers, thus a drop in demand, and a resulting drop in prices.

Analyzing Your Market

Use the MAD Method

There are many complicated ways to analyze the market conditions in your local area, enough to confuse and boggle the novice investor's mind. However, you can keep things simple by using our "MAD" method. This means paying attention to three important factors and noting whether they're going up or down:

- **M**—Median housing prices
- **A**—Active listings on the market
- **D**—Days on the market

By paying attention to these three simple factors, you'll get a good snapshot of the state of your local market.

Median housing prices. The median home price is the exact middle of the scale, meaning that half the houses sold for less and half sold for more. Compare this with the mean or average, which takes the total number of dollar sales and divides it by the number of homes sold.

What Does Median Price Mean?

Let's say you had seven properties in a neighborhood and they sold for the following amounts:

- $87,000
- $110,000
- $112,000
- $115,000
- $118, 000
- $120,000
- $122,000

The median price of these properties is $115,000. The mean or average price is $112,000, which is logically closer to splitting the difference between the high and low sales.

Generally, the median price is considered a more reliable indicator of the state of the market than the mean price. Why? Because if more homes on the extreme high end or low end of the spectrum sell (as in this example), it can throw off the whole equation and provide a misleading figure. Therefore, using the median price is a better yardstick to measure your local market.

If median house prices in your area are rising, this can be a good indicator that your market is on the way up. If prices are rising, you can ride the appreciation of the properties. In this kind of market, you won't have to buy houses as cheaply, depending on your exit strategy (discussed in Chapter 7). However, if they have been rising for several years and the rise in price is slowing, it can be a sign that your market is flattening or getting ready for a fall. That requires you to be more defensive in your buying—that is, you would buy properties at a lower price and assume no market appreciation (or possibly anticipate falling prices in the short term). Also, keep in mind that many areas are seasonal, so housing prices may be higher in the spring and summer than in winter (or vice versa in ski resort areas, for example).

Our Advice: Use Housing Tracker to Find Median Prices

Web sites such as Housing Tracker (**www.housingtracker.net**) can help you keep abreast of the latest median prices of homes in your market. You can also use this Web site to compare past prices and other markets.

It's important to keep in mind that even if a real estate market is reaching a peak in prices within a particular area, this doesn't necessarily mean it will collapse. The fact that real estate values in a specific city have climbed at twice the rate of inflation last year and only half the rate of inflation this year doesn't mean the bottom is falling out because markets inevitably rise and fall in price.

A temporary excess of demand over supply causes a rise in prices, but supply almost always catches up. When it does, prices level off; sometimes they drop for a period and then rise again, with the next peak being higher than the last peak due to inflation. However, just because a boom in housing prices exists, a bust doesn't necessarily follow. A likely scenario may be a "cooling off" where prices remain flat, appreciating just above average inflation.

Keep in mind that just because your city's average real estate values or home sales may have declined, it doesn't mean this was true for the entire city. Unfortunately, people see headlines like "Median Real Estate Prices Falling" and they panic. You need to look specifically in the price range and location of houses you're buying. For example, the mass overbuilding of new $750,000 homes in your market may not affect the older $200,000 homes that you're buying. On the other hand,

What Causes a Real Estate Bust?

The "bubble" theorists claim that if housing prices rise too rapidly, a bust or sudden drop is likely to follow. However, the bubble theory is full of hot air, according to a report published by the Federal Deposit Insurance Corporation (FDIC) in 2005. A 25-year study of nationwide housing prices shows that only 17 percent of local markets "busted" (experienced a 15 percent decline in five years) after a boom period (experienced a 30 percent increase in three years). The vast majority of "busted" markets could be explained by local economic conditions that resulted in mass unemployment or a mass population decrease in that city. In other words, once hysteria subsides, most real estate markets tend to flatten or fizzle after a boom, rather than crash (absent other contributing factors such as a recession in the local economy).

To invest defensively, keep an eye out for local or national events or issues that could potentially kill a market, such as:

- rising interest rates,
- drastic tax or zoning law changes,
- a major local employer leaving town or downsizing,
- a local industry (such as oil or high tech) that is substantially affected by world events, and
- environmental issues such as lack of water supply, pollution, or public health issues (e.g., "cancer clusters").

it's certainly possible that a particular development or sector within a market (such as high-priced condominiums) could fall in a market in which median prices are otherwise stable or rising. In short, know your market on multiple levels—national, local, and microlocal.

Housing prices alone may not be an accurate indicator of the local market. Sellers often give buyers concessions at closing rather than drop the price, which can skew the math. For example, a concession may include paying some of the buyer's loan fees or allowing a credit for items that are in need of repair. In the case of new homes, housing prices don't always reflect builder concessions, such as favorable financing or upgrades.

In addition, housing prices don't reflect the amount of money sellers spend to renovate the property before the sale. In a seller's market, homes will sell quickly regardless of their condition. In a buyer's market, sellers may spend as much as 10 percent of the price of the home doing renovations before placing it on the market. Thus, for example, if the price of a house rose 5 percent in the last year, it's really a net loss of 5 percent for that area. You need to look not only at numbers, but also at the houses for sale. Go to open houses and talk with real estate brokers in a particular area to get a reality check of what's really going on.

Active listings on the market. This is the second factor to track in our MAD method of determining the state of your local market. The changes in the number of properties available for sale provide a good sign of the state of the local market. The basic economics of supply and demand determine whether the local housing market is rising or falling. When demand exceeds supply, prices rise—and the real estate market is said to be rising. When supply exceeds demand, prices fall—and the real estate market is said to be falling.

Most residential properties for sale are listed on the Multiple Listing Service (MLS). The number of active listings on the MLS today compared to six or 12 months ago (adjusting for seasonal changes) can tell you if the market in your area is rising or falling. A good real estate broker can provide you with the numbers for listings by searching the local MLS.

In addition, you can check your local building department for the number of permits for new buildings to see if more development is coming. Being active in local politics can give you the inside track on upcoming projects that builders are involved in to get housing developments approved. Also, it never hurts to make friends with people who are in ancillary businesses such as the subcontractors who supply goods and services to home builders. They often can provide prospective and "inside" information that the statistics won't show.

Economic Factors Behind the Math

Instead of focusing on price and inventory trends, take time to study the local economic factors that cause trends. Weather, cost of living, taxes, and overall "livability" can all play a factor in driving population statistics, but jobs are generally the main factor. If the job market is good, it will drive people to move into a particular area. If it's poor, people will move away.

If housing supply is limited, find out why. Is it because of unanticipated demand or because of geographic limitations, such as lack of land or zoning restrictions? In some parts of the country, water supply, highway infrastructure, or political factors limit growth.

Keep in mind also that nationwide migration of the existing population will play a big factor as baby boomers retire.

Boomers may move to retirement-friendly areas and many will purchase second homes and condominiums in resort communities. This increases demand without increasing population. In addition, immigration from Mexico and other countries may affect housing prices, especially in border states where people come to work and live. Finally, "wildcard" factors such as terrorism, hurricanes, earthquakes, and weather may drive people in and out of certain parts of the country.

Days on the market. This is the third factor to track in the MAD method. It will help you determine the state of your local market, after median housing prices and active listings on the market. This factor is the average number of days it takes to sell a house in the relevant price range. For example, a market in which a house sells for $250,000 in three weeks is quite different from a market in which the same house sells in six months (the latter is known as a soft market). In a soft market, sellers can drop prices, give concessions, or wait longer for their houses to sell. The vast majority of homes are owner-occupied, so there's generally not a negative impact to sellers who can't sell their houses because they can continue to live in them unless sellers are in dire need to move because of a foreclosure, job transfer, or other firm deadline they're likely to hold out for more time to get their prices. If sellers have enough equity in their homes, they can refinance their loans and take their homes off the market.

You can find the average days on market for a particular-priced home by asking a real estate broker to search through the MLS. Make sure you're comparing apples to apples—that is, the average days on the market for houses in the same area and in the same price range. If the broker has access to the right information on the MLS, you can compare renovated versus nonrenovated homes to get a more detailed analysis. The more information you have, the more accurate your assumptions about the market will be and the more solid your resulting investing plan will be.

Our Advice: Watch for This Listing Trick

Because an old listing can spell trouble for a seller who doesn't want to appear too motivated, real estate brokers often cancel listings, wait a few weeks, and then relist a property that hasn't sold. Make sure you take this possibility into account when you're analyzing days on the market data.

Work Your "Farm" Area

Real estate brokers generally have particular neighborhoods in which they work, rather than an entire city. Brokers refer to this as a "farm" area. You'd be wise to adapt a similar approach to your business. The goal is to become an expert on one specific farm area, roughly 3,000 to 5,000 homes. In some locations, this will be easy because the homes are divided into subdivisions or developments.

You'd be wise to learn the neighborhood inside and out and become familiar with every detail about it.

Values. Become familiar with the high and low range of the neighborhood. If all the homes are similar and were built in the same time period, this task should be quite easy. You should be able to rattle off value estimates almost instantly upon hearing a few pertinent details about a particular property in your farm area, such as the style and size of the home. In older neighborhoods (usually 50 years or older), a particular geographical area may have a wide variety of homes, making it difficult to determine values. Novice investors should avoid these areas until they have more experience.

Schools. Schools, particularly elementary and middle schools, are an important factor for people with families who are considering moving to an area. Get to know the local schools and determine which are the most desirable.

Zoning and homeowners' association restrictions. Learn the restrictions on building and remodeling as well any homeowners' association (HOA) rules or covenants for the neighborhood that may affect its salability. For example, there may be a covenant restricting how many unrelated people can live in a home within that neighborhood.

Local shopping and developments. A new road, highway, or commercial development nearby can affect property values in a positive or negative way. For example, a new shopping center or highway nearby may improve values or be so close as to create undesirable traffic and noise. Get to know what's in the works by following local news and attending local city council and HOA meetings or by visiting the local zoning and planning department.

Failed communities. Many new developments that rely on a golf course, ski resort, shopping mall, or other attractions for value can tank quickly if the attraction closes, is becoming run down, or isn't as great as it was predicted to be. Be especially careful of the risk if the attraction hasn't yet been completed, such as a new country club.

Our Advice: Always Use Common Sense

While statistics, calculations, and economic factors are relevant, so is common sense. Look around. Observe what's really happening in your farm area right now. Talk to your local real estate brokers, investors, and lenders for a better picture of the local market. Don't focus solely on broad nationwide, statewide, or even citywide statistics. Be concerned with the median prices in the particular neighborhoods in which you buy houses; the average time on the market; the changes in sales prices, inventory, sales concessions, and days on market from last year to this year.

You need more than a snapshot of your farm area—you need thorough, up-to-date insight on the housing situation in your farm area.

Different Markets, Different Strategies

Once you learn how to analyze where your market is and the direction it's probably going, then you can plan your investment attack.

Certain strategies work well in a rising market, others work better in a flat or falling market. Many strategies will work in *any* market, as long as you know your market and adjust your investing accordingly. Here are some of your options.

Flipping works in every market. Frustrated investors often complain that specific real estate techniques such as flipping (buying low and selling quickly for a profit) won't work in their market. We call this the "not in my market" myth. The reality is this: Flipping works in any market, depending on how you do it. For investors who buy dilapidated properties, rehab them, and sell them quickly, the market appreciation or decline isn't relevant to profit because the holding period is typically only a few months. If your plan is to flip houses, you only need to know what the resale value is for that type of house in that neighborhood and approximately how long it will take to sell (days on market).

If you're in a hot market, you can sell properties faster or, if you keep them, you can ride inflation—that is, realize gains from inflation over the years. Flipping in a hot market means you won't find as many incredible bargain properties, but you'll be able to get top dollar on any resale. If you time it right, the property may appreciate in the few months you've owned it.

Our Advice: Keep in Touch with Sellers in Denial

Buyers and investors are often more receptive to noticing the signs of a weak market than sellers may be. Sellers have a tendency to stay in a state of denial for a while, refusing to believe the market is taking a turn for the worse. They'll convince themselves that any slowdown is a temporary fluke or won't affect an "irresistible" property like theirs. Such a seller will be reluctant to consider a low offer. In this case, it's best to move on to the next deal rather than wasting time trying to get a reluctant seller to "see the light." Nevertheless, keep this seller in the back of your mind and check back after a few weeks or months. By that time, the seller may have accepted the reality of the market and might be more agreeable to discussing your offer.

Market timing. Without a doubt, price inflation is the easiest way to make money in real estate because you don't need to struggle to find a super bargain; you only need to hold on to the property long enough to ride the market. Markets generally go up and down in price cycles, about every seven to ten years from bottom to top to bottom again, with the next top being higher than the last. There are two problems with using this approach:

1. Your local market may move inconsistently with your retirement plans—your retirement age may end up in the middle of a bad market trough and you won't be able to sell or rent your properties for what you anticipated.

2. You may be wrong about the top or bottom of the market. Be sure to apply the market factors we discuss in this chapter to any market in which you choose to invest.

While there is no crystal ball, educated investors can make some good investments in places other than their own backyards *if* they're armed with the right information. (You'll find a list of sources for this data in Appendix 1.) However, keep in mind that market timing by itself isn't enough. You must learn how to make an investment within a particular market that makes sense.

The following chapters provide more guidance and formulas to help you make prudent investment decisions—whether your market is rising or falling in the short term.

Long-term investing works in any market. If you buy and hold property for the long term (15 years or more), you're not likely to lose. Real estate values go up and down in cycles, but they generally go up in the long run, with few exceptions. (The same is generally true of the stock market in the long run, but there's one problem: You have no guarantee that a company in which you invest will be in business in 15 years!) Therefore, if you try to time the market in the short term and make a mistake, you may end up doing just fine if you hold on to your investments long enough. Historically, median real estate prices outperform inflation over the long haul. At the risk of beating a dead horse: Be a defensive investor. That means have a solid plan as well as a good backup plan with an exit strategy if the first plan doesn't work. (Chapter 7 discusses multiple exit strategies in more detail.)

The Great Debate: Flipping versus Holding

Some investors focus on flipping—that is, turning properties over quickly, rather than keeping them long term. In some cases, holding property generates more long-term wealth for you than flipping. Therefore, you may consider flipping some properties and holding others. On the other hand, you may consider using the flipping strategy awhile, and then begin holding properties later. The big question is, "When should you hold versus when should you flip?"

The advantages of flipping. The main advantage of flipping is that you get your cash out immediately rather than later. For many people, the certainty of getting a paycheck right away is highly appealing. Flipping takes the real estate market *per se* out of the equation. If you buy a property correctly, whether the market is rising or falling is almost irrelevant, except for how long it will take you to resell the property. (Of course, if you buy cheap in a soft market, you can afford to hold a property longer.)

Flipping is generally good for your cash flow, which is important in any business. If you purchase houses and acquire too much equity and not enough cash, you may get into a cash crunch if you don't have additional income. (We'll discuss the importance of cash flow more in Chapter 6.)

Don't forget that you can flip houses as a part-time or full-time business. You can do as much or as little as you want and you can also afford to take a break from your flipping business. In short, once you empty your inventory, you're not tied to your business; you can take long vacations or up and move to another city and start over.

The disadvantages of flipping. The main disadvantage of flipping is that it's "hands-on" income: Once you stop flipping, you stop making money. If you're young and like to work for a few months and then take a few months off, the flipping strategy can work for you. However, at some point, you'll realize that if you keep spending the profits, you won't accumulate wealth.

In addition, if you flip, you lose the benefit of market appreciation. While market timing is a risky venture, a good market timer can gain wealth quickly with little effort by buying properties at the right time in emerging markets (developments, cities, or parts of the country that are ripe for economic growth and new jobs, thus new home building). On the other hand, if you buy a property in the wrong place at the wrong time, particularly for the wrong price, you can end up with a property you can't get rid of quickly enough. You could also get in over your head in a rehab project and have to bail, risking the loss of thousands of dollars.

Finally, if you don't spend all your income on living expenses, what will you do with it? A diversified portfolio is a good idea—you could put some of this cash in bonds, money markets, or mutual funds—but you might earn a better return by leaving your profits in real estate rather than taking them out.

The advantages of holding. Property holders can generate true wealth over the long term. Historically, property values appreciate at a rate greater than the rate of inflation in the United States. If you buy in the right neighborhoods, your annual appreciation may reach double digits. You can use properties with equity as collateral. You can provide rental income for your retirement years, and you can pass property down to the next generation. Once your rental properties are owned "free and clear," you have passive income from rents paid that gives you an income even when you're not working.

The disadvantages of holding. The main disadvantage to holding on to property is that your assets aren't liquid. Unlike stocks or bonds, real estate isn't easily converted to cash. When selling real estate, you have to locate a buyer and then pay transaction-related costs.

If you must sell when the market is down, you won't get the best price. If you have tenants in your property under a lease, you can't simply kick them out without notice. You have to wait until the lease expires, pay the tenant to leave early, or hope to find a buyer who doesn't mind having someone living in the property. Moreover, of course, the future is always uncertain. While real estate may have appreciated in a particular area an average of 10 percent over the past 20 years, it doesn't mean it will do so in the future.

If you hold properties, you also risk running into negative cash flow. There may be times when your properties are vacant or need repairs. That's when you have to dip into your savings to feed the proverbial "alligator at your door."

What's Right for You?

The important question isn't whether flipping is better or worse than holding, but which strategy is right for you. To discover the answer for yourself, ask these questions:

- Do I need additional income now or in the future?

- Am I in a high-income tax bracket that would be adversely affected by more income now?
- Does my local real estate market present opportunities to acquire bargains, yet still command high rents that would cover my expenses if I need to hold on to the properties?
- Do I have other income or savings that I could tap into in case my rental properties become vacant or need major repairs?
- Do I have the time and patience to deal with tenants and landlord issues?
- Is the local real estate market rising or falling at this time?
- Does bringing in income now or later fit into my short-term and long-term financial goals?

Most investors start out flipping houses, and then gradually work into managing rental houses or becoming involved in larger, more complex real estate projects. Some people don't have the temperament to deal with tenants and the headaches that come with rental properties. Some look for side income by flipping. Others want to quit their jobs and make flipping houses their full-time business.

As you can see, many investors were once in your shoes making these decisions. Be sure to consider all options, including a mixture of flipping and holding properties. Reevaluate your financial goals on a regular basis and adjust your real estate strategies to support these goals. Moreover, of course, make sure your strategy is appropriate for your local market.

Being defensive may mean adjusting your strategies on a regular basis, as well as re-evaluating your goals to work within market conditions. Sometimes the market works for you and sometimes it may be in conflict, but smart investors know how to make any market work to their advantage.

Key Points to Remember

The most important concepts addressed in this chapter are:

- Focus on one limited farm area and learn everything you can about that market.
- If you use the right approach, any type of market can offer great opportunities.
- Use our MAD approach to determine market conditions.
- Market timing alone isn't likely to work—you need to apply the principles of successful investing to any market.
- Consider a mix of flipping and holding properties.
- Whatever strategy you choose, be sure it supports your long-term investing and financial goals.

CHAPTER

3

Learn How to Valuate a Property

"Country clubs and cemeteries are the biggest waste of prime real estate."

—Rodney Dangerfield, from the movie *Caddyshack*

How do you know if you have found a good deal? You can't determine whether you have a good deal unless you know what the property is currently worth. In the stock market, the current day's trading price will give you an idea and you can compare that to the earnings report of the company. In real estate, the current valuation isn't so cut and dry. The third principle of defensive investing is learning to valuate a property.

Most novice investors are either ignorant or downright delusional when it comes to property values. A defensive investor does extensive research, verifies all assumptions, and is extremely conservative when estimating property values.

The Art and Science of Valuating a Property

To valuate a property, some people look at appraisals, others look at the tax assessor's value, and others say that a house is worth what someone will pay for it. Further confusing the issue, we can look at the income the property generates or the insurance replacement value. In some cases, the land is worth more than the house itself and any improvements are ignored.

All these factors have importance when you valuate a property so we'll discuss how to apply each factor and in which circumstances. Keep in mind that valuation is more of an art than a science, but by using a few formulas and practicing them, you can learn to valuate any property correctly.

Warning! Don't Ask the Person Who Has a Stake in the Property

The worst way to find out a home's value is to ask someone who has an interest in the deal. For example, asking the listing real estate broker for advice on what the property is worth is like asking your barber, "How's my haircut?" In both cases, they'll tell you what they think you want to hear. A bad deal burns many novice investors because they trusted someone for advice and that person was biased by the potential profit of the deal.

Common Methods to Estimate Property Value

Generally speaking, a good appraiser can pinpoint a home's value within 1 to 2 percent. As an experienced investor, we recommend you shoot for the same accuracy rate.

Appraisers typically use the following three ways to estimate a property's value:

- Comparable sales approach
- Replacement cost approach
- Income approach

Comparable sales approach. This is the most common method to valuate single-family homes and condominiums. The comparable sales approach (also known as *using comps*) involves comparing a specific property to other similar properties in the area that have sold recently.

Ideally, all the properties you consider should be roughly the same size and style. They should have the same number of bedrooms, bathrooms, and other rooms, and it's important that they're in the same neighborhood. Comparable sales are considered a very good indicator of the market because the market is always changing. Comps reflect these changes (More details about using comps are explained later in this chapter.).

Replacement cost approach. Using this method of valuating a property, you add the value of the land, the age of the building, and the cost to reconstruct the building. It's important to go by today's costs, not original construction costs, because it would most likely be more expensive to construct the building at current prices. The goal is to figure out what it would cost today to replace the building if a fire, natural disaster, or other unexpected event destroyed it.

The cost replacement approach is not as accurate as comps because of the variations of land values. For example, a "shack" on the beach that can be replaced for a few hundred thousand does not take into account the value of the land.

Income approach. The income approach is particularly useful when you're valuating commercial property and multifamily rental property with more than four units. The valuation of income properties is based on its capitalization or cap rate, which is the value of property compared to the income it brings in. Cap rates are a measure often used on income properties to make comparisons to other income properties. When using this approach, you base your figures on the building's actual current revenue.

It's important not to be misled by a seller's representation that he's renting the property for less than market because he doesn't want tenant turnover. In addition, don't go by "full occupancy" estimates either—vacancies are a real factor determined by the market and the condition of the property. While using the income approach does make sense for income properties, it's generally not as accurate as the comparable sales approach for single-family units because owners, not tenants, occupy most single-family properties. Thus, the comparable sale for an owner-occupant is more accurate than a sale to an investor who will rent the property. For two-unit, three-unit, and four-unit properties, it's best to look at both comparables sales and income. For lending purposes, the comp standard is generally used for four units or less.

Comparable Sales Method

The comparable sales method is the most commonly used—and the most accurate method—to determine the value of single-family homes, condominiums, and small rental buildings (two to four units). Therefore, the rest of this chapter describes how you can implement this formula in your investing activities. Much of the legwork noted here is what a professional appraiser would do. (We've provided a sample appraisal report in Appendix 2.)

When doing comparables sales, make sure you compare actual sales, not listings. Remember, a listing price is an asking price. Novice investors often look at listing prices to determine what a house is worth, but this isn't as accurate as looking at properties that have sold within the last six to 12 months.

Listing prices *become* relevant, however, if they're substantially different from the sold prices because it may indicate a trend (for example, a rapidly appreciating or declining market). Furthermore, when you look at sold prices, compare them to the original asking prices. This will give you an idea of where the marketing is heading.

Real estate brokers are notorious for choosing the highest priced listings and sales, then using them as your comparables. Not all brokers who do this are dishonest, but brokers are trained to be optimistic. Appraisers are more conservative and realistic about the amount for which the home will sell. Still, it can be helpful to take a peek at newer listings as a market barometer; if the new listings are substantially lower than existing home sales, for example, this may indicate a falling market.

In addition, you can have high-tech help when it comes to determining a home's value. Start by researching information about sold properties on your local government Web sites for your target area. Many tax assessors' offices and county courthouses have searchable online databases where you can view the prices for properties within a specific area. They usually list some information about the properties, including square footage. Subscriber Web sites such as **www.dataquick.com** and **www.electronicappraiser.com** can give you detailed information, particularly in areas where online data is scarce.

Free Web sites such as **www.zillow.com** that offer property data are available, but the information is less detailed than for the paid Web sites. For example, the seller's name may be missing, which could be relevant if the seller was a bank (as in the case of a foreclosure sale). If that's the case, it can't be considered a comparable sale because this property was sold in distress.

Be careful using Web sites that offer a computer-generated valuation. These are automated valuation models (AVMs), which are statistical models of many comparable sales of reportedly similar comparables. Many times they're not similar, but they're generally accurate within 10 percent. Remember, we advised you to become an expert in your farm area. If you're becoming an expert in your area, 10 percent isn't good enough. AVMs are useful for preliminary research and for getting a rough idea of value, but they aren't nearly as accurate as using your own eyes, driving by properties, and applying experience and common sense to create your own comps.

The most useful computer database for getting information about comps is the local Multiple Listing Service. This database shows the number of days on market and includes notes that indicate whether the property was updated, whether the seller offered concessions, and so on. This additional data is generally not available through other sources and most MLS systems aren't accessible to the general public, so having a real estate broker help you will be crucial.

Be forewarned: Comps provided by a broker who is listing the property may not be the best indicator of value. Agents carefully select the comps, providing the ones that best suit their own purposes.

While many factors come into play when you're evaluating a residential property's value by comps, the three key factors are location, size of the home, and the number of bedrooms and bathrooms. Obviously, you'll need to look at many other aspects before you can pinpoint the exact value of a property, but these are the "big three." You should be able to look at comparable sales involving properties with the same three factors and get a good idea of the value of properties you may invest in.

Location, location. This factor is extremely important when you're comparing sold properties. A professional appraiser typically looks at houses in the same subdivision and so should you. In the case of a subdivision where the houses are all similar and built in the same time period, you only need to compare similar houses with similar styles to get an accurate valuation. If there's a wide mix of properties in the subdivision, you may need to go outside of it to get comparable sales, but be careful with "dividing lines." Geographic dividing lines such as different sides of the river, the park, or a main highway may put the property in another school district and may not give you accurate comps.

Look Within a One-Mile Radius

Appraisers and loan underwriters generally look at comparables sales within one mile of the subject property. However, in populated cities, one mile may be too far. In rural areas, one mile may be too close.

Within a subdivision, you'll find variations in lots that affect privacy, road noise, or sunlight. These lot variations won't affect the valuation unless an extreme difference exists. For example, if a row of houses backs up to a major road, this may drop the value of the house as much as 10 percent. If a row of houses backs up to power lines or a garbage dump, the discount may be even more substantial. On the other hand, a great view may affect the lot substantially—in a positive way, of course. A location on a golf course, lake, ocean, or simply having a spectacular view may push values up by 25 percent. Take note of the assessed land value versus the improvements, then note what the average lot premium or discount amounts to. You can check the lot premium in new home developments by asking the builder. In older areas, the home sales records of similar houses in the neighborhood will be reflected in the prices of houses sold that are the same model, but have different lots. Amateur investors often make the mistake of comparing houses that are across the street from each other, overlooking the fact that the lots have significant variations.

What Is Assessed Value?

County tax assessors value property for tax purposes. This is called the *assessed value*. This figure usually has some bearing on market value, but don't rely on its real market value. Instead, look at the assessed value as it compares to the selling prices on the comparable properties as a reference point.

In some parts of the country, *assessed* value is a formula based on real value so the amount is more reliable. In either event, only use the assessed value as a benchmark. For example, if the assessed value of homes in your farm area is generally 90 percent of market value and your subject property is listed for double the assessed value, something may be wrong!

Square footage. When determining a home's value be sure to evaluate the home's square footage. Note that appraisers typically look at homes that are within 20 percent more or less in square footage as comparables. Doing the same shouldn't be a problem for you and your farm area. Generally (especially within a subdivision), most homes fall within a fairly limited size range. Granted, nearly every neighborhood has one or two homeowners who try to outdo their neighbors by building a behemoth that towers over all the other homes—and a few tiny homes may dot the neighborhood—but the majority will fall in the middle of the spectrum, often at several size increments. Therefore, you should be able to develop a good gauge for the selling price of homes in those particular sizes.

Not all square footage is created equal

Most people think that if a house has 1,000 square feet and is worth $100,000, then the 1,100-square-foot house next door would be worth $110,000. Wrong; the extra 10 percent in square footage equals only a few percentage points in value. If these two houses offer the same location, style, and number of bedrooms and baths, the 10 percent additional square footage won't change the valuation much because there is a fixed cost on a house based on the value of the land, cost of construction, sewer, subdivision plans, and more. An extra few hundred feet of space involves very little cost—only wood, nails, carpet, and possibly some minor electrical and plumbing costs.

Below-ground space. While finished basements can add value, the amount of value is less than it is for above-ground living areas. In addition, this greatly varies depending on different regions of the country. In humid areas, below-ground living space isn't as valuable to homeowners as in dryer areas of the country. Thus, the American National Standards Institute (ANSI) uses above-ground construction as the national standard for comparing values.

Sometimes homeowners refinish basements (or add other space) without obtaining proper building permits from the county. Be sure to check public records to see if the finished square footage represented by the seller matches the county's file.

Bill's Advice: Know the Local Laws

A client rented an illegal basement apartment to a woman who had stopped paying rent. We filed for an eviction in court for nonpayment of rent, but the judge dismissed the case. He said my client wasn't legally permitted to collect rent in the first place! In some parts of the country, added or renovated space requires a certificate of occupancy from the local building department before you can close on the sale of the home. In other areas, this sort of thing is overlooked. In short, get to know what's customary in your area.

Bedrooms and baths. To determine a home's value using comps, also look at the quality and number of bedrooms and bathrooms. After studying the farm area awhile, you'll become familiar with the price levels for the most common bedroom and bathroom combinations:

- two bedrooms and one bathroom ("two-one"),
- two bedrooms and two bathrooms ("two-two"),
- three bedrooms and one bathroom ("three-one"), and
- three bedrooms and two bathrooms ("three-two").

When comparing bathrooms make sure you understand the different types of bathrooms and compare them correctly. A full bathroom includes a shower, bath, toilet, and sink. A three-quarter bath has a toilet and a sink plus a shower but no tub. A half bath has a toilet and sink but no tub or shower. A three-quarter and full bath have roughly the same value, particularly if another bathroom in the house has a tub. A half bath has less value unless there are enough other bathrooms in the house. In addition, a five-piece bath (separate shower and tub) generally doesn't add more value than a regular full bathroom with a combination shower and tub.

Other factors that affect the value of the home. There are other factors to consider that will affect the value of a home, but generally you'd give these less weight than the location, size, and number of bedrooms and bathrooms.

Some houses have one-car or two-car garages, some have carports, and others have neither. The garage factors in some value, depending on the rest of the neighborhood. For example, if the neighborhood comps all have two-car garages, this can affect value as much as 10 percent on the subject property if it only has a one-car garage or no garage. However, if the houses are all small and there's a mix of garage options, the garage won't be as big an issue. Likewise, a four-car garage in a three-car garage neighborhood probably won't count for much either.

One exception is with condominium developments. Parking spots or garages are generally sold with condominiums and can have substantial value, particularly in large cities where parking is limited to the street.

In most cases, a swimming pool won't affect the value of a property. In fact, in most regions of the country, a pool may actually diminish the value because it's considered a safety issue and may take up precious backyard space. In hot regions like Arizona or southern Florida, though, a small dipping pool is a nice feature. However, it still won't affect the value to a large degree.

A House Is Its Own Best "Comp"

An appraisal is a certification by a licensed professional that a house is worth a certain amount based on comparable sales. It is, however, an opinion of value based on one person's analysis and experience. The actual "market value" is the amount a buyer is willing to pay and for which a seller is willing to sell under normal circumstances.

Investors often misunderstand the phrase *market value*. Here's a good way to understand this: Imagine that a home has been on the market for several months. Typically, homes in this particular market sell within a few weeks; if the seller doesn't receive a single offer, then you have to assume the property is overpriced. Several factors may contribute to the problem, including the condition, location, and layout of the house. However, all of these factor into the asking price. In short, if the house is priced right for its location, condition, and features, it will sell within the same time frame as other houses in the neighborhood.

Many times the real estate broker takes a listing at a higher price than "market" with full knowledge that the home is listed too high. Sometimes brokers do this to win the listing over competing brokers by telling sellers what they want to hear. Like the barber who says, "It's a great haircut," they'll say, "I'll get you a higher price." Most often, having an asking price that is higher than market is the seller's fault (rather than the broker's) because the seller has unrealistic expectations about the property's value. However, you can't always blame sellers. They get their information from other brokers, the sales prices of other homes in the neighborhood, information and misinformation from neighbors, and the most recent appraisal. Therefore, your job as an investor is to sift through the information and determine the real value of the property.

In the real estate business, the subject property is often its own best "comp." This means that the final sales price agreed upon by the buyer and seller is generally the property's true market value. It doesn't matter what the real estate broker, appraiser, neighbor, or mortgage broker have said. *The actual selling price will often determine the property's value.*

A common trap for novice investors is the so-called "bargain" property. For example, a house is appraised at $200,000 and available for only $150,000. Certainly, there are cases in which a property is available for a real discount of 25 percent, particularly if the property is in disrepair or the seller is extremely motivated as in the case of a divorce or foreclosure.

Absent motivating circumstances, however, if the property in question sells for $150,000, the comp has been established for this house. The value of the property is what it sold for, regardless of what the appraisal shows. Many houses are listed on the MLS as "priced below appraisal" and, in fact, sit for months without selling. If a property was listed on the MLS at $150,000 for six months when the average number of days on market in that price range is 96 days, does the $200,000 appraisal mean anything? Obviously not!

A word to the wise: When you're doing comparable sales, look at the sales history of the property itself. Knowing if it was previously listed, relisted, or sold helps a great deal in determining a property's true value. Don't buy a house you think is worth $200,000 just because it's appraised for $200,000. Do your due diligence.

Estimate Repairs Accurately and Carefully

One area in which both new and experienced investors often run into trouble is estimating the costs of repairs and how this affects the current and potential value of a property. Looks can be deceiving. What appears to be a minor problem can often end up costing a lot to fix. Even if you don't plan on doing any of the work, you still need to know how the current condition of the property affects its market value. Obviously, two identical houses side by side are not worth the same amount if one needs substantial repairs.

Be sure to follow these rules:

- Do the math correctly.

- Don't do the work yourself.
- Estimate high on repairs.

Do the math correctly. If a house is listed for $180,000 and needs $20,000 in repairs, it should be worth $200,000 when fixed up, correct? Theoretically the answer is "yes," but then why bother with the headache and risk of a rehab? You should look at the least to double your money on the rehab, thus you should pay $160,000 (or less) for the house. The bottom line is that you need to know the current "as is" value as well as the "after-repaired value." The as-is value of a house should be a lot less than its value after it's repaired, less repair costs, because a house that needs $20,000 in work lacks market appeal and attracts fewer buyers. In other words, you want to discount the property more than the dollar value of repairs needed.

Our Advice: Get Appraisals for "Before" and "After" Values

When you purchase a property using institutional financing, the lender requires a professional appraisal. Ask the appraiser for two values: an "as is" value and an estimated value after certain repairs are completed. Be prepared to give the appraiser a written list of repairs you intend to make on the property.

It's important to do research that will give you a basic idea of the cost of common home repair projects. At the very least, spend time browsing home repair stores to become familiar with the costs of building supplies. Call a few contractors or "handymen" to estimate labors costs.

Don't do the work yourself. Many novice investors evaluate the cost of the labor by assuming they'll do some or all of it themselves. This is generally a mistake for several reasons. First, your time is more valuable than a contractor's time, so it's best to hire out the help. If you get a particular "Zen" from plumbing, that's great, but replacing toilets isn't the best use of your time.

Second, most investors are unskilled or lack the necessary time to devote to rehab projects; this causes frustration with an extended rehab project. Finally, what if you're injured or have a family emergency and can't complete what you started? Always assume you'll hire people in the trades to help and figure this cost into your purchase price.

Estimate high on repairs. Novice investors often delude themselves about the necessary rehab costs. The following story illustrates how investors should approach estimating a rehab project.

Legend has it that Tiger Woods was playing golf in a tournament with the late Payne Stewart, another great golfer. They were tied at even par. On one particular hole, they both hit their drives down the fairway and their balls landed about 100 yards from the green. Payne's ball was just a few inches behind Tiger's, so he would take the next shot. Payne asked his caddy how far he was from the hole. "One hundred yards," his caddy replied, handing him a club. Payne hit the ball, which landed ten feet from the hole. Tiger turned to his caddy and asked, "How far?" His caddy replied, "Ninety-seven yards," and then handed Tiger a club. Tiger hit his ball six inches from the hole. Payne turned to his caddy and angrily demanded, "Why did you give me a round number and Tiger's caddy gave him exact yardage?" Payne's caddy replied, "Because you're not as good as Tiger Woods."

The lesson here is that most investors are not good enough at estimating repairs to guess exact numbers. Instead, it's best to think in increments of $5,000 or $10,000, always rounding high. For example, an investor who's talented at estimating repair costs may come up with the figure of $7,200 to rehab a property. A "guestimating" investor may come up with a similar number, but should round it up to $10,000 to play it safe.

Bill's Advice: Be Very Conservative on Old Houses

If you're looking to purchase older homes, consider the "Hoffa Factor," that is, the odds that when you open up the walls, you might find Jimmy Hoffa buried there!

Joking aside, rehabbing old houses frequently comes with surprises that you don't discover until you start taking things apart. Therefore, we suggest that novice investors estimate as high as 50 percent more on repair budgets for older homes.

Ideally, you already have a trusted contractor on your side. Good contractors have the experience and expertise to provide a quick, accurate estimate of needed repairs. Even so, always estimate high on repair costs and cost of materials. Our experience has consistently shown us that two things are inevitable when rehabbing a property:

- It always *costs more* than you think it will.
- It always *takes longer* than you think it will.

As with market conditions and property values, be defensive. Estimate conservatively on repairs and you will be pleasantly surprised if it costs less.

It's essential to know how to valuate a house quickly and accurately because you can't determine whether you have a good deal unless you know what the property is currently worth. Being defensive means being as dead-on accurate as you can with the realistic value of a home in its present condition and what it will be worth after repairs or renovations.

Key Points to Remember

The most important concepts addressed in this chapter are:

- Comparable sales are generally the best way to assess a home's value.
- Knowing the costs of repairs is essential when determining a house's value.
- Always be conservative and estimate high on repairs.

CHAPTER

4

Determine Your Profit Before You Buy

"Look before you leap."

—Confucius

In this chapter, you'll learn the cardinal rule of real estate: *You don't make your money when you sell; you make your money when you buy.* This means that, as an investor, you shouldn't buy houses with the assumption that you'll figure out how to make a profit later. Instead, you need to ensure that you get a good deal—better yet, a great deal—when you buy a house so you see your profit up front. This chapter addresses determining your profit before you buy.

The Past Doesn't Equal the Future

Many people make the mistake of counting on earning a profit because of something that might happen *after* they buy, such as the property appreciating in value. While it's true that most properties generally do go up in value over time, this isn't always the case, especially in the short run. Unforeseen events may depress property values in the area.

Beware that many investment gurus use this emphasis on appreciation as a tactic when they're trying to persuade prospective clients to accept their advice about investing. They'll often use a pitch along this line: "If you had used this strategy of ours ten years ago, you would have realized a 100 percent return on your money." Hindsight is always 20/20 and every economist is a genius when looking back.

When you're investing in real estate, never presume that a property will increase in value. Don't be controlled by the blind hope—based on the fact that the property's value rose in the past—that it will continue to appreciate if you hold it for another few years.

Over the long run, the real estate market always seems to correct an investor's mistakes. Values go up and down in cycles in the short run, but over 20 or 30 years, the market tends to go up at a steady, conservative pace. History has shown that real estate has almost always outpaced inflation over the long term. However, if you're looking at the short term and counting on a three- to five-year strategy because real estate values went up over the past few years, you may be taking an unnecessary risk. A more defensive strategy is to make your profit from the start by getting the proper discount when you purchase a property.

Comparing real estate investing with the stock market. To grasp the idea of up-front profits and their importance in a real estate deal, it's helpful to compare real estate and the stock market. When you buy a stock below value, you assume that it's undervalued. Thus, for you to realize a profit, your stock must go up in value.

With real estate, the concept of value is different. Value is regarded as what a property will sell for today. For example, if similar houses are selling for $100,000 in a neighborhood, buying a property for $50,000 is a bargain because you can realize a profit by selling it quickly at its current value: $100,000.

In real estate, a particular investment is a deal in one of four cases:

1. You can buy it below it's current market value
2. There is some upside potential, such as a change of use, better management or additions and improvements that can be made to the property
3. It will provide sufficient income in relation to the purchase price
4. Future market appreciation.

The latter two cases are very similar to the stock market in that they are driven by earnings per dollar invested or future speculation, both of which are market-driven. The first two cases are generally based on seller distress or mismanagement, neither of which have much to do with the local real estate market.

In the stock market, a business may have a good plan but lacks capital; therefore, an investor can supply the necessary capital in exchange for future profits. In real estate, a seller's distress can mean profits for a buyer. Certainly market timing opportunities exist in real estate, but regardless of the market, one thing is constant: Individuals are often in distress.

Reasons for their stress might include:

- Divorce
- Job loss
- Foreclosure
- Death
- Lack of interest in the property

Thus, even if you think there are no deals in your town because it's a seller's market or there's no growth opportunity, *someone* always fits in one of the categories. Someone always exists who will sell you a property for less than fair market value. These people are called *motivated sellers*.

Find Motivated Sellers

The key to getting great real estate deals in any market is finding motivated sellers. After all, only those who absolutely need to sell are going to price their homes well below market value or accept unusual financing arrangements.

Generally, motivated sellers are facing some kind of crisis or hardship such as divorce, unemployment, or financial instability. In these cases, the property and the expenses of owning that property are one of many problems these people must deal with. Therefore, they're usually eager to get rid of their properties.

Here is your dream scenario: A property owner says, "That's it, I want out. I can't take it anymore. I've got to sell right now. I've just got to get rid of this house."

How do you find these motivated sellers? Fortunately, that isn't difficult to do these days because many motivated sellers exist out there. Start by scanning the classified ads for "For Sale by Owner" properties. Look for key words that signal distressed sellers such as "must sell" and "needs work." Basically, look for anything that implies desperation or urgency on the seller's part.

You can also take a proactive approach by advertising that you're looking for properties. It's important to emphasize that you'll pay quickly for homes. The lure of fast money will help you reel in distressed sellers.

When it comes to finding distressed homeowners, a little detective work also comes in useful. Search public notices and courthouse records for owners who are delinquent on their property taxes or are in some stage of the foreclosure process. There's a good chance these people are having money problems and may be eager to sell their homes before a foreclosure is complete.

How to Analyze a Potential Deal

When you find a motivated seller, consider whether that person's property is a good deal or not. Before you can do this, determine your plan for this property. Too many novice investors just assume, "Everything in this area has gone up, so I ought to invest." In other words, before you buy a property, construct a viable plan including an exit strategy. (You'll learn more about exit strategies in Chapter 7.) The key point here is this: *Never go into a deal without knowing exactly how to exit it.* The lower the purchase price relative to the current market, the higher your profit potential will be.

A "Good Deal" Can Vary from Place to Place

When it comes to determining a good deal, no cut-and-dry formula works for every market. In some areas, you can pay 90 percent of market value and still make a substantial profit, especially when demand is high. In other places, you may need to obtain a property for 70 percent of market value or less to be confident that you'll do well. Once you become familiar with an area and have completed a few deals, you'll get a feel for the market and know exactly what kind of discount is necessary to consider buying a property and calling it "a good deal."

Unfortunately, this means that you'll be less likely to spot a good deal when you first start out. Therefore, if you're a novice investor, we suggest you accept the fact that you'll miss out on a few good deals by taking a defensive stance. Being too aggressive can lead to borderline deals—deals that don't provide much profit. It's better to let a few deals slip through your fingers rather than take a chance on properties that end up costing you money.

Knowledge Is Power

The keys to analyzing a good deal are *knowledge* and *education*. In real estate investment, a strong correlation exists between knowledge and risk. The more knowledge you have about properties, markets, mortgages, financing, neighborhoods, local rent rates, repair costs, and so forth, the less you risk losing on a deal.

CLEAR System of Analyzing Deals

A great way to determine whether a deal is good is to use our CLEAR system. CLEAR stands for:

- **C**ash flow
- **L**everage
- **E**quity
- **A**ppreciation
- **R**isk

Let's analyze each of these concepts.

Cash Flow

Cash flow is an important consideration when you evaluate a potential deal. Your first priority is to determine whether a property will provide you with positive cash flow. This depends on a number of factors such as the state of the local rental market, the amount of financing, and the interest rate you'll be paying. Be sure to compare the cash flow potential of a particular property against that of other properties you're considering.

It's important to do "real math" on income properties. What do we mean by this? Let's look at "fool's math" for income properties. Novice investors generally do the following math for rental properties:

Monthly rent	$1,000
Monthly mortgage payment	$ 800
Monthly profit	$ 200

However, when you apply for a loan, most lenders will discount the rental income on your existing properties by 25 percent because there are other costs (see below) involved in operating a rental property. Therefore, using the above figures, you'd be in the hole by $50 a month (that is, $1,000 - $250 vacancy - $800 mortgage payment). Our experience shows that a 25 percent discount is generally correct. Rental properties involve much more than "rent versus mortgage payments" because expenses include:

- Taxes
- Hazard insurance
- Vacancy
- Repairs
- Management (there's a cost, even if you manage it yourself)
- Evictions and legal fees
- Maintenance
- Utilities
- Advertising

With multiunit residential rental buildings, these expenses can be as much as 50 percent of the rental property's income. Of course, they'll vary depending on local vacancy rates, the type of neighborhood (for example, there may be more vandalism, repairs, and turnover in low-income areas), and the age and condition of the property when you bought it. As with repairs, always estimate high on expenses. (Refer to the sample expenses in Property Cash Flow Analysis form in Appendix 3 to get a better idea of the real math involved.)

Several traditional income formulas for real estate are applied to income properties, although less commonly to single-family rentals. We suggest you take time to become familiar with these common formulas and use them to compare income properties.

Gross operating income. Gross operating income refers to the scheduled income of the property minus allowable vacancy. If the property is currently vacant or rented below market, you could use the potential income amount, using conservative figures. Don't compare rents to a building much nicer or in a better location, but rather a property that is similar to yours. You can send a "spy" (friend) to check out the property and act as a potential tenant, or check online Web sites like **www.rentclicks.com**.

Operating expenses. Operating expenses include just about everything else except paying mortgage debt. This includes maintenance, management, insurance, taxes, and all the other expenses listed in the Property Cash Flow Analysis form in Appendix 3.

Net operating income. Net operating income is gross operating income less operating expenses, as explained earlier.

Capitalization rate. Capitalization rate (also called the cap rate) is the net operating income divided by the value of the property. This doesn't take into account the financing and is a measure of a property's value compared to income it will provide. For example, if you own a property worth $100,000 that has a net operating income of $10,000 a year, your cap rate is 10 percent. If you own it free and clear without a mortgage, you have more cash flow than if you paid a mortgage each month, but doing that only changes your cash flow, not your cap rate.

Cash on cash return. Cash on cash return is the annual rate of return you're getting based on the cash you invest. This number will be higher the less you pay for the property and the less money you have invested in the deal. As an example, let's use the same $100,000 property that has a net operating income of $10,000 a year. If you invested $10,000 down on this property and have a $90,000 mortgage with an annual payment of $9,000, your cash flow annual is $1,000 and your cash on cash return is 10 percent. If you put $40,000 down and have a $50,000 mortgage, your cash flow would increase, but your cash on cash return would go down.

These are just formulas; they don't take into account anything other than the income of the property. However, they provide useful benchmarks for comparing one property against another for income potential.

Leverage

Next in our CLEAR system for determining a good deal (after cash flow) is leverage. Because of inflation, a dollar today will generally be worth less in the future. Thus, while real estate values may increase, an all-cash purchase may not be economically feasible because you could use your cash in more effective ways. As you can see from the previous cash on cash return example, more cash invested into a deal may increase cash flow, but may not maximize the return on your capital.

Understanding the Concept of Leverage

Leverage is the concept of using borrowed money to make a return on an investment. Let's say you buy a house using all your cash for $100,000. If the property increases in value 10 percent over 12 months, it is now worth $110,000. As a result, your return on investment (ROI) is 10 percent annually. (In actuality, you would net less because you would incur costs when you sell the property.)

However, if you purchase a property using $10,000 of your own cash and $90,000 in borrowed money, a 10 percent increase in value would still result in $10,000 of increased equity, but your return on cash is 100 percent ($10,000 investment yielding $20,000 in equity). Of course, the borrowed money isn't cost-free; you incur loan costs and interest payments when you take on a loan. However, you could also rent the property in the meantime, which would offset the interest expense of the loan.

Please note that ROI is not the same as cash on cash. As you can see in the examples, appreciation on the investment was considered in the equation. Cash on cash return is simply the cash you get each year versus the cash you have invested. The return on investment (ROI) calculation considers the total profit including appreciation.

Taking the concept of leverage a step further, you could purchase ten properties with 10 percent down and 90 percent financing. If you could rent these properties for breakeven cash flow (that is, actual expenses and mortgage payments not exceeding actual income), you would have built up a large nest egg in 20 years when you pay off the properties. Balance that with what you could make by investing the cash flow on one free-and-clear property for 20 years; you would have maximum cash flow each year, but your total portfolio would not increase nearly as much.

Why is leverage important when you invest? Because the less cash you put down on each property, the more properties you can buy.

Many investors ask us, "If leverage is so important, what about the 'no money down' deals?" Many people like to buy real estate with no money down because it's the ultimate form of leverage. In addition, this may also be their only option if they have no cash available at the moment. Keep in mind, though, that there's nothing special about buying a property with no money down; the deal must also make sense in terms of profitability at some point.

On the other hand, if you can purchase the property at a substantially below-market price and with no money down, you have the perfect combination for a good deal. This is buying 100 percent loan-to-purchase (LTP), not 100 percent loan-to-value (LTV). Figure 4.1 illustrates the difference between LTP and LTV. Investors should strive for high LTP and low LTV.

FIGURE 4.1 LTP versus LTV

Price	Value	Loan	LTV	LTP
$100,000	$100,000	$100,000	100 percent	100 percent
$ 80,000	$100,000	$ 80,000	80 percent	100 percent

If you can buy below market and close to 100 percent loan-to-purchase (LTP) with breakeven or positive cash flow, you'll go to real estate investor heaven!

The problem with buying a property at a below-market price is that lenders tend to "penalize" investors with their loan regulations. Fannie Mae (FNMA) conforming loan guidelines usually require you to put up 20 percent of your own cash as a down payment. The 20 percent rule applies even if the purchase price is half of the property's appraised value. Thus, the loan-to-value (LTV) rules are based on appraised value or purchase price, whichever is less.

Seasoning May Be Necessary When You Refinance a Property

Refinancing is generally based on loan-to-value (LTV), not loan-to-purchase (LTP). Thus, if you can buy a property below market using cash (using a source such as your home equity line of credit), you can refinance the property based on its appraised value and be close to 100 percent loan-to-value on the property with little or no money in the deal. To refinance based on the property's value (assuming it's higher than the recent purchase price) a lender generally requires six months or more of ownership. This is called *seasoning*. Some lenders will refinance a property without seasoning if you have excellent credit.

Leveraging real estate deals is great if the properties go up in value because the rate of return on your money goes up exponentially. However, if the properties go down in value and you have a lot of debt on them, the result will be negative cash flow.

Is negative cash flow necessarily a bad thing? Well, yes and no. If you have other sources of income and are looking for long-term appreciation, you can consider negative cash flow the equivalent of payments into a retirement plan that will eventually pay off. This leads to a discussion on equity, the next concept in the CLEAR system after cash flow and leverage.

Equity

Remember, our goal with the CLEAR system is to determine if purchasing a specific property is a good deal. Therefore, you need to determine how much (if any) equity the property has. You can find equity in many forms, including a foreclosure or other distress situation in which a property has a discounted price, a fixer-upper offering lots of potential, or a poorly managed income property. You can also create equity by rezoning a property—changing its use from commercial to residential or vice versa. For example, buying a house on a main street may not be appealing, but if the area gets rezoned for commercial use, this house can be converted into an office or a retail storefront and prove to be a good investment.

With financing involved, equity can take the form of a paydown on debt. For example, a rental property with income can be used to pay down financing, known as *amortization*. Each mortgage payment is part principal, part interest. As you collect rent and make mortgage payments, the principal payment increases your equity in the property, even if the value does not increase.

Appreciation

The fourth concept in our CLEAR system is to determine the property's probable appreciation. Jumping into the right neighborhoods at the perfect time can result in appreciation and profit. However, it can be tricky to time this exactly right.

Depending completely on appreciation for your profit is risky. Instead, buying for moderately long-term (ten to 20 years) appreciation is safer and easier. Study the long-term neighborhood and citywide trends to choose areas that will hold their values and grow at an average 5 to 7 percent annual rate.

Calculate Appreciation as Net of Inflation

Note that appreciation should be calculated net of inflation. For example, if inflation is 3 percent annually, a 5 percent increase in property values translates into a 2 percent gain. In inflationary terms, this is described as "nominal" (numbers) versus "real" (inflation-adjusted) or "net" value.

You can find information on annual inflation at the U.S. Department of Labor Statistics at **www.bls.gov**.

Risk

The final concept in the CLEAR system to assess the risk involved in a particular property investment. Unfortunately, many investors don't spend nearly enough time considering risk. Virtually every real estate deal involves at least some element of risk, no matter how "safe" it may seem. Because real estate purchases most often involve debt, an initial investment of cash can turn into a huge liability if an investment turns bad. There are also potential legal liabilities involved in real estate, which are discussed in Chapter 8.

We suggest you always have a Plan B in case your initial plan goes awry. Know the answer to this question: If you buy a property for short-term appreciation and it doesn't appreciate in value, can you rent it for positive cash flow until the market rebounds?

Also take financing into account when you're considering risk. Many novice investors buy properties with adjustable rate loans assuming that they'll sell the property for a profit before the loan payments increase. If you do that, consider this question: If you buy a property with an adjustable rate loan and the rates go up, will this put you out of business? If you have a few vacancies, can you handle the negative cash flow or will it break the bank? In other words, expect the best but prepare for the worst.

Bill's Advice: Look at a Wide Range of Risk Factors

When considering risk, also consider the headache and liability involved in your investments.

At one time, I considered investing a few hundred thousand dollars in properties in Kansas City, Missouri. An investor was liquidating a portfolio of 22 houses that he owned free and clear, and would owner-finance with a sizeable down payment. The houses were worth about $30,000 each, and each one rented for about $300 a month. On paper, it seemed like a great deal because it would yield $6,600 a month in income. After careful consideration, however, I passed on the deal to buy one single-family rental in Boulder, Colorado, and one condominium in Denver, Colorado. They rented for a total of about $2,500 a month.

Why didn't I go for the deal in Missouri that seemed more lucrative? First, the Kansas City properties were older than those in Colorado were and located in poor neighborhoods. While the income was better for these 22 houses, so was the potential for crime, management hassles, liability, and repairs. Remember, putting a roof on a $30,000 house in Kansas City costs the same as putting a roof on a similar house that's worth $200,000 in Boulder or $500,000 in Boston.

Second, it's much easier to manage two tenants than 22 tenants. Regardless of the property values, dealing with more tenants and more properties means more headaches and more liability.

When you're considering risk, also pay attention to possible tax law changes. Rental properties can provide a good tax break for those who qualify because of their depreciation factor. While real estate does increase in value, the IRS allows a large deduction for the theoretical depreciation of the property improvements, which can often create a loss, at least on paper. For some investors, a negative cash flow is a large loss that offsets other income.

However, as many investors learned in the 1980s, "what the government giveth, it can take away." With the Tax Reform Act of 1986, the U.S. Congress suddenly and drastically changed rules on deducting losses on rental property. Before that time, many investors bought properties that did not make financial sense, except for the tax write-offs. When the laws changed, many investors simply walked away from these properties, causing massive foreclosures that significantly hurt the housing market. We hope that investors learned from this debacle and won't make the same mistake. In other words, don't just buy a property because it's a good tax break because that risk factor could change overnight.

Balance Your Business with Your Personal Goals

You must balance using the CLEAR system with your personal goals. For some investors, cash flow isn't as important as retirement income or equity growth. For others, they need income right now to quit their job and, thus, owning rentals may not provide enough income. If you have a full-time job or business, rentals or rehabs may be too time consuming. In short, do the math and consider all the implications of your real estate investments.

Gary's Advice: It's Critical to Follow Your CLEAR Plan

Over the many years I've been in this business, I have encountered numerous successful investors and many others who struggle. I can boil down the difference into one statement: The successful investors had a CLEAR plan and followed it through.

I advise first-time investors to purchase one good house a year for ten years using the CLEAR formula and hold them. At the end of ten years, they would have a million dollars in net worth. This advice is as valid now as it was 30 years ago. I know this because investors who tried to buy the latest hot property in the latest fad areas are now struggling to be successful.

It doesn't matter what your plan is; what matters is that you approach each property using the CLEAR formula. Keep in mind that it's more about *quality* than quantity.

Key Points to Remember

The most important concepts addressed in this chapter are:

- As an investor, you can never take profits for granted. Be sure to analyze and go for the best deal at the onset of a transaction.
- The ability to locate (and deal with) motivated sellers is critical to realizing profitable deals.
- The CLEAR system can be an efficient way to analyze a potential deal quickly.

CHAPTER

5

Always Invest in "Safe" Deals

"Take calculated risks. That is quite different from being rash."
—George S. Patton

People who've always put their money in blue-chip stocks, bonds, and money-market accounts commonly think of real estate as being an inherently risky investment. While real estate can be risky, you can certainly limit that risk by educating yourself. Our experience shows that certain types of investments in real estate can be inherently safer than others, particularly where there is uncertainty in the future of the market, whether it will go up or down.

After all, real estate is a survival game—anyone can make money in rising markets, but those who survive the down markets retire wealthy. Stick to this fifth principle—always invest in "safe" deals—and you'll survive long term in this business. Remember, there is no 100 percent "safe" deal, but being thoughtful, conservative, and defensive will increase your odds of long-term success in real estate investing whether markets are up or down.

Invest in Deals, Not Markets

Too many novice investors try to time the market and ride the waves of market appreciation. Certainly buying and selling at the perfect time (when the market peaks, for example) is the easiest and most lucrative way to invest in real estate. It's also the most risky because few people have enough foresight to figure out where the top and bottom of the market are.

Instead of trying to guess the bottom and top of a market, stick to particular deals that make sense. In any market, by applying our CLEAR formula from the previous chapter you can find particular bargains in solid neighborhoods that make sense.

Buying houses at great bargains is easy when the market is soft and sellers are flexible. Even if you're in a hot market, you can still find homeowners who want to sell below market for reasons other than money, including the stress of a divorce, a death in the family, a job transfer, or other life changes. At times like these, people can be highly motivated to sell their houses quickly. If you're in a flat or falling market, you can either invest elsewhere or stay in your farm area and buy extremely cheap. Even if you seek emerging markets around the country, you can still end up with a bad deal that won't make you money. In short, each deal must stand on its own.

The late Will Rogers said, "Buy when others are selling and sell when people are buying." This may work for stocks because you can get in and out of a deal in a short time. However, in real estate, you can't expect to time the market in terms of days. Unless you're in a market where bidding wars occur and prices go up in a matter of days, plan your strategies in terms of months and possibly years.

Stick with Metropolitan Areas

As mentioned earlier, housing markets are driven by people and people tend to go where there are jobs. The more people who live in an area, the easier it is to sell or rent a property, so stick with major areas that have a large, diverse population. As a rule, stay away from resort areas or smaller towns that have one major employer. (You may recall what happened to Flint, Michigan, in the 1980s when General Motors laid off a large part of its workforce, causing mass unemployment and long-term depression of the local housing market.)

College towns are usually an exception to this rule. They tend to do well because of the built-in population that lives there temporarily year after year. College rental properties tend to cost more, are seasonal, and are prone to high turnover and damage (remember the movie *Animal House*), but there's no shortage of college and graduate school enrollment across the nation.

Another good idea is to invest in towns that have the employer-equivalent of Disney World or a local government (e.g., the school system) that employs a significant percentage of the population. These people aren't moving anywhere soon.

Watch the latest trends when looking for metropolitan areas in which to invest. The revival of urban neighborhoods is a growing national trend. Once considered the haven for the poor, laden with crime and plagued by poor schools, these areas are coming back with a vengeance. Art galleries and restaurants are replacing burnt-out buildings. Boarded-up housing is being refurbished into stylish town homes. Many empty-nester baby boomers are selling their large, suburban homes and moving downtown to experience a hip urban way of life. Thus, proximity to the downtown areas in many cities has become more desirable than sprawling, suburban, middle-class neighborhoods.

Every city has certain neighborhoods that are more desirable than others are. These areas always seem to hold their property values in down times and increase exponentially in good times. It may be because of proximity to downtown or the strength of a particular school district, but pound for pound, properties in desirable areas are worth more than houses in areas that don't have the same features. You may not find great bargains, but they're always safer investment bets over the long run than newer developments or super cheap areas.

Buy the WOB in the MOB Near the Blob

As a rule of thumb, the worst house on the block in a median-priced neighborhood (or below) is generally a safe bet for investing. We call this buying the WOB in the MOB near the Blob. Spelled out, this is:

- buy the WOB (**W**orst **O**n the **B**lock)
- in the MOB (**M**edian price **O**r **B**elow)
- near the Blob (see explanation below).

Now, let's break this down, step by step.

Worst on the Block (WOB)

The worst house on the block in a good neighborhood is always a better investment than the nicest house in a lesser neighborhood for two reasons. First, most people would rather live in a better neighborhood than be king of a slum. They like to brag that they live in a particular neighborhood, even if it's the cheapest house in it.

Second, there's always more room to push the values on the low end of the spectrum than on the high end. As we discussed earlier, appraisers look at comparable sales within a particular neighborhood. If your house is already the highest priced for the area, there's not much you can do to improve its value. However, if your house is priced on the low end for the area, you can fix it up and stretch its value. Appraisers are more comfortable stretching the price per square foot of a cheap house than stretching the total price of a house that's already at the high end of the neighborhood. Remember: *Market value is what someone is willing to pay for a house.* A nicer house will generally sell for more per square foot than a bigger one that's not as nice.

Median Price or Below (MOB)

As you may recall, the median price marks the "middle of the pack," with half of the housing in that area selling for less, half for more. The below-median price range within a metropolitan area is generally a safe investment because there's a growing shortage of these houses.

New homebuilders have certain fixed costs involved in building new subdivisions. These costs include paving roads, installing power and sewer lines, and maintaining a large staff. While more expensive homes can take longer to sell, in the long run, those builders make more money because of the economies of scale. It only takes a few extra two-by-fours to make a house that's 3,000 square feet versus a house that's 2,000 square feet and the profit margin on the extra size is all gravy to the builder.

Because of land restrictions and costs, most of the newer developments are being built farther and farther from the center of town. As discussed earlier, the inner-city housing demand has increased; many smaller houses are being knocked down, refurbished, or rebuilt. Thus, what we have is a shortage of affordable housing. With mass immigration into the United States, the demand for affordable houses within proximity of the metropolitan areas will continue, particular for rental properties. Investors who own housing in the MOB will find their properties retaining value in the long run.

The "Blob"

Remember the movie *The Blob*? In this movie, a giant monster oozed from place to place, taking everything and everyone in its path. The same effect often happens in neighborhoods. If a particular area is hot and desirable, it will eventually run out of room and the closest geographical neighborhood will generally be next. In some cases, hot areas may greatly exceed the median price, thus possibly increasing the investor's risk because it's not the desired median price or below. Investing in more reasonably priced homes in close proximity to this desirable Blob neighborhood may be a safer bet.

When considering the Blob effect, take into account neighborhood dividing lines. In some cases, it's simply a road. In others, it may be a hard, impassable line, including a railroad track, major highway, or body of water. Paris is a good example of a city with a strong dividing line. If you've visited Paris, you've seen the neighborhoods on the Right Bank and the Left Bank of the Seine River. It's clear to see how the neighborhoods on either side of the river differ.

All things being equal, the worst house on the block in the median-price neighborhood or below near a hot and growing area is your safest and best investment in any market. Certainly when prices are rising, a new condo by the beach or a 10 percent appreciation on a million-dollar house seems like a good way to make a fast buck Nevertheless, being a defensive investor means going with the lowest-risk investment on a consistent basis, not shooting for the moon. Ask any good football coach the key to consistently winning and it's not the "hail Mary" pass. It's making first down over and over by moving the ball down the field a few yards at a time.

Look Where a New Starbucks Opens

Have you noticed that Starbucks coffee shops are popping up in "up and coming" areas? Big companies like Starbucks do a lot of research before they open a store that sells four-dollar cups of coffee. Why should you reinvent the wheel? Let the pros do your initial research. They're probably more experienced than you are! If you see a Starbucks going up in a transitioning neighborhood, that may be your green light to go ahead and buy there.

Fixer-Uppers

Fixer-uppers are almost always a safe bet if you buy them right. As we mentioned earlier, fixer-uppers generally have less market appeal than houses that are in good shape. This translates into less demand and a lower purchase price. However, be extremely careful about what kinds of projects you take on—not all fixer-uppers are worth the effort. Despite what you see on the cable television shows, a fix-and-flip property isn't just about fixing things. It's about knowing what things to fix, how to estimate the repairs, and whether such an endeavor is even worth the effort.

What Should You Fix?

While you should be systematic in your approach to rehabs, keep in mind that every property is different. Location, age, potential value, and the architectural style of a property all affect how to approach any renovation. The condition of the property and the scope of the needed repairs will also affect the rehab process.

Certain improvements will always give you the most bang for your buck—namely, kitchens and bathrooms. Remodeling kitchens and bathrooms and adding bathrooms will give you the most return on your money. However, if you plan to keep the property as a rental, adding more livable space may get you more rent, depending on how much existing space is in the house already. For example, if the house is a small, two-bedroom ranch, converting the garage into one or two bedrooms may be worthwhile if plenty of parking is available other than in the garage.

Generally, decks, pools, patios, landscaping, and expensive flooring don't add much value. Certain "overkill improvements" don't add much value either. This includes spending more money than necessary on appliances, roofing, heating, plumbing, and sprinkler systems. For example, if the house has an old roof, you must fix it, but adding a roof with a 30-year warranty versus a ten-year warranty won't get you more money when you sell the house. Likewise, an energy-efficient appliance that costs you twice as much as a typical appliance isn't going to bring you more money for the house. If something is old or broken, fix it, but don't overspend unless the extra money visibly adds to the marketability of the house. In many cases, if it looks clean, replacing an ugly or broken appliance with a newer used one works fine. Kitchen cabinets can often be painted over or refaced instead of replaced entirely. Moreover, if you do choose to replace the cabinets, spend a little extra on the handles for an extra designer's touch.

Appraisal versus Appeal

It's important to understand the difference between improvements that will affect the appraisal value versus the marketability or "appeal" of the property. For example, using granite slab countertops versus Formica will not significantly affect the appraisal of the property. The issue for the appraisal is whether the kitchen was remodeled or not. Granite slab may cost you $3,000, but add only $1,000 to the appraisal. Therefore, why would any investor add such an extravagance if the property won't appraise for more? The answer is "appeal."

While appraisers look unemotionally at facts like a house's square footage, buyers are emotional people who can get hooked by a classy-looking kitchen countertop. If a buyer loves your house and is willing to pay more for it, then it should appraise for the actual purchase price. That's why appraisers consider comparable sales of similar homes in the neighborhood. Technically, they are required to consider the details of the sale and are provided with a copy of the sales contract, which includes the price and details of the sale.

Human nature being what it is, appraisers tend to appraise to the contract price unless the price is completely out of line for the neighborhood. This is why it's crucial to remodel houses on the "inexpensive" end of a neighborhood than on the high end. If the house you are selling is on the high end and you attempt to push the price beyond the highest comp, it gives the appraiser nothing to justify your price. On the other hand, if your house is on the low end, there are other sales to justify the price even if comparable houses are bigger than yours is. Appraisers can record notes in their reports that your house was better remodeled than similar houses in the neighborhood that sold for less.

Keep in mind that if you're getting an appraisal for a refinance, you have no buyer in love with your kitchen to push up the house's value. Appraisers are human beings who are impressed with nice-looking houses, but they won't be swayed like a buyer who thinks about calling this house "home" and wants a higher value to it.

Bill's Advice: Be Cheap, but Don't Make Your House Look Cheap

You can spend a minimal amount and still make a house look inviting. We typically spend less than $15,000 on a complete renovation of a 1,200-square-foot home, which is generally half what other investors spend. The key is to spend the minimum on items that are expensive, and the maximum on things that are inexpensive, but visible, as noted next.

Doors, electrical switch plates, faucets, door knobs, and light fixtures. Overspend on these hardware items because they will add "pizzazz" without affecting your total budget much. For example, a $100 light fixture will look incredibly nice in a basic house compared to a

$30 fixture. Will $70 break your budget? Of course not! Use fancy $15 door handles instead of plain ones. After all, there are only about seven doors in a small house. If your house has only one level, replace old brown doors with new six-panel hollow-core doors. It shouldn't cost you more than $200 a door, including materials, labor, handles, and paint. Instead of using cheap plastic switch plate covers, upgrade to nice ones for about $60.

Upgrade the tile. If you are replacing the kitchen and bathroom floors with new tiles, spend extra for really nice ones. If the total square footage of the kitchen and bathrooms is 200 square feet, then using $2 tiles versus $1 tiles will affect your budget by only $200.

Watch for hidden hazards. Be sure to go through an extensive inspection process before closing on a property. Sometimes what seems like an easy rehab will turn out to be an environmental nightmare. For example, water damage can lead to black mold, which threatens health and can be expensive to get rid of. Lead-based paint, which was used before 1978 but has been phased out, can be expensive to remove. Asbestos is another hazard. If insulation made with asbestos is discovered on ductwork over dirt, the dirt needs to be tested to see if it has been contaminated by pieces flaking off, which usually happens. Radon is common in certain parts of the country and houses should be inspected for this.

Finally, be aware of "meth" houses, that is, houses in which methamphetamine was prepared or stored. Your county health department may have a list of houses that were identified as meth houses. Once flagged as a meth house, a house must be completely renovated by an OSHA-certified (U.S. Department of Labor Occupational Safety and Health Organization) contractor, which is an expensive process.

How nice should the house be? Before you get involved in a fixer-upper, assess the neighborhood carefully to determine the scope of your repairs. Do you want your house to be consistent with those in the neighborhood, or do you want to make it a little nicer? You can easily overdo this if you're not careful, so don't go overboard regarding quality of materials, time spent on minor details, or unimportant prob-

Gary's Advice: Look Out for Fixer-Upper Cost Killers

Some minor but expensive hazards you may have to deal with include single-strand aluminum electrical wire, polybutylene water supply pipe, termites, hidden water damage, and Masonite Woodruf roofing. Always hire a qualified home inspector who has experience in these issues and other building code issues before you buy a fixer-upper.

Make sure you hire a professional inspector to assist you with the inspection of the house until you become more experienced yourself. A professional inspector charges between $300 and $500 for a thorough inspection of a house from top to bottom. Choose an inspector who has experience with the particular neighborhood and model of house you are considering purchasing.

lems. *Focus on repairs and improvements that add value and make the property more marketable.*

Beginning investors commonly spend time and money on unnecessary projects. As a result, these beginners are pressed to ask premium prices for their properties, wasting time and money as they wait for their houses to sell. A rule of thumb is to tackle only projects that will bring you at least double your money back in profit. For example, if you spend $10,000 in repairs or improvements, you want to yield an extra $20,000 or more in net profit when you sell.

Remember, "net profit" includes what you have after paying all of your costs. Many novice investors mistakenly assume that buying a house for $90,000 and investing $10,000 in repairs means the house can be sold for $110,000 and bring in $10,000 in profit. This is not quite true. Here are a few "hidden" costs to be aware of:

- **Acquisition costs**—When you purchase a property, you may pay for various escrow fees, transfer tax (as high as 3 percent of the sales price in some areas), appraisal, inspection, and lawyer fees.

- **Loan costs**—The cost of funding a loan to purchase the property can be substantial for an investor. It could include points, "processing" fees, prepaid interest, and lender escrows for property taxes.
- **Holding costs**—The cost of carrying a property is more than you think. Calculate at least six months of insurance, property taxes, and utilities.
- **Broker commissions**—Statistically, 95 percent of all properties sell on the multiple listing service (MLS), which requires using a real estate broker. You can use a flat-fee listing service to save money, but you will likely have to pay a 3 percent commission to the broker who brings you the buyer.
- **Closing costs**—When you resell the property, you will have another set of escrow fees, title insurance, recording fees, and other miscellaneous charges.

In short, estimate at least 10 percent of the total purchase price to cover these charges, possibly more, depending where you invest. If you are unsure, ask a local real estate broker for a good estimate.

Our Advice: Know the Mathematics of Renovations

Many television home improvement shows and magazine articles cite statistics about the dollar return on an investment for different home improvement projects. Generally, we find they are correct in terms of what items are worth fixing and not. The confusing part is that they might say, "For every $10,000 you spend on the bathroom, you will increase the value of the property $8,000." Remember, investing is a for-profit business, so spending $10,000 to bring a return of $8,000—or even $10,000—simply isn't worth the effort. The key is to buy right, which means you must buy for substantially less money than the repairs will cost you.

It's crucial to understand that the renovation *itself* doesn't make you a profit; rather, it gets the home into "marketable" condition. The more repairs a home needs, the less appealing it is, and therefore the fewer potential buyers will be attracted to it. More than that, the market dictates that sellers must drop their prices to attract more buyers who are mostly investors. Most novice investors can handle cosmetic repairs like painting and carpeting, but any major projects usually discourage all but the most experienced rehabbers. That further drives down the "as is" market value of the house. Therefore, instead of thinking, "What can I fix to improve the value of this house?" it's better to think, "How cheap can I acquire this miserable piece of junk that nobody else wants?"

The key advice here is to *make your money when you buy.* Sound familiar?

Conversely, you never want to purchase the most expensive house in a neighborhood—just the cleanest. Standard items should be consistent with those in other nearby homes. For example, window air conditioners may be the norm in one neighborhood, but central air may be standard in another. That means you don't need to install central air conditioning in a window-unit neighborhood. Items such as sprinkler systems, security alarms, and storm doors aren't usually worth the cost and effort to install. On the other hand, be generous on the inexpensive items, such as ceiling fans, doorknobs, switch plates, toilet seats, faucets, trim, bushes, and other cosmetic items that add appeal without adding much total cost. New windows can sometimes be worth the price you pay, particularly in parts of the country where heating and cooling are big issues.

If you plan to buy a house for a rental, only spend money that will make the house safe or command more rent. As previously discussed, knowing the cost of the repairs is a crucial factor in the equation of how to approach fixer-uppers. Whether you do a complete rehab and resell it, do a light rehab and rent it, or resell the property "as is" to another investor, understand how to evaluate repairs (e.g., the scope and cost of the whole project) and how repairs will add value to the property.

Condominiums

Condominiums are traditionally the most volatile of real estate investments. Ask anyone who bought one in the 1970s or 1980s (your humble authors are no exception) and they'll show you the financial scars on their backs.

Condos have made a strong comeback in recent years because of the popularity of purchasing second homes, particularly in resort areas. Whether this trend will continue is uncertain, but keep in mind that condos are generally a tougher sell in most areas than single-family homes. Moreover, because condominiums involve a homeowners' association, you'll have to deal with management issues, rules, and costs that may be out of your control.

When buying a condo, consider your prospective tenant or buyer when you resell. Is it priced so high that your pool of buyers is limited? It may be in the median price range or below, but how many people live in one-bedroom condos? Is the development so old that the HOA (homeowners' association) dues are high and will continue to rise as the development ages and needs repairs?

For the most part, condos tend to fit into two categories: rentable and livable. Cheap condos that rent well often don't appreciate much in value. Using our CLEAR formula in Chapter 4, you can get away with buying a $50,000 condo and renting it for $500 a month forever. In 20 years, it may barely have appreciated above inflation. Yet a different condo near downtown or the beach may rent for negative cash flow and appreciate 10 to 15 percent a year.

In short, the normal formulas that apply to single-family homes aren't as consistent with condos, which is why defensive investors need to approach buying condos with extreme caution.

Our Advice: Look for Limitations When Buying Condos

Be aware that some homeowners' association rules restrict the rental of units, so make sure you check the limitations before you purchase a condo that you plan to rent out. In addition, many lenders have limitations on financing condos, including a requirement that owners occupy a certain percentage of the units. Find out all these details before you buy.

Multifamily Housing

Investing in multifamily housing can be a blessing or a nightmare, depending on whether you're cut out for management. While it's possible to hire a management company, few are good at dealing with small buildings. The cost per unit of multifamily housing is much lower than single-family homes, but the management factor and liability is exponentially higher. Moreover, financing is more difficult for multiunits, especially for buildings with more than four units that cost less than $3,000,000 in total.

In short, the normal formulas that apply to single-family homes are not the same with multiunit buildings, which is why defensive investors need to approach them with more caution than single-family homes.

Properties to Avoid

The WOB in the MOB near the Blob is a good rule of thumb for safe investments, but it is just that—a rule of thumb. Some investments may be an exception or a calculated risk, but general rules like this provide guidelines that both novice and experienced investors live by.

Likewise, pay attention to the rules of thumb for avoiding certain investments. Certainly exceptions exist, but the following tend to be more speculative and riskier for novice investors. You can certainly make good money at these, but it takes more experience and research. If you're a novice investor, we advise you to proceed with caution and be particularly defensive in your approach to these types of investments.

New or Preconstruction Properties

Properties are often sold before they are built during the "preconstruction" phase. Preconstruction properties, particularly condos, have been popular in many markets over the last few years. Some speculators have made a bundle buying up preconstruction condominiums in hot markets, and then selling them for 25 to 50 percent profit upon completion of the project, often a year later. Properly timed, a preconstruction condo purchase can be lucrative if there is limited supply (such as beachfront property) and a strong local market.

However, the basic premise of such activity violates one of our cardinal rules: *Make your profit when you buy, not when you sell.* If you're paying full price at what could be the top of a saturated market, you may find yourself stuck buying an overpriced property or bailing on a large earnest money deposit.

Bill's Advice: Find Out Builder's Policy on Reservation Fees

Builders generally require a certain amount of the selling price (anywhere from 1 to 5 percent of the sales price) as a "reservation fee" before the development is built. Most often reservation fees are refundable, but in such cases the builder may reserve for himself the right to back out and refund your fee.

It can be a Catch-22 because if you're *not* committed, neither is the builder, but if you *are* committed, you can lose money. The builder contract generally requires an additional earnest money deposit of anywhere from 5 to 10 percent of the purchase price when the building reaches substantial completion. Most often, this earnest money is not refundable.

If you sign a contract to purchase a preconstruction property, make sure the builder doesn't prohibit you from flipping the property after it's complete. Also, have Plan B ready. For example, if you can't sell the property, can you complete the purchase and rent the property to ride out a market cycle? Check the fine print to see what you're committing to and how much money you have to put up now and before the project is completed.

Keep in mind also that construction projects often get delayed for a variety of reasons, so make sure you're dealing with a reputable builder.

Properties in Weather-Dependent Resort Areas

Investing in seasonal resort properties that depend on weather, such as ski resorts and beach properties, can be risky if the weather doesn't cooperate. Most investors who profit from resort properties do so by appreciation, but that requires good timing—and a little luck. However, these tend to be risky ventures unless you don't mind owning a resort property as a second home and making payments out of your own pocket during the hard times.

Bill's Advice: The Math on Vacation Homes Doesn't Usually Work

Too many people talk themselves into buying vacation homes as a way to save money or as an investment. In fact, they are rarely a good idea.

For example, my family goes skiing an average of 12 weekends per year, which is about every other weekend during the season. A two-night stay averages $600 for the weekend, which ends up being $7,200 for the entire season. The typical condo we rent (we find it at www.vrbo.com) costs about $400,000 to buy. With 10 percent invested, a $360,000 mortgage costs about $2,400 a month, plus HOA dues, utilities, maintenance, taxes, insurance, wear and tear, and cleaning fees. That totals well over $3,000 a month or $36,000 a year. The condo would have to be rented every night from November 15th until April 15th to come close to breaking even in terms of cash flow. This is nearly impossible; ski condos generally rent for long weekends and a few holiday weeks. It doesn't take a complicated calculator to figure out that the math doesn't work unless the condo is in a rapidly appreciating market and is rented every weekend—which means I wouldn't get to enjoy it!

Upper-Middle-Class Homes

Traditionally, the type of house that first loses value when a market turns downward is the upper-middle-class home. If you purchase this kind of house as a rental property, it can be difficult to rent for even close to breakeven cash flow because of the limited market for renters who can afford high rents. Generally, when the economy turns downward, these homes get foreclosed and the occupants take one step down when they need to rent or purchase a house. That's where you should be buying—in the MOB (median priced or below)—and not the upper-middle-class homes.

Ironically, this trend doesn't apply to very high-end homes, which hold their value in soft markets. The super-expensive properties that are second-home and even third-home playgrounds for the rich are frequently owned free and clear. Therefore, these owners aren't as vulnerable as upper-middle-class, white-collar workers who live in their overleveraged homes as their primary residences.

Properties in Small, Rural Towns

Small rural towns that are far from major metropolitan areas and lack a college or resort attraction aren't the best bet for most investors. Many of these towns have one major employer that could lay off a large workforce or pack up and leave, crushing the town's economy. In addition, the potential pool of buyers or renters is small.

If you live in this type of town, you have two choices—invest elsewhere or be extremely conservative in estimating vacancy rates or resale time—and, of course, buy *really cheap*!

Mobile Homes

Mobile or "manufactured" homes can be risky, unless they're on their own parcel of land. If your home is in a park, you're at the whim of the park rules, which means your lot rent could increase or the lot owners could change the standards and not allow renters. If you read between the lines, owning a mobile park can be a safe bet; you collect rent for the lots and you can also sell homes in your own park.

Be careful to distinguish between *modular* and *manufactured* houses. A modular home is generally a prefabricated home that is built in pieces, shipped to a destination, and constructed as a unit. Modular homes are craned on-site and set on permanent foundations; once they're set in place they can't be moved. These homes are generally classified the same as regular "stick-built" homes for the purposes of financing.

Manufactured homes, which look similar, are built on frames and tied down. They can, in theory, be transported to a new location, so they're generally treated like mobile homes and are harder to finance.

Gary's Advice: If It Quacks Like a Duck...

Many investors make the mistake of taking the word of a seller or real estate broker that a house is a modular home when, in fact, it's a manufactured home. Here's one easy way to tell the difference: By law, a manufactured home must have a tag issued by the U.S. Department of Housing and Urban Development (HUD) on it. The manufactured tag is located in two places: on the outside of the home and under a sink in the kitchen.

As you're probably gathering from this chapter, we recommend keeping your investment business simple if you want to succeed. Stick to reasonably priced, single-family homes in good neighborhoods that you can buy at a discount because they need a little work. Keep the base of your investing portfolio in "the WOB in the MOB near the Blob" category. Once you've mastered this, you can move on to the more exotic investments.

Key Points to Remember

The most important concepts addressed in this chapter are:

- Invest in deals, not markets.
- Buy the WOB in the MOB near the Blob!
- Fixer-uppers can be a good bet—if you fix the right things.
- If you're a novice investor, avoid risky deals.

CHAPTER 6

Manage Your Cash Flow

"Cash is king."

—Anonymous

Ask anyone who has spent a long time in real estate (or any other business) about the secret to surviving and the response will probably be these two words: cash flow. To remain a successful investor over the long term, it's imperative to master the art of managing your cash flow, which is the sixth principle of defensive investing.

Many investors start out with little cash, and then what cash they do have, they often sink into one property. They go broke in the process because they don't understand the importance of managing their cash flow.

The Importance of Cash Flow

Many businesses fail in the first few year mainly due to poor cash flow management.

According to a recent survey, the number-one thing small business owners say they wish they'd have done differently was have more startup money. Even experienced companies file bankruptcy, not because they don't have a good business model but because they run out of cash.

Consumers, too, don't often manage their cash flow effectively and this can lead to foreclosures. True, the catalyst may have been an unexpected layoff, a change in the economy, a divorce, or some other crisis, but with sufficient cash reserves, consumers can overcome virtually any problem.

The same principle applies to any business. Something can go wrong or business can become slow because of a down cycle, but as long as the business manages its cash flow, it will survive. Real estate investing is no exception. The reason most investors fail is because their plans and investment strategies don't include effectively managing their cash flow.

For example, let's say an investor (we'll call him John) buys a house as a rental property investment with no money down. If John has no cash reserves, what happens if he experiences a 20 percent vacancy rate—that is, he doesn't rent the house for several months? What happens when there are repairs and unforeseen problems that may result in the need for thousands of dollars in repairs or improvements? John will have real problems if any of these events occur *if* his cash flow is low or nonexistent.

Bill's Advice: Unexpected Repairs May Blindside You—and Cause a Cash Crunch

Although I plan for repairs, vacancies, slow months, and a down market, I've had more than my share of unexpected cash crunch issues.

For example, several times a local municipality made me repave a driveway, remove an abandoned car, or rebuild a fence. My insurance company made me re-concrete a long walkway because of what they considered safety issues. More than a dozen plumbing problems have caused major water damage to my properties—damage that was less than my insurance deductible.

Every investor at some time gets blindsided by an unexpected repair cost, so be conservative when establishing your cash reserves.

In essence, real estate investors are no different from average Americans who struggle to get by and live paycheck to paycheck, then suddenly get hit with an unexpected medical bill or car repair expense. The bottom can fall out from underneath quickly, so you'd be wise to set up a financial safety net.

How Much Should You Keep in Reserve?

There's no magic formula you can use to determine how much you should keep in reserve in the real estate business. When we rent properties, the four key factors to consider are strength of the local rental market, eviction time line and cost, the age of the property, and the type of neighborhood.

Strength of the Local Rental Market

The lower the vacancy rates in your area, the fewer reserves you'll need for vacancies. Your local newspaper or your city's housing department may have articles or statistics on vacancy rates. You should, at a minimum, have enough cash reserves to pay for one month of vacancy per unit, which is only an 8 percent vacancy rate.

Even in a good market, you'll deal with problem tenants who may stop paying rent and require an eviction. Good tenant screening will help solve this problem. If you plan to rent properties, you should always, without exception, do a rigorous background check on tenants. This includes reviewing credit reports, employment verification, references, and calling current and previous landlords. (You'll find a list of resources for tenant screening in Appendix 4.)

Eviction Time Line and Cost

The length of time it takes to evict a tenant is relative to your cash reserves. In pro-tenant states like New York and Massachusetts, it could take months and thousands of dollars in legal fees to evict a tenant—all while you're paying the mortgage. In addition, in our experience, collecting back rents or damages from tenants who've been evicted can be futile.

Age of the Property

With newer and recently renovated properties, you won't need to anticipate many repairs in the first few years. As noted earlier, we recommend that you always hire a professional property inspector before you buy. Inspectors will go through the property with a fine-tooth comb, which helps ensure you'll have no surprises later on. Another thing to keep in mind is that many utility companies offer a fixed monthly payment option so you don't experience payment swings each season if you're paying for heating, water, or other utilities as the landlord.

Gary's Advice: Homebuyer's Warranty Is a Good Bet

When you buy rental property, purchase a homebuyer's warranty to cover everything from the furnace and air conditioner to appliances. These warranties are available from many reputable insurance companies and often cost less than $500 a year.

I know of an investor who buys properties in South Carolina and lives in California. He instructs his tenants to call a toll-free number when a repair that's covered by the insurance plan is required. I purchased a home warranty for approximately $300 and later discovered that the home needed a new furnace and hot water heater at a combined cost of nearly $2,400. Was the warranty a good investment? You bet!

Type of Neighborhood

If you're renting properties in low-income neighborhoods, you can expect the turnover to be much higher than in high-income areas. In addition, multiunit buildings with small units and one-bedroom condos will attract more single people who tend to move more often than families.

Cash Flow Applies to Fixer-Uppers and Flips Too!

Too often, inexperienced investors will buy houses, fix them up, and decide to sell them. At this point, the investors have all their money tied up in these houses. What happens if the houses on the market for six months? The investors embark on a downward spiral, which can lead to full-blown panic. Unfortunately, these investors can't blame anyone else for this situation; they should have planned for this possibility and had the foresight to accumulate enough cash reserves to get through this period. Lessons learned?

- Always price the property reasonably to move it quickly.
- Don't overspend on repairs.
- Plan for it to take twice as long to sell as the average property in the neighborhood.

Cash Flow versus Cash Reserve

Don't look at your cash flow in a vacuum but look at it in relationship with your overall financial strategy, the amount of cash you have available, and your return on investment. For example, if you buy rental houses for 100 percent cash, you probably won't have a negative cash flow, but you may not be maximizing leverage. On a similar note, the size of your down payment will affect your cash flow on rental properties.

The following examples can shed some light on cash flow versus cash reserve.

Cash flow example 1: Purchase a $100,000 property with $20,000 down—Your $80,000 loan at 6 percent interest (including taxes and insurance) is about $600 a month. Assuming you can rent the property for $800 a month, you have $200 a month cash flow or $2,400 a year. The cash flow is good, but the $20,000 down payment may have wiped out your cash reserve.

Cash flow example 2: Purchase a $100,000 property with no money down—Your $100,000 loan at 8 percent (this higher rate is common for zero-down loans) would make your payments close to $900 a month. Again, let's assume you can rent the property for $800 a month. With zero down, you have $100 a month *negative* cash flow—but you still have the $20,000 in reserve.

Which is better? Well, it depends on your goals and the rest of your financial picture.

Let's say you intend to hold the property for ten years. In the first example, you have $200 a month cash flow, but no cash reserve. In the second example, you have $100 a month negative cash flow, but you have $20,000 in reserve. Some people automatically assume that the first example is safer, but is it really?

Think about it this way: In the first example, if your property becomes vacant for one month, you'd be out of pocket $600. Once you rent the property, it would take three months to make up that $600. In the second example, you have $20,000 in a cash cushion to make up the deficit. With $20,000 in the bank, you could handle $1,200 a year negative cash flow for 16 years. If the property is in an appreciating market, you'd come out fine, even with negative cash flow.

Another factor in cash flow is the choice of loan. You could buy a property with nothing down and an interest-only loan fixed at 5 percent for three years. If your exit strategy was to sell within 36 months, then why select a fixed-rate loan for 30 years?

The point here is that you shouldn't automatically seek positive cash flow as the only goal when choosing financing. Likewise, you shouldn't buy properties just for leverage and/or appreciation with nothing down, experience a negative cash flow, and assume that short-term market appreciation will be the only source of your profit.

Do you see how cash flow and cash reserve are important considerations in your real estate investing plans and strategies? (See Appendix 5 for a sample form that records cash flow.)

How Cash Flow Affects Your Decisions

By now, you're getting the idea that to continue investing in real estate over the long term, you need cash reserves. Buying real estate with nothing down is easy. However, handling negative cash flow, repairs, and other expenses once you purchase the property is the real test. In fact, if you can make it through the bad times in real estate investing, you'll always come out on top. Lack of cash reserves—and the related fear of vacancies—puts unnecessary pressure on landlord-investors to do substandard repairs, accept unqualified tenants, and give in to tenants' demands. When these cash-strapped investors sell fix-and-flip properties, this situation forces them to drop the price and leave too much equity on the table because they can't wait for the property to sell to recoup their investment.

On the other hand, if you have the security of a sufficient cash reserve, you can act rationally and afford to play the waiting game, holding out for a higher sales price. You can also afford to wait for a qualified tenant and even leave properties vacant rather than renting to undesirable tenants. You can take care of necessary repairs and improvements on properties. In short, when you have cash in your pocket, it's a whole different ballgame than trying to operate with a lack of cash.

The bottom line: You can buy real estate without money, but you simply cannot survive in business without cash reserves. Thus, it's important to consider accumulating cash reserves before you invest in rental properties.

Generate Both Cash Flow and Cash Reserves

From a long-term perspective, rental properties can be a good source of steady cash flow and equity buildup. As an investor, you can buy a rental property and aim to break even, perhaps even provide some cash flow, but with repairs and vacancies, this can be an up-and-down process and most people won't be able to retire on rentals until these properties are paid off or have increased substantially in value. Therefore, you need to plan other ways to generate cash flow or cash reserves to protect your real estate investment business.

If you have a good-paying job, a spouse who works, another source of income, or other cash reserves, rentals can be a good long-term investment play. If you don't have any of these cash-generating "weapons" in your arsenal, consider the following popular options to generate some quick cash or build cash reserves.

Wholesale deals. A popular strategy is to do a lot of fix-and-flip deals to generate cash and build a cash reserve. However, inexperienced investors can get in over their heads quickly when a fixer-upper won't sell. Some cable television shows make it seem that rehabbing is easy, but it's a lot harder to make a buck than it looks. Investors who are new in the business, crunched for cash flow, or already involved in several fix-up projects may consider wholesaling deals to another investor.

The wholesale usually involves flipping a fixer-upper property "as is" to another investor who'll do the lion's share of the fixing. As the wholesaler, you'll only make a small profit ($5,000 to $10,000 per deal), but there's virtually no risk because, typically, you would accomplish the transaction by using a double-closing or contract assignment.

Basically, a double-closing (or simultaneous escrow) means holding two closings, back to back. The funds from the second closing are used to fund the first closing. The double-closing is an effective way to buy and flip properties without using your own funds. Despite rumors and urban myths to the contrary, there's nothing illegal about double-closings. However, many title companies and lenders won't do double-closings because they fear potential fraud, but this is generally more of an issue when flipping to owner-occupant buyers.

A contract assignment is an alternative transaction to a double-closing. Here, the buyer/investor assigns the purchase contract to another investor who closes in his or her place. In the case of a contract assignment, there's only one closing. A contract assignment is similar to endorsing a check to a third party.

Bill's Advice: Don't Be Greedy

When figuring your profit on a wholesale deal, don't expect too much. Many novice (and some experienced, albeit foolish) investors expect more profit than they deserve out of a deal. You must be realistic. If you want to sell a property quickly to another investor who'll do a lot of work and incur some risk, you can't expect to make as much as he or she will. While it's possible to negotiate a great price and make a strong profit, remember that most deals don't have enough room for two investors to "make a killing."

For a detailed discussion of the wholesaling process, refer to *Flipping Properties—Generate Instant Cash Profits in Real Estate*, 2nd Edition (Kaplan 2006).

Partner on Deals. If you don't have the cash reserves, consider partnering on a deal with someone who does. For example, a house in an expensive area may rent for less than the mortgage payments, even if you buy it at a tremendous discount in an appreciating market. Bringing in a partner to cover the down payment requirement and to feed the monthly negative cash flow could be profitable for both of you if you split the profits when you resell the property.

Make sure you verify that this partner actually has the money and consider forming a partnership or legal entity that has a bank account where the money is deposited. (Chapter 8 discusses legal entities in more detail.)

Bill's Advice: Half of Something Is Better Than All of Nothing

I know of a particular investor who had millions in equity. When the local rental market went sour, he was stuck on negative cash flow on hundreds of rental properties. His solution was to sell half of his equity, at a discount, for cash to a partner. He used that cash as a reserve to feed the negative cash flow the properties were demanding. As a result, he still has plenty of equity and plans to sell the properties when the local market rebounds in price.

The lesson he learned is a good one that many investors would be wise to follow: half of something is better than ALL of nothing is! If you can't handle negative cash flow, your equity won't matter much when you lose your properties to foreclosure.

Save Your Money. If your grandparents were like ours, they used to scrimp and save every penny they could. Consider doing the same and even wait awhile before investing until you have some cash in the bank. If you have a good-paying job, we suggest setting up an automatic debit of 10 percent or more of your income into a forced saving account.

Have Backup Sources of Funds. Having backup sources of funds for emergencies doesn't necessarily mean cash or other income. It can be (at least in part) access to credit cards and credit lines. Many businesses have access to lines of credit for emergency purposes.

Many banks offer business credit lines up to $200,000, but these are expensive to get. Often this will cost as much as $5,000, even if you don't use it. Don't fret, though; you may already have more available credit than you realize. Credit cards and other existing revolving debt accounts can be quite useful in real estate investing. Most major credit cards allow you to take cash advances or write checks to borrow on the account. The transaction fees and interest rates are fairly high, but you can access this money on 24 hours' notice. In addition, you won't have to pay loan costs that are normally associated with a real estate transaction such as title insurance, appraisals, pest inspections, surveys, and so on. Often, you're better off paying 18 percent interest or more on a credit line for six months than paying 8 percent interest on an institutional loan, which has up-front costs that would take you years to recoup.

Promotional interest rates are often available on your credit cards, but again, beware. These rates often skyrocket after several months. Chances are if you have a good credit history, you'll be able to raise your credit limits on your existing cards. Creditors don't need to know you'll be using your credit cards for the business of real estate investing. Ironically, these creditors would rather see you using credit-line increases for typical consumer purchases that depreciate in value and produce no income.

Keep in mind that you must approach high-interest debt cautiously. Your personality type may not embrace the idea of owing tens of thousands of dollars in revolving debt.

You can also benefit by using home improvement store cards with no cash advance features. These cards are available through the major lumberyards, hardware-store chains, and home-improvement stores.

They allow you to finance your material costs that can involve many thousands of dollars. The interest you pay for the use of this money is generally deductible, so be careful to separate your business credit card use from your personal credit card use.

A home equity line of credit (HELOC) can be an excellent financing tool if you use it properly. Basically, a HELOC is a credit card secured by a mortgage or deed of trust on your property. You only pay interest on the amount you borrow on the HELOC. If you don't use the line of credit, you don't have any monthly payments to make. You can access the HELOC by writing checks provided by the lender. Note that, in most cases, the HELOC will be a second lien on your property.

Key Points to Remember

Cash flow management is the bedrock of survival in any business, with real estate being no exception. Defensive investors must be careful not to run out of cash or they will be soon out of business.

The most important concepts addressed in this chapter are:

- Having little or no cash reserve is a surefire way to financial disaster.
- Lack of cash flow can cause investors to make foolish, risky decisions.
- Wholesaling properties can be a good way to generate cash flow.
- Line up sources of backup funds, such as credit cards and credit lines.

CHAPTER

7

Have Multiple Exit Strategies

"We must dare to think 'unthinkable' thoughts. We must learn to explore all the options and possibilities that confront us in a complex and rapidly changing world."

—J. William Fulbright

As mentioned earlier, we suggest you avoid entering a deal without having a clearly defined exit strategy. Walking into a deal blindly is a foolish move that will likely cost you dearly in the end. Many sorry investors have regretted jumping into deals without taking the time to think them all the way through to the finish line. For an investor to simply rely solely on Plan A is a risky approach. You must also have a Plan B and, ideally, a Plan C and D, as well. Our seventh defensive investing principle is having more than one exit strategy.

As discussed in earlier chapters, market timing is difficult to predict, and many investors get into a market too late. This is fine if you buy in areas where real estate appreciates over time and you actually stick it out for the long run. In the stock market, there's a concept called, "dollar cost averaging," which means if you keep buying consistently, you will make out long term because some of your purchases will be at the bottom of the market and some at the top. However, because the market will always go higher in the long run, all of your purchases will average out.

We believe the same concept applies to real estate—*if* you can survive in the long run. We don't suggest that you throw caution to the wind and just buy blindly. To the contrary, we advocate being defensive—that is, plan carefully, consider the risk, know your market before you buy, and have a backup plan if your assumptions turn out to be incorrect. In fact, defensive investors have several backup plans if the first one doesn't work out.

Choices, Choices, Choices

No single exit strategy is inherently better than any other is. The best choice for you in a given situation varies depending on numerous factors including your long-term plans, the local market, your cash-flow situation, and the condition of the property.

Let's discuss a variety of real estate investment strategies that could be your Plan A. Later in this chapter, we'll discuss appropriate backup plans you can turn to when Plan A doesn't work.

The Fix-and-Flip

In the rehab deal, an investor intends to buy a property in need of repair, fix it up, and then sell it to an owner-occupant. This property will likely be listed on the Multiple Listing Service and involve a real estate agent. Investors call this selling *retail*.

Always figure on paying a real estate commission when you sell property retail. The standard commission in most parts of the country is about 6 percent. Many novices make the mistake of thinking they can cut out the broker's commission and sell property on their own. However, more than 95 percent of all retail properties (new homes excluded) sell on the MLS so don't assume you can beat the odds.

The Wholesale Flip

As you learned in the previous chapter, you can flip a rehab property "as is" to another investor. With this exit strategy, keep in mind that there must be enough profit to go around here. Don't try to work

Bill's Advice: Consider Using a Flat-Fee Listing Broker

If you have extra time on your hands, you can go with a flat-fee listing broker. Most properties involve two brokers: the listing broker and the selling broker (a.k.a. the *buyer's broker*) who split the commission when the property sells. For a $200,000 house, a 6 percent commission is $12,000. A flat-fee listing broker will charge you $500 or less to list the property on the MLS. You'll still need to pay the selling broker's commission (about $6,000 in this example), but you'll save a lot of money—about $5,500 in this example. However, you'll have to conduct your own open houses, show the property, and prepare contracts yourself. If you're uncomfortable with the paperwork and legal details, hiring a good real estate attorney is a lot cheaper than a listing broker!

on the "greater fool" theory—that is, a novice investor who knows less than you, buys it thinking he can make a profit. This is hardly a way to make a living, is unpredictable, and will not leave you feeling good about yourself at the end of the day.

The Partial Rehab

In strong markets, you can flip properties directly to the retail sector with little or no rehab work involved. This an excellent exit strategy in strong markets because if the property is in decent shape, you may only need to do basic redecorating to prepare it for resale.

Even when the property needs more work, you can often make essential improvements quickly and then sell it as a minor fixer-upper. This is often referred to as a *partial rehab* or a *flip/fix combo*. In this situation, a thorough cleaning and some painting may be sufficient to get this property ready for sale. You can complete those tasks within a few days so you'll be able to offer this type of property for sale quickly.

The Rental

You can buy and hold a property as a rental, or you can buy, fix, and hold a property as a rental. With this strategy, you must be familiar with the rental market in your area (particularly in your farm area), the appropriate expenses, and the rental laws. Keep in mind that rentals require time management so you should be able to devote the appropriate time. Hiring a property manager for one single-family home is economically unfeasible and usually unnecessary. Property management isn't easy and you should learn how to do it properly. An old saying goes like this: "What you don't know about landlording, your tenants will teach you." We highly recommend these books:

- Goodwin, Daniel et al. *The Landlord's Handbook*, 3rd ed. Kaplan Publishing (2003).
- Robinson, Leigh. *Landlording: A Handymanual for Scrupulous Landlords and Landladies Who Do It Themselves*, 10th ed., Express Publishing (2006).
- Taylor, Jeffrey. *The Landlord's Kit: A Complete Set of Ready-to-Use Forms, Letters, and Notices to Increase Profits, Take Control, and Eliminate the Hassle*. Kaplan Publishing (2002).

The Lease/Option Strategy

Another popular exit strategy option is to rehab a property, refinance it, and then lease it to your renters using a lease with an option to buy. Lease/option is a popular format because it allows the seller to get top dollar for the property without paying a broker's fee while covering mortgage payments on the property until the tenant exercises his option to purchase. Generally speaking, you can get a higher price for a property if you offer creative terms (e.g., give a partial rent credit to tenants against the purchase price of the property, which allows them to generate equity if they can't afford a down payment at the time). If tenants do exercise their option to purchase after 12 months, you'll fare better with your tax situation than if you had flipped the property quickly.

Bill's Advice: Take Time to Learn the Pros and Cons of the Lease/Option Strategy

If you hold a property for 12 months or more, the gain on the sale is considered a long-term capital gain and taxed at a lower rate than if you sell the property within 12 months. (We'll discuss taxes in more detail in Chapter 8.)

However, a lease/option transaction does involve inherent risk. If tenants choose not to exercise their option to buy, you're left with the property. The market may have taken a downswing since you first obtained the property, meaning you'll either need to lower your asking price or hold on to the property awhile. In addition, if tenants put down a substantial deposit or did repairs and improvements, they may be able to claim an "equitable interest" in the property, making eviction more difficult. Good paperwork is essential to making any lease/option strategy go smoothly. For more details, check out the "Big Profits with Lease/Options" system, which is available at **www.legalwiz.com**.

Owner Financing

As the investor and seller in an owner-financed sale, you'd take all or part of the purchase price in the installment payments after closing instead of taking all cash. Remember, "all cash" doesn't necessarily mean the buyer is using 100 percent cash to purchase the property; it may mean the buyer gets a loan. Both result in the seller receiving all cash for the purchase price.

Three top benefits of doing an owner-carry installment sale rather than a cash sale are:

1. **Highest price**—As the seller, you can insist on and receive the highest price when offering flexible owner-finance terms. In many cases, you can receive more than the fair market value of the property by offering these "soft" terms. People are always willing to pay a premium for nonqualifying financing.

2. **Cash**—Nearly every seller says he or she wants all cash, but few really need it. Instead, the typical seller wants the most *net* cash from the deal. Often, the seller must pay closing costs, title insurance, broker fees, and the balance of the existing financing. In addition, you may need to pay capital gains tax to Uncle Sam. In many cases, the sale of a property by an installment sale will net you more future yield than any source from which the cash proceeds were reinvested.
3. **Fast closing**—Nothing holds up a sale more than new lender financing. In some areas of the country, it can take months for a buyer to qualify and close a new loan to purchase your property. Because most standard real estate contracts contain a financing contingency, you may end up back at square one if your buyer doesn't qualify for a loan.

There are few assumable loans available to buyers and few sellers offer these soft terms. Thus, an owner-carry sale makes your house unique. Furthermore, an owner-carry transaction can be consummated in a matter of days. That's because there is no appraisal, underwriting, or survey involved. In many cases, you'll be able to sell the property with owner financing and save thousands of dollars in real estate brokers' fees.

Pitfalls and risks of owner financing. The main risk of offering owner financing is that the buyer may default, requiring you to go through a legal proceeding to get the property back. An unrecorded land sale contract (a.k.a. "contract for deed") is often a viable strategy to allow you to sell the property and quickly remove the buyer for nonpayment. It can be challenging, though, because the process is not well defined in many states, resulting in uncertainty as to the legal process and thus the cost and time involved.

A foreclosure on an owner-financed deal may take several months and cost many thousands in legal fees; all the while, you're paying your existing loan payments, property taxes, and so on. It's important to discuss the process with a local attorney before proceeding with an owner-financing sale.

Exit Strategies and Financing Options

As a real estate investor, your exit strategy will play a major role in deciding the kind of financing option you may need or want. The main factor will be your anticipated time from loan initiation to loan payoff.

Short-Term Financing

Short-term financing is a temporary source of money that you may use, assuming you'll refinance or resell the property quickly. Short-term financing generally has a higher rate of interest and a balloon or payoff deadline within six to 12 months. Generally, you access short-term financing through smaller commercial banks or private hard-money lenders (called equity lenders) who make their money on up-front points and fees.

Short-term financing is useful even when long-term financing may be a better deal for two reasons: availability and speed.

Availability of financing is often more important than cost. Although short-term loans are often costly, even a high-interest loan can make sense when you plan to keep the property for a short time before selling or refinancing it. This does involve some risk, though—if something unexpected happens and you can't sell or refinance the property quickly, you'll be forced to endure that high interest rate.

You can quickly obtain funds with short-term financing. Generally, long-term financing takes more time and requires more documentation, which potentially means a lost opportunity for a good deal. With short-term financing, equity lenders are more concerned with the collateral they are lending against than the credit or income of the borrower so funding can be completed in a matter of days. Availability of quick financing can be important to your real estate investing business because decisions are made by a smaller, more flexible lender who will finance deals that the big players won't.

While equity lenders won't go as high on loan-to-value as the credit-based lenders, they base their loan-to-value calculation on whichever is highest: the purchase price or appraisal. Remember, credit lenders generally base their loans as a percentage of whichever is less: the purchase price or the appraisal price. This means that even if you purchase a property at 50 percent of value, you can't do this type of loan with no money down.

Bill's Advice: Buy "Subject to" Existing Financing

If possible, try to buy the property "subject to" the existing financing as an alternative to short-term financing. Buying "subject to" means you get the seller simply to deed you the property without paying off the existing loan. As the buyer and investor, you would make the payments until you sell or refinance the property. Buying "subject to" existing financing is fast, less costly (no new loan costs are involved), and doesn't tie up your credit.

In most cases, the mortgage or deed of trust securing the existing loan contains a due-on-sale restriction, allowing the lender to call the balance owed immediately due and payable. Some misinformed real estate "professionals" will tell you that it's illegal to transfer ownership of a property without notifying the lender. This is hogwash. First of all, most lenders could care less, especially if the payments are being made on time. Second, by the time they find out, you'll have paid off the loan by reselling the property or refinancing the debt. It's a good idea, however, to make sure there is full disclosure in writing to the seller about the implications of leaving the loan in his or her name. Some states have a mandated disclosure for taking "subject to" properties in foreclosure.

Keep in mind also that if you sell a property by a lease/option or land sale contract (a.k.a. "contract for deed"), it will also trigger the due-on-sale process on your underlying loan. However, most lenders don't find out because the agreement is not recorded. In most cases, lenders don't even care as long as the loan is being paid; their only incentive to enforce the due-on-sale is financial. If market interest rates are higher than the existing loan, it makes sense for the lender to make you pay it off so they can refinance you (or your buyer) at a higher rate. Therefore, it's recommended that you place some sort of "out" position (e.g., a balloon date or option expiration date) so you aren't tied to the deal indefinitely and risk the lender calling in the loan.

Long-Term Financing

Long-term financing will give you more options if you're not pressed for time to close, when loan-to-value isn't an issue or you plan to keep the property as a rental. Many options for long-term financing are available if you have good credit. These include fixed-rate, adjustable-rate, and interest-only payment loans, and the option adjustable rate mortgage (ARM).

In a rising interest rate market, fixed-rate loans may be the way to go if you plan to keep a property for a long time. However, a 30-year fixed-rate loan is generally the most expensive type of long-term loan in terms of fees and interest rates. Adjustable-rate and interest-only payment loans can be a cheaper option, depending on your back-end strategy. Generally speaking, a loan that adjusts based on the market rate of interest charged is less risky for lenders because it hedges their bets against rising interest rates. Accordingly, they'll offer you a cheaper starting rate than if the rate were fixed over 30 years.

Of course, the same risk works *against* you if interest rates rise in the future. Many adjustable rate loans are fixed for a certain time period (e.g., three years) and/or can only adjust a certain percentage per year. You don't want any big surprises. If you plan to sell the property on a lease/option within a few years, then an adjustable rate mortgage may be the way to go.

One of the most misunderstood loans is the called the option ARM. With an ARM, the interest rate is based on an index like the London Interbank Offered Rate (LIBOR). The loan has four payment options, each of which can change monthly based on the interest rate the loan is indexed to.

These options are:

- Interest only
- Amortized for 15 years
- Amortized for 30 years
- Minimum payment

Depending on the market interest rate, the minimum payment may create a negative amortization, which means the loan balance may increase with time. Carefully used, an option ARM can be an excellent way to hedge your bets with rental properties because this provides a low-payment option if you have unexpected repairs or vacancies. The ARM is particularly effective in a rising price market because it gives you some breathing room if your loan balance is increasing.

Prepayment Penalties

Carefully check when you get a loan to see if there's a prepayment penalty. Often, loan reps quote you a better rate than their competitors; you find out why when you go to sell the property and discover that there's a prepayment penalty. A prepayment penalty is a fee you must pay to the lender for paying off the loan early. In most cases, the penalty only applies in the first few years of the loan. A prepayment penalty is typically three to six months of interest payments based on the original amount of the loan.

Prepayment penalties are not always a bad thing. If you have no intention of selling or refinancing the loan within the first few years, then having a prepayment penalty won't be a problem. In fact, it may allow you to pay less in loan fees or have a lower interest rate. If you're uncertain of your exit strategy and want the most options, you may have to pay a fee up front to get rid of the prepayment penalty.

Gary's Advice: Don't Be Tricked!

Two types of prepayment penalties exist: "hard" and "soft." The soft prepayment penalty applies whenever you refinance the property and don't sell it. A hard prepayment penalty is paid for the term of the penalty, whether you transfer title in any manner or refinance it. No matter what your mortgage broker says, read the documents carefully at closing. Many investors get tricked into signing documents with a prepayment penalty. When they realize the mistake, it's often too late, so beware!

Remember, the lending business changes often, and this can affect your exit strategy if you had planned to refinance the property a few years down the road. You need to work with a knowledgeable mortgage professional before you go into a deal.

What to Do When Plan A Doesn't Work

When your primary plan of action doesn't work, you need to have a backup strategy. This may involve switching gears from a retail sale to a rental or rent-to-own deal. However, before you give up, here are a few tricks that may work and a variety of backup strategies.

Stage It

The cheapest way to create appeal for your property is to stage it—that is, dress it up so it doesn't look empty. The idea is to upgrade the appearance of the property, so you wouldn't use cheap-looking items or those that might appear too personal in taste. You may feel qualified to make all the decisions regarding your décor and presentation, but it would be wise to get second opinions from an interior decorator, friend, or real estate expert. Visit show homes in new neighborhoods to gather ideas. You can even borrow a few items from your home if you don't have sentimental attachment to them.

Professional staging companies will decorate the house and bring the furniture with them. Depending on the size of the house and price range, this may make sense. It isn't uncommon for sellers to pay $10,000 to decorate a $1,000,000 home professionally. Of course, this may be overkill in a small starter home or condominium priced under $250,000. Although the term *home staging* is trademarked, it has become a common expression in the industry and refers to the process of decorating houses for resale.

Visit these Web sites to learn about easy ways to stage your properties for sale:

- **www.simpleappeal.com**
- **www.stagedhomes.com**
- **www.homestagers.com**

Offer Attractive Sales Terms

Every type of business acknowledges the value of offering attractive financing terms to attract customers—especially in cases involving a backlog of inventory that needs to be sold. Auto dealers frequently employ this strategy, especially at the end of the year when they need to clear out last year's models to make room for the coming year's models. This is when you'll see commercials promising "zero-percent financing" deals or similar offers.

It's no different in real estate. Investors who have properties that haven't been selling can often increase a buyer's interest by offering attractive financing options. For example, you can offer to pay the closing costs or you can "buy down" the buyer's interest rate by offering to prepay six months of payments on the buyer's loan. Another strategy is to offer to carry back 10 percent or more of the purchase price with a note secured by a lien on the property. By making arrangements in advance to help buyers with financing, you can attract more buyers.

Bill's Advice: Don't Cross the Line from "Creative" to "Criminal"

Whatever creative financing you do, make sure it's aboveboard and disclosed on the settlement statement (HUD-1 form) at closing. Sometimes sellers (at the suggestion of the buyer, the buyer's real estate broker, or mortgage broker) mark up the sales price and give the seller his or her down payment back after closing. In this way, the buyer can get 100 percent financing. This is illegal—don't do it.

Change Your Exit Plan

Your exit strategy may have been to sell the property retail, but if that doesn't work out, you could refinance and rent the property awhile. On the other hand, you could offer a lease/option or owner financing. You might also consider the advantages of wholesaling to other investors, not only for cash but also for alternative terms.

Bill's Advice: It Pays to Be Flexible

I once put a rehab property under contract and tried to flip it wholesale, only to find out there was a slim profit margin for a fix-and-flip. The investor who bought it from me gave me a note, which was paid when he resold the property. The total cash in my pocket wasn't substantial, but I only spent a few hours on the deal. Sometimes it pays to be flexible and receive your profits on a marginal deal, which is better than losing a deal altogether.

Bring in a Partner

Sometimes a partner can bring something to the table that you don't have. The missing resource could be credit (the ability to borrow to refinance the debt), cash, or experience. Bringing in a partner to rework the deal can be effective, particularly if there's enough equity to share. For example, if your credit is shaky, you're overextended, or you simply ran out of cash, a partner can help fund negative cash flow or lend his or her credit to refinance the property in exchange for a percentage of the back-end profit. Remember, there must be enough equity in the deal for a second person to profit; otherwise you won't find too many willing partners.

Bail Out and Cut Your Losses

Sometimes the only option is to bail out and cut your losses. It takes a big person to look in the mirror and say, "I made a mistake." Too many investors let their egos get in the way and hold on longer than they should and the bleeding never stops. If it's a retail deal, then drop your price, even if it means losing money. If it's a rental, drop your rent low enough to attract a solid tenant. If your monthly carrying cost is

$1,000 on a unit, it makes sense to drop your rent by $80 a month rather than have a vacancy. In fact, if you're offering the property on a lease with the option to purchase, you may consider dropping the rent below market and taking a monthly loss to make it up on the back end, assuming there's enough equity to justify the monthly loss.

For example, suppose you buy a house for $150,000 and it's worth $200,000, but because of a poor financing choice, your monthly payment is $1,300 a month. Even if market rents are $1,100 a month, that doesn't mean you must hold out for $1,300 a month. Rather, it makes sense to rent it for $1,100 or even $1,000 to get a qualified tenant who can eventually buy it for $200,000 in two years. A loss of $300 for 24 months is only $6,800, which is justified when you make $50,000 profit on the back end. Words of caution, though, never compromise your rental standards because it will cost you more in the long run for evictions and repairs.

Over the past few years, many novice investors got into preconstruction deals, anticipating a huge increase in prices by the time the development finished. Instead, the values flattened or dropped. Rather than walk away from their deposits, many insisted on completing their purchases, hoping the market would come back. They were often wrong, and ended up selling the property for less than they bought it for. If they had stayed in the game long term or had devised a viable alternative exit strategy (such as renting in the meantime) then they may have come out on top. More often than not, however, the best course of action may be to cut your losses early.

Real-Life Story: Sometimes Cutting Your Losses Is Best

An investor we know put up over $100,000 in deposits on new construction condos in Las Vegas. By the time the first half of the development was half built, "reservation" prices on the second preconstruction phase were higher than the first phase prices. The investor figured that the difference between the so-called "market" prices of reservations on the second phase and the prices he had reserved in the first phase amounted to about $500,000 in equity.

We tried to explain to him that this equity was like fool's gold because neither phase of the construction was complete and by the time he'd actually resell those units, the true market price could be lower than his acquisition price due to competition from other condo projects.

When the time came for the next required payment on the condo units (over $250,000), we suggested he either sell one-half of his interest in his "equity" to a partner for $100,000 (limiting his risk to zero) or walk way. He was incredulous, insisting that he had $500,000 in equity. Unfortunately, many novice investors don't think defensively when it comes to real estate. Time will tell who's right on this deal, but there's a lesson to be learned. As the old expression goes, "pigs get fat, hogs get slaughtered."

Renegotiate the Debt

If you end up owing more on a property than it's worth (or on several properties for that matter); you could be in a real pickle. There's no room to drop your prices if the market value of your houses is less than your debt.

In this case, you can either wait out the market or negotiate with the lenders who hold the liens on your properties. Your likely options are short sale, forbearance, and deed in lieu, discussed next.

Lenders realize that taking back properties in mass isn't good for their portfolios. Often, they're willing to take a discount on what is owed. Called a *short sale*, the lender essentially accepts less than the full amount as a payoff, contemporaneously with a sale. The lender won't allow you to profit from the deal so a refinance isn't possible; you need to sell the property to a buyer at an arms'-length transaction (that is, to someone who's not related to you by family, friendship, or business). Make sure the debt is settled in "full satisfaction"; otherwise, the lender could sue you for a deficiency. Keep in mind, also, the extent that the debt is forgiven by the lender because you may have taxable income. We strongly suggest reviewing this exit strategy with your tax advisor before proceeding.

If all you need is more time to try to sell a property, sometimes you can work a forbearance with the lender. A forbearance happens when the lender agrees to work with you on back payments. If you have the property actively listed, the lender may delay proceeding with foreclosure on the property, which gives you more time to sell it. Remember, the more contact you have with your lender, the more the lender will be willing to work with you. Silence is the worst tactic when you're in default on a loan with your lender.

If the lender is willing, another option is to accept a deed in lieu of foreclosing the property. This involves simply deeding the property to the lender in exchange for the lender's promise not to sue you for a deficiency.

Buy It Right

As stressed earlier, *you need to make your money when you buy*. Thus, you can see how your exit strategy is often dictated by two factors: your purchase price and your local market. The better deal you get when you buy, the more options you'll have on your exit. Too many investors make the colossal mistake of paying too much for a property and assuming they'll "make it up" on the back end of the deal.

The following common mistakes shed light on how investors can fail to "buy it right."

The "Skinny" Rehab

Let's say your rehab strategy is to buy at 75 percent of the after-repaired value, less repair costs. The property is worth $200,000 in perfect condition and needs $20,000 in repairs. The maximum you want to pay is 75 percent of $200,000 ($150,000) minus $20,000, which equals $130,000. You offer $130,000 and the seller counters at $150,000. You arrive at a negotiated price of $143,000. It's more than you wanted to pay so you figure you'll spend a little extra in repairs to make it extra nice so you can sell the property for $205,000. However, when you get into the project, you realize it will cost $30,000 in repairs. Then you'd have to list it for $209,000—without a single comp in the neighborhood to support that price. You end up holding the property too long, dropping the price, and selling the property for $193,000. After loan costs, holding costs, seller concessions, and real estate broker commissions, you barely break even. This is a common tale.

The moral of this story is that you have to be conservative in your repair estimates and your resale price on rehabs. There's rarely such a thing as a "skinny" rehab unless you are keeping it as a rental or are lucky enough to be in a hot market where properties sell no matter what their condition.

The "Skinny" Lease/Option

You buy a property worth $200,000 for $180,000. It only needs carpet and paint, or so you think. Your strategy is to sell it on lease/option for $209,000. Once you fork over $4,000 in loan costs to acquire the property, you realize the small "carpet and paint" job also involves replacing a furnace and hot water heater, totaling $8,000. The property sits vacant for two months while you look for a tenant. This brings your total acquisition cost to $200,000. To top it off, your tenant/buyer leaves after three months. Your property is once again vacant and you're losing money.

The moral of the story is that you shouldn't pay top dollar for a property just because you have a built-in back end, because that back end may not work. Instead, develop multiple exit strategies in case your initial plan doesn't work out. Certainly you'll save a few bucks by not having to advertise for a tenant and pay monthly mortgage payments in the meantime, but that doesn't justify paying $20,000 more than you should.

The "Greater Fool" Deal

You're trying to wholesale fixer-upper properties to other investors without a clue about what other investors want to pay. You get a $200,000 fixer-upper property under contract for $166,000, then attempt to find someone who'll buy it from you. Three investors tell you that you're asking too much. On top of that, you want $10,000 to assign the contract. You figure you'll advertise it in the paper and flip it to a novice investor. Once in a while, you can justify it by saying,

"Well, that person is just less discriminating than I am." The point here is you need to have ethics in this business; taking advantage of others should not be a basis for your investing practices.

We see these mistakes every single day in our business; they're all too common. The bottom line is that you need to obtain a property that's cheap enough to leave yourself multiple exit strategies. If you buy a cheap enough property but it won't sell, drop the price. If it won't rent, you'll have enough room to sell it cheap—and the more equity you have, it's easier to bring in a partner or refinance the property.

Gary's Advice: Shoot for 20 Percent Equity

The magic number for investor financing is *80 percent*. As long as you have a bona fide 20 percent equity position (or better), financing is generally fairly easy. Once you try to go higher than 80 percent loan-to-value financing, your options are limited.

Key Points to Remember

The defensive investor is always thinking "exit strategy." Better yet is having a backup plan, making you a really smart investor. The name of the game is "risk" and the more contingencies you plan for, the better your chance of success.

The most important concepts addressed in this chapter are:

- Never get into a transaction without having a plan to get out of it.
- Having one exit strategy isn't enough. You also need to have a Plan B as a backup.
- Sometimes your only option is to cut and run.
- Buy right and you'll have multiple exit strategies.

CHAPTER

8

You've Earned It, Now Learn How to Keep It

"A lawyer with his briefcase can steal more than a hundred men with guns."

—Mario Puzo, author of *The Godfather*

Unfortunately, we live in a litigious society where many people seek to place blame on others. Some people believe that if you treat people right and carry sufficient insurance, you'll be fine, but that's naïve thinking, which can get you into a lot of trouble. One lawsuit can ruin everything you've worked hard to create, which is why it's critical to apply the eighth principle, learning how to keep your wealth.

Real estate is a high-risk business, particularly when dealing with rental properties, tenants, and rehab projects. There are a lot of ways to mess up a deal and lose your investment—and potentially more if someone has a good lawyer. Every investor needs to learn some defensive strategies to keep what they have, including limiting taxes and avoiding lawsuits.

Know the Laws

Start by knowing the laws as they apply to your real estate business. The old expression "ignorance of the law is no defense" is true. You're expected to know the law as it applies to your business. Your state, city, or municipality may have particular laws, codes, and regulations with which you must become familiar. Discuss your business practices regularly with a local attorney and other investors in your business. Review your forms, agreements, and contracts to make sure the disclosures and clauses are appropriate for the particular way you do business.

Common Investor Legal Mistakes

You can't expect to reduce your risk of getting sued to zero, but you can take steps to reduce your risk as much as possible. In any situation where your money is at risk, ask yourself, "Is there a better way?" Know the legal and financial risks of the situations in which you place yourself, your business, your family, and your assets.

Without covering every issue involved, here are a few common mistakes that investors make, novice and experienced alike.

Poor legal forms. It's amazing how short-sighted novice investors can be when it comes to shelling out money for good legal contracts. They often buy contracts at discount office supply stores, from Internet Web sites, or borrow them from friends. However, a real estate deal is only worth the paper it's written on. Like the old expression, "every tax strategy works until you get audited," it can be said that "every contract works until you have a dispute." Therefore, invest in a good set of legal forms that apply to your practice and ask a local real estate attorney to review them. Also, make certain you fill in the forms correctly—a good real estate attorney will review contracts for just a few hundred dollars.

Too many people rely on real estate brokers to fill out contracts, which is fine for a "standard" deal. However, most brokers aren't trained in legal matters and often create long contract addendums that are insufficient to protect your interests.

Illegal discrimination. The Fair Housing Act of 1968, as amended, prohibits discrimination on the basis of race, color, religion, nationality, familial status, age, and gender. Many state and local laws also forbid discrimination on the basis of sexuality or source of income and the Americans with Disabilities Act makes it illegal to discriminate against disabled people. If you harbor any such prejudices and would allow them to come into play when renting a housing unit, then you're probably not cut out to be a landlord. However, many sincere real estate investors make honest mistakes that result in discrimination lawsuits. The best way to avoid these lawsuits is to be informed.

The Fair Housing Act may appear to be common sense and most people would never think of discriminating against people of different races or religions or on the basis of gender. However, it's important to note that the Act extends beyond the screening process and into advertising as well, so watch the wording in your ads. This is where many landlords and property managers make critical mistakes. Some people scour the classifieds looking for inappropriately worded ads so they can pounce on them and threaten a lawsuit. While someone must have standing to bring suit, these scoundrels often work in coalitions to ensure that all of their bases are covered.

For example, if you own a rental property in a predominantly Jewish community, its proximity to the local synagogue could be a major feature. However, if your ad says "within walking distance of the synagogue," you could be sending the message "Gentiles need not apply"—even though this wasn't your intent. Keep in mind also that you may not discriminate on the basis of whether a couple is married and whether children are to live in the unit. You may also not discriminate on the basis of age. Often, novice landlords aren't aware of these areas of concern—and while it's good that citizens are more aware of their rights today, it can create a bad situation for well-meaning landlords who are out of step with the law.

Be aware of your local laws and use good business sense. State law and local ordinances can extend similar protections granted under the Fair Housing Act to other groups. For example, California, Minnesota, and North Dakota prohibit discrimination based on source of income. In other words, landlords can't discriminate against would-be tenants who rely on public assistance. Putting the political perspective of the landlord aside, such discrimination makes little business sense because people on welfare or social security are virtually assured of a fixed income.

The Americans with Disabilities Act (ADA) prohibits discrimination against the disabled and also requires landlords to make "reasonable accommodations" to disabled tenants. Who decides what's reasonable? Typically, courts, if it comes to that; but while most landlords are aware of the ADA and would never stoop to discriminate against a person in a wheelchair. However, many are unaware that the ADA also protects mentally disabled tenants. A mental disability could also include recovering alcoholics and drug addicts.

Improper disclosures. Improper disclosures are a common mistake for investors. It's critical to be aware of the federal and state requirements for disclosures. For example, federal law requires a lead-based paint disclosure on the sale or rental of properties that were built before 1978. State laws may have additional regulations.

It's become common practice for real estate brokers to use a property disclosure form for all aspects of the house. Even if you're selling your house on your own, be sure to use one of these forms (refer to the sample in Appendix 6). Whenever in doubt, disclose what you know, especially something the buyer or tenant may not know about, such as dangerous conditions, water damage, electrical issues, or plumbing problems.

Illegal solicitation of money. Many novice investors try to solicit money for investing via public advertising or mailings. This is commonly referred to as *syndication*. You may inadvertently cross over a variety of federal and state securities regulations when trying to raise capital. Chatting with friends over the dinner table about a real estate deal is one thing, but advertising to the public in mass may be considered a "public offering". Before soliciting money from strangers, review your marketing, paperwork, and solicitation strategies with a local attorney well versed in this area of law. You may be able to get away with a good set of written disclosures if you solicit money on a limited basis, but it's better to be safe than sorry.

Independent contractor liability. The IRS and your state department of labor are on the lookout for employers who don't collect and pay withholding taxes, unemployment, and workers' compensation insurance. If you have employees that are "off the books," you're looking for trouble. If you get caught, you'll have to pay withholding taxes and as much as a 25 percent penalty. Intentionally failing to file W-2 forms will subject you to a $100 fine per form.

If you hire people to do contract work for you on a per-diem basis, the IRS may consider them employees. If any workers fail to pay their estimated taxes, you may still be liable for withholding.

To protect yourself, you should:

- Hire only contract workers who own their own corporation or get the business card and letterhead of any unincorporated contractors you may use so you can prove these workers aren't your employees.
- Require proof of insurance (liability, unemployment, and workers' compensation) in writing.
- Get written contracts or estimates on workers' letterhead that states they'll work their own hours and that you don't have direct supervision over the details of the work. (Refer to the sample independent contractor agreement in Appendix 7.)
- Have letters of reference from other people for whom the contractors worked to show that the contractors didn't work solely for you. Keep these in your files.
- File IRS Form 1099 for every unincorporated worker to whom you pay more than $600 per year.

In addition to possible tax implications, an independent contractor can create liability for you if a court determines the contractor is your employee. For example, if your independent contractor is negligent and injures another person, the injured party can sue you directly. If facts show that you exercised enough control over your contractor, a court may rule that this contractor is your employee for liability purposes. As you may know, an employer is "vicariously liable" for the acts of his or her employees—the employer is liable as a matter of law without proof of fault on the part of the employer. Make certain you follow these guidelines when hiring contractors and pay particular attention to the issue of control.

Finally, under your state's law be aware which duties are considered inherently dangerous, such as providing adequate security for tenants in a multiunit building. These duties can't be delegated to an independent contractor without liability on your part, regardless of whether the person you hire is considered an independent contractor or an employee.

Insurance—Your First Line of Defense

We suggest you insure each property you buy with plenty of liability coverage. Most investors don't specifically ask for liability coverage so they get a standard policy that may have adequate replacement coverage but minimal liability coverage. We recommend you get $1,000,000 in liability coverage for each property, even if it's a cheap property. Investors often fall into the trap of thinking, "Gee, it's just a cheap little condo," when, in fact, an injury can result in the same liability as an expensive property.

You may even consider a "builder's risk" policy if you do a lot of rehab projects. If you're concerned about cost, get insurance with a large liability portion and a high deductible. If you carry your property liability, personal residence, and business insurance with a single carrier, they will offer you an umbrella policy for several million dollars of additional coverage at a reasonable price. Be aware that certain claims—such as breach of contract, discrimination, and misrepresentation—aren't covered by insurance. In fact, most insurance won't cover any intentional act. Therefore, while having insurance is a good thing, it's only your first line of defense to lawsuits.

Corporate Entities—Your Second Line of Defense

You can know the laws and carry lots of insurance, but if you do enough business, you'll end up with a lawsuit that won't be covered by insurance. Setting up a corporation or LLC creates a barrier of protection from liability.

Avoid Being a Sole Proprietor

Most people starting their own businesses do so as sole proprietors. This means they are doing business as individuals or under fictitious "Doing Business As" (DBA) names. This scenario offers absolutely no liability protection. If your business gets sued, all your personal assets are at risk as a sole proprietor—your home, savings accounts, cars, and more. If you're the buyer or seller on a real estate contract, you (not your fictitious DBA) will be sued in the case of a breach of contract. If you sign a warranty deed as seller and any problems with title arise, you can be sued personally for breach of warranty, even if you paid for title insurance. If workers are injured on your property while you're rehabbing it, say hello to their lawyer. The fact is, there are dozens of scenarios that can lead to liability, and you're fully exposed when you conduct a real estate investment business in your own name.

The best way to protect yourself is to avoid getting sued personally—that is, form a legal entity to wedge between yourself and the liabilities that your business creates.

Set Up a Corporation or LLC

For less than $100 in most states, you can form a corporation or limited liability company (LLC) to do your business or trade. If properly maintained, a corporation or LLC will shield your personal assets if your business gets sued or goes bankrupt. A corporation can also provide you with some tax benefits, if used properly. Furthermore, a corporation or LLC gives you a more professional look when dealing with people in business. A corporation can be formed with a single owner, as can an LLC.

Some people may think that incorporating your business to limit your financial exposure is somehow unethical. Others think lawsuits are the equivalent of legal extortion. How you want to limit your liability is a call you'll have to make, but if you do incorporate your business, you'll have greater protection.

Bill's Advice: Know the Difference Between an LLC and a Corporation

Both a corporation and an LLC are formed under state law by filing papers with your state department of corporations or secretary of state. Both limit the liability of their owners, but these entities are taxed differently. You should discuss appropriate tax issues with your CPA or tax advisor before proceeding. For example, a C corporation, if used properly, can save you tens of thousands of dollars in taxes if you know how to use it. Most people believe a C corporation is bad because of double taxation. While this is true, an S corporation or LLC isn't necessarily better than a C corporation. For example, a C corporation can give you the ability to deduct 100 percent of your medical expenses and medical insurance through your company. You may also save thousands of dollars in federal income taxes if you learn how to "split" your income between your corporation and your personal return or other entities.

For more information on C corporations and how they can work for you, you can order "How to Create a Bulletproof Corporation" program from www.legalwiz.com.

Gary's Advice: Another Benefit of Corporations and LLCs

There's a Catch-22 when starting out as a real estate investor. If you go to the bank for financing, the lender will require that you have two years of real estate investing experience. How do you get a loan to begin investing if you don't have investing experience? One of the first items of business is to set up a corporation or LLC that's registered with your state. After two years, lenders will recognize that you've been in business the required minimum time.

Doing Business with Partners

When it comes to liability, doing business with a partner can be even worse than doing business as a sole proprietor. A partnership is formed when two or more people decide to do business together for profit. It doesn't require a formal partnership agreement or filing of any official documents, although it's often formed that way. Moreover, you can create a partnership even if you didn't intend to! (We explain this in a following section.)

Here's the problem with partnerships: If your partner does something foolish, you're liable. If you allow your partner to commit the partnership to a contract, the partnership and its partners can be held liable for that debt. If your partner slanders someone, commits a negligent act, or incurs a debt on behalf of the partnership, you're on the hook—even if your partner files for bankruptcy. This is the doctrine of "joint and several liability." Regardless of the percentage of fault between you and your partners, a judgment by a creditor for any tortious acts is 100 percent collectible from any one of the partners. Joint and several liability can be particularly disastrous if you're the silent partner with all the money.

Another problem is the accidental partnership. Here's an example: Harry finds a good business deal. He needs capital so he approaches Fred. Fred agrees to invest with Harry as the silent partner. Harry deals with the public, often referring to his "partner" Fred. Fred and Harry do business, make money, and part ways. A month later, Harry gets into financial trouble. Creditors come knocking on his door, but he has no money to pay them, so these creditors come after his "partner" Fred. Is Fred liable? In some cases, the answer is yes if the public thought Harry and Fred were partners and Fred did nothing to stop Harry from presenting them as partners.

If you only want to do a one-shot deal with a partner, consider drafting a joint venture agreement. (Refer to the sample joint venture agreement in Appendix 8.) Basically, a joint venture is a partnership for a specific purpose. If you intend to do business with partners for the long term, consider forming a corporation or limited liability company.

Release Yourself from Liability

Legal disputes can often lead to lawsuits; smart investors stay out of court and away from expensive, risky lawsuits. However, most people forget one simple step that's crucial to the process of settling a dispute: a written release of liability. Omitting this simple step could result in a future lawsuit against you even if you settled the claim.

Consider an investor who settles with a tenant who was delinquent on his rent: the owner accepts the keys, waives the tenant's back rent, and allows him to move out quietly. Nevertheless, the tenant can come back and sue the owner at some point in the future, claiming damage to his furniture because of a leaky pipe.

In another example, an investor accepts an earnest money deposit on a real estate contract. However, the closing never happens and the investor keeps the earnest money. Believe it or not, the investor can be sued for breach of contract.

The secret to avoiding future liability on transactions such as these is shockingly simple: Get a written release of liability. This release, also known as a *general release*, is a simple document by which someone agrees to release someone else from all liability. A properly drafted release prevents the signor of the document (the releaser) from bringing any claims against you in the future for any claims before signing the release.

Keep this in mind: If you have a dispute with another party that is eventually settled, it's imperative that you have the other party sign a general release form before giving any money or consideration.

While we're on the topic of consideration, you must actually give a consideration for the release to make it legally binding. In other words, you can't just ask someone to sign a release with nothing in return. A promise by you to waive your own legal rights against the releasor may be insufficient consideration. Even if you don't think the other party deserves it, giving someone a few hundred bucks may be a good idea to have a sufficient release. (Refer to the sample General Release form in Appendix 9.)

Get Educated on Tax Issues

The foolish investor waits until April 15 to file his or her taxes, and then hands a shoebox full of receipts to the accountant. Be sure to plan for your taxes at the beginning of the tax year and consult with your tax advisors throughout the year. People who say the tax system isn't fair are just ignorant of the rules. Taxes will eat up a large percentage of your income over your lifetime so learn how to make the rules work for you!

Basic Taxation Rules

You must become schooled in the basic rules of federal taxation as they apply to real estate. The biggest expense you'll pay in your life is taxes. We suggest you learn how to reduce your taxes, which is the easiest way to have more profit in your business.

Take time to learn the difference between capital gains and ordinary gains. Ordinary income is taxed at ordinary rates, which is the same rate as wages earned from an employer. This can prove to be unfortunate for those who work extra hours and get taxed on their wages. The system is set up to penalize wages and reward investments. If you buy an investment property and hold it for 12 months or more, this is considered a long-term capital asset. When you sell the property then this long-term capital asset results in a long-term capital gain. The long-term capital gains tax rate as of January 2007 maxes out at 15 percent, depending on your income. This rate is significantly lower than regular personal income tax rates, which can be as high as 35 percent.

Learn how to use depreciation to your advantage. If you hold a property as a rental, you can deduct mortgage interest and property tax payments as well as other operating expenses. You can also take depreciation for the structures; in fact, you're required to do so under IRS rules. For example, if a property is valued at $150,000 and the land is valued at $50,000, you would depreciate the $100,000 structure over 27.5 years according to the federal income tax rules. The annual depreciation deduction for a $100,000 structure according to the IRS schedules is about $3,600. In this example, you can have $3,600 a year in positive cash flow without owing any taxes on this income. If you have less than $3,600 in income from this property,

Flipping Properties Doesn't Incur Tax Penalties

Many people wrongly assume that flipping properties causes an investor to incur a tax penalty or other negative tax consequences. This assessment isn't completely accurate. A flip generally means the property is bought and sold within 12 months or less, which means the property is taxed as an ordinary gain (same rate as personal income) versus a long-term capital gain (maximum 15 percent). In other words, the federal income tax rates on a flip are the same as your ordinary income tax rates you pay on income from wages.

you'll end up a "loss," at least on paper. You can use this loss to "wash" other income you have as long as you meet certain rules. For example, if you make $100,000 a year from your business or job, a loss from your real estate activities will reduce your taxable income so you end up paying fewer taxes on that income when your taxes are due the following year.

To be able to take a loss on your taxes from rental properties, the first rule you must meet is "active participation." That is, you must show you're actively involved in managing the property, which usually isn't hard to do when you're showing properties to tenants.

The second rule is that your gross income doesn't exceed $100,000 for the particular tax year in which you're trying to take the loss. If you meet these two rules, you can deduct up to $25,000 in losses. If you're considered a real estate professional, you're not limited by the $25,000 loss cap. Therefore, if you begin investing full time, it'll be easy to meet this rule—as long as you can show you work the requisite number of hours (750 a year) and it's more than 50 percent of what you do with your work time.

If you sold a rental property and took depreciation, the depreciation is "recaptured" at sale, resulting in a gain. The depreciation recapture is taxed at 25 percent. This reflects federal taxes only; don't forget about state income taxes!

Some states charge additional gains tax on the profit, giving a lower rate for long-term investments. Most states charge a documentary transfer tax based on purchase price, but this is the equivalent of a sales tax and is generally paid by the buyer.

Our Advice: Learn the Rules and Maximize Them in Your Favor

Because the rules are somewhat complex, take time to discuss them with your tax advisors at the beginning of each tax year. That way, you can plan to maximize these rules in your favor. Remember, *it's up to you to learn the rules*. No one will do it for you.

Installment Sale

An installment sale is when the seller accepts any part of the sales price after the closing date. For federal income tax purposes, the definition is modified slightly—*it's when the seller gets any part of the sales price in the tax year after the sale*. In this case, the seller only gets taxed to the extent that principal is received in the year that it's reported. Thus, if you sell on an installment basis, you can defer paying gains until later tax years while still enjoying a good return on your investment. However, the interest payments you receive are taxable in the year you receive them. (Installment sales are discussed in more detail in IRS publication 537. You'll find content from this publication in Appendix 10.)

The 1031 Exchange

Under Section 1031 of the Internal Revenue Code, you can defer paying taxes on the sale of real estate by doing a "like-kind" exchange.

The 1031 exchange allows you to "park" the proceeds of a sale of property with a qualified intermediary, then roll the money into another property or properties without paying any capital gains tax. The tax basis in the property you sold (called the *relinquished property*) is rolled into the new property (called the *replacement property*). You have 45 days from the sale of the relinquished property to identify your replacement properties, then a total of 180 days to close the transaction. The rules are stringent and technical. We strongly advise you to use a professional company to accomplish this task.

Bill's Advice: Carefully Select Your Intermediary

The 1031 process involves parking your sales proceeds with a company that is not related to you, called an "intermediary." Obviously, if you are not in control of this company (by law, you really can't be), it should be a reliable operation with sufficient backing.

Make sure your intermediary is bonded and uses segregated accounts. Many investors have learned this lesson the hard way—after their intermediary went out of business, taking all the money with them. Furthermore, ask your intermediary if he or she will pay you interest during the period between the relinquished property sale and the replacement property closing.

The Real Estate Dealer

A flipper is defined as someone who buys properties with the intent of immediately reselling them. The IRS uses a similar definition for a real estate dealer. If you're actively buying and selling real estate on a regular basis, you may be considered a dealer in real estate properties. On the other hand, if you're an investor, you buy with the intent of holding for "productive use" (for example, rental income or appreciation). The Internal Revenue Code doesn't have a magic formula to determine who's an investor and who's a dealer. However, the IRS will balance a number of factors to determine this. These factors include:

- The purpose for which the property was purchased
- How long the property was held
- The number of sales by the taxpayer in that year
- The amount of income from sales compared to the taxpayer's other income
- How many deals the taxpayer made in that year
- The amount of gain realized from the sale

If the IRS pegs you as a dealer, then you can't use the installment sales method. The installment sales will be disallowed and the entire paper profits you report count as ordinary income in the year of sale. Furthermore, the sale of property will be subject to self-employment tax, which is currently 15.3 percent. If the IRS recharacterizes this income several years after the transaction, you may also be subject to additional interest and possibly a penalty. Again, we strongly recommend that you work closely with a tax advisor, preferably someone with expertise in real estate transactions.

Bill's Advice: Avoid Schedule C

If you do business as an unincorporated sole proprietor, you report your income and expenses on Schedule C of your federal personal income tax return. However, we don't recommend that you do real estate business on a Schedule C as a sole proprietor because your liability is unlimited, you're subject to self-employment tax on earnings, and your chances of being audited as a small business are higher than if you're incorporated.

As we discussed previously, consider forming a corporation or LLC. Find a good tax accountant knowledgeable in real estate transactions to be a key player on your team. When choosing an accountant, make sure he or she serves many real estate clients and, ideally, owns investment real estate too.

The Death Tax

You spend a lifetime acquiring property to enjoy it and die wealthy, passing your estate on to your heirs. There's only one problem—more taxes! The "death tax" is one of the most onerous and expensive taxes you'll pay during your lifetime (well, not exactly, because it's paid on your death). While some of your estate may be exempt (up to $2,000,000 as of 2007), as an investor you can quickly amass several million dollars in your estate from appreciation. The tax rates for estates are almost 50 percent, which can be staggering for heirs if there's no cash in the estate to pay the tax. Often, heirs must liquidate properties from estates to raise money for estate tax—a shame if it's your estate. (However, this can be a source of bargains, if you're looking for one as an investor!)

Consider adding a good estate-planning attorney to your investing team. No one knows when his or her "number will be up" so the earlier you plan, the better. In addition, make sure your heirs are aware of what you have and how everything runs. A sudden tragedy that results in your demise or severe disability could impose a huge burden on your family if they have no idea how to manage your real estate empire. Make sure they know what to do!

Bill's Advice: Another Way to Keep More of What You Earn

Consider forming a family LLC or family limited partnership as an estate-planning device. Simply owning rental property in one of these entities can reduce the valuation of your estate by as much as 25 percent, potentially saving hundreds of thousands of dollars in estate tax. For more information on this topic, read *Wealth Protection Secrets of a Millionaire Real Estate Investor* by Bill Bronchick (Kaplan Publishing 2003).

Good Records

It's important to maintain good records for your property dealings. Plan ahead and document everything in case you're ever audited. In addition, many businesses fail due to poor accounting practices, so keeping your books up to date will help you succeed.

An off-the-shelf accounting program such as QuickBooks® is good for this, particularly because of the ability to attribute expenses to specific properties. The key to keeping good records is to start by setting up simple procedures. A good CPA or bookkeeper can help you set up your accounting so your records are clean and follow generally accepted accounting principles. You can also purchase real estate software packages and models that work with QuickBooks such as the *KISS Guide to Real Estate Accounting* available from Legalwiz Publications (**www.legalwiz.com/KISS**).

Key Points to Remember

Defensive investors must master how to keep what they make while avoiding lawsuits, liability, and excessive taxes. As with any small business owner, you want to avoid these pitfalls to preserve wealth.

The most important concepts addressed in this chapter are:

- You must learn as much as possible about the tax and legal issues involved in real estate investing.
- Consider forming an LLC or corporation to reduce your liability.
- Know the tax laws, especially estate tax, and plan for these tax issues with a qualified tax advisor.

CHAPTER

9

Avoid Common Investment Scams

"Be wary of the man who urges an action in which he himself incurs no risk."

—Joaquin Setanti

As noted in Chapter 1, many people seek the easiest way to riches. Unfortunately, many promoters have figured out ways to appeal to this weakness, resulting in a new crop of real estate scams that you must avoid. Avoiding common scams is the ninth principle of defensive investing.

The "Too Good to Be True" Deal

Our email inboxes are filled every day with special offers that read like this:

- "New condos for only $5,000 down"
- "Buy 25 percent below appraisal"
- "$50,000 cash back at closing"

These deals sound too good to be true, don't they? That's because most of them aren't what they sound like. You have to read the fine print to understand what they're truly selling. Keep reading to learn more about the most common "too good to be true" deals.

Little or Nothing Down

A deal that requires a minimum cash investment sounds great because it promises high leverage and high return on the cash you've invested, but understand that just because you can buy with little or no money down, it doesn't qualify as a good deal. Many promoters of marginal deals know that novice investors are lured by "no money down" deals and play to the relative ignorance of these investors. As discussed in Chapter 4, consider the loan-to-purchase price not just loan-to-value. So if you can buy a property with only $5,000 down and get it at a price well below market, then this may be a good deal if it otherwise meets our CLEAR formula described in Chapter 4.

Also, keep in mind that a $5,000 investment in real estate isn't the same as a $5,000 investment in a security. If you sign your name to a $200,000 loan, you can lose a lot more than just your $5,000!

The Car Dealer Pitch

One of the most common pitches that car dealers use is the "only $X/month" hook. It requires you to study the fine print in order to discover the down payment and actual purchase price. Most people who buy cars don't negotiate the price of the vehicle; they negotiate how much they'll put down and how much they'll pay per month. You need to check all the math to see what makes sense when you buy a car. Likewise, you need to do all the math on your real estate investments. Don't just consider your down payment and monthly payment amounts.

Cash Back at Closing

Wow, getting cash back at closing is even better than putting nothing down! These promoters would have you think that you can actually buy real estate without putting any money down and walk away with more money in your pocket when you purchase the property. How can this be possible?

Essentially, to get cash back at closing, you're borrowing more than the purchase price. If the purchase price is 70 percent of value and you borrow 80 percent of value, you can walk out of the closing with cash. Of course, the difference isn't profit—it's borrowed money.

Getting cash out at closing isn't necessarily a bad idea because you can put that cash into the bank and save it for a rainy day. To the credit of many real estate promoters, they do pitch the deal this way. Unfortunately, most investors aren't disciplined enough to save the cash and they end up spending it like income. Moreover, here's the caveat: In many cases, the low purchase price isn't really as low as the investor first thought because it's based on appraised value not real market value. As discussed in Chapter 3, appraised value isn't necessarily what a property is really worth.

Be Mindful of How You Get Cash Back at Closing

Any money that gets distributed through closing must be disclosed on the HUD-1 settlement statement. Remember that when you sign your name on the bottom of that HUD-1, you're making a statement of fact that, if untrue, can result in criminal prosecution.

The "Wholesale" Deal

As we mentioned earlier, investors should look for wholesale deals. The problem is, most novice investors don't know what a wholesale deal is and a number of operators out there scam new investors with what they represent as wholesale deals.

Here's a common scam perpetrated on novice investors: Scam-Investor makes a deal with a builder on 30 new homes that are "appraised" at $215,000, but really worth only $200,000. Scam-Investor can buy them "wholesale" from the builder for $185,000.

Scam-Investor approaches Newbie-Investor with this deal: "You can buy a wholesale home with no money down." Scam-Investor buys the home from the builder at $185,000 and flips it to Newbie-Investor for $195,000. Using a charade of fake down payments and passing money back to the buyer under the table (which is loan fraud), Newbie-Investor ends up with a property worth $200,000 and a "no-money-down" loan for $195,000. Scam-Investor walks away with $10,000, and Newbie-Investor has a house with almost no equity,—although he thinks he has $20,000 in equity.

Newbie-Investor can't rent his house for breakeven cash flow so he tries to sell it for $215,000. When it doesn't sell after being on the market for several months, he finally realizes that the property is only worth $200,000. Newbie-Investor can't afford the payments so he dumps the property for $180,000. The bottom line: He lost $15,000 on the deal.

This type of activity is profitable for fast-talking scam artists who prey on uneducated novice investors. Keep in mind the old maxim: "buyer beware." There's no shortcut to getting rich in real estate, and there's no substitute for hard work, education, and doing your homework. If you trust others to find wholesale deals for you without knowing what "wholesale" really is, you'll get lousy deals. Always do your own independent research and due diligence on a real estate investment.

Letting Others "Borrow" Your Credit

Partnerships can work out if one person puts up his or her credit to get financing and the other puts up cash, labor, or finds the good deals. If you're the person putting up the credit, be careful. Your credit is extremely important. It can be ruined if you're not in control of the deal.

If you put up your credit on a deal, don't let someone else make your payments. Instead, make the payments yourself or set up an online payment system with your bank to make sure you can verify the payments are being made. Just being a few months late can result in a severe hit to your credit score, so make sure you have full access to your mortgage accounts to make sure they are being paid on time.

Real-life Story: Credit Is More Important Than Cash

Dave, an experienced investor, approached Bruce, a novice investor. Dave asked Bruce to put up his credit to partner on a rental duplex. Dave put up over $20,000 in cash and managed the property; Bruce was the "silent" partner. A few months later, Bruce received a call from the mortgage company notifying him that the mortgage was several payments in default and about to go into foreclosure. Dave had disappeared—with all the rent payments. He had never made a single mortgage payment. Luckily, Bruce's name was on the deed so he was able to sell the property quickly for the balance of the mortgage. Dave had walked away from his $20,000 down payment, but Bruce's credit was damaged for years. The lesson here: Credit is more important than cash because cash can be recouped a lot faster.

Mortgage Elimination Scam

You've probably seen this type of claim: "Legally eliminate your mortgage!" Can this possibly be true? No, not quite.

The claim is that you can legally eliminate your mortgage based on an accounting loophole that goes something like this: "If the lender who funded your loan used borrowed money to fund your loan, then the loan isn't valid. In addition, because the loan isn't valid, the security (mortgage or deed of trust) isn't valid either. All you do is simply march into court and ask a judge to void your mortgage lien and you don't have to pay it back." For a fee of just $2,500 to these promoters, they'll show you how to do it!

A common sense approach would tell you that the entire premise of this argument is patently absurd. Think about it—most lenders use borrowed money to fund loans. That's the nature of the business. If these "mortgage elimination" promoters were correct, then millions of mortgages would be void. Perhaps our entire economy would collapse.

The mortgage elimination argument reminds us of the tax protestor scam where people claim they don't owe income tax because the U.S. government doesn't have the constitutional authority to tax them. On a philosophical level, some people appreciate discussions about how the dollar isn't backed by gold, the government doesn't have the constitutional right to tax Americans, and the like. But, no sensible person would recommend someone ruin their life by trying to make these arguements in court.

In the end, the tax protestors always lose in court, pay large fines, and sometimes go to prison. Similarly, the government is going after the promoters of the mortgage elimination scam. Obviously, it's critical that you avoid these scams—and their promoters.

Syndication Scams

Many investors get sucked into investing resources that will be pooled with other investors in a syndication project. Syndication is a means of raising money from various private sources to fund large real estate projects. In many ways, it is much like investing in securities, such as buying shares of a publication corporation. Real estate investment trusts (REITs) have been around for years, pooling capital to buy large commercial projects such as shopping centers, large apartments, and office buildings.

There are basically two kinds of REITs—public and private. Shares or units in public REITs are traded on the stock exchanges and their values fluctuate daily just like any other stock. The market price is not necessarily based on the actual values of the properties the REITs own, but rather the market for the REIT shares. A publicly traded REIT is verifiable because the information is public and highly regulated by the government. It is also liquid, because it can be sold like shares of stock.

A private REIT is offered directly to individuals and can have more lucrative potential than a public REIT. Although subject to regulatory scrutiny set up by the Securities and Exchange Commission, a small private REIT can often pass under the radar of regulators, opening it up for potential abuse to misrepresentations, unsuitable investments, mismanagement, and downright fraud.

Our Advice: Avoid Affinity Marketing Scams

A common scheme to watch out for is "affinity marketing"—that is, people who market to you because they claim they are just like you. Scam artists often use their affinity to you (such as religion, race, nationality, age) to gain your trust so your guard goes down. Imagine someone from your own church trying to scam you!

While you should do business with people you know and trust, you can't necessarily trust someone just because they are like you, particularly if they keep reminding you of that fact!

Join the "Club"

A real estate investment club can be a great place to meet other investors, get good advice, and find good deals, but not all real estate clubs are alike. Real estate associations can offer many different things such as education and networking as well as the opportunity to invest in deals. Be careful about joining clubs that primarily offer "inside access" to real estate deals promoted by the club itself.

Just because you meet people at a real estate club meeting doesn't necessarily mean they behave ethically. First, make sure they are members of the group. Many group meetings and seminars attract scam artists who hang around, pass out flyers in the hallway or parking lot, and try to solicit business from the group. Second, ask around about them. Ask for references from other people with whom they've done business. Run their names by the group leaders to see if they know them.

No matter what, it's your money and credit on the line, so do thorough due diligence on any real estate transaction.

Bill's Advice: Beware of "Insider Deals"

Beware of the promise of special "insider deals" from any a real estate club or promoter. Any organization that promotes a pipeline of wholesale deals with membership in their club is suspect, to say the least. Finding true wholesale deals takes hard work, discipline, and a little luck. Belonging to a network of other investors is worthwhile because it can give you access to individual people who may have particular deals here and there.

However, the vast majority of these investors are novices who wouldn't know a good deal if it fell on their lap. This isn't to say you won't find good deals by joining a real estate club, but you'll have to sift through a lot of mediocre ones first. The deals should come from the individual members of the club, not the promoters of the club itself who promise you "special wholesale pricing" if you're a member. Remember, don't ever trust a stranger's opinion on the value of an investment—always do your own due diligence and check your own comps.

Gary's Advice: How to Identify a Good Contact

To identify credible people to work with, make sure you check out the vendors who offer loans, consulting, or opportunities to invest in deals. Go to the club meetings for several months, determine which vendors you may want to use, and see who's there most of the time. Ask them how many deals they've done and whom would they use as a referral source. If you ask enough people and the same person's name comes up, then this vendor may be a good contact.

Learn What's Not a Scam

As important as it is to learn common scams and how to avoid them, it's equally important to learn what is *not* a scam.

Often, investors are told by uneducated real estate brokers, loan officers, escrow agents, and, yes, even lawyers that a particular investing technique is illegal when in fact it is not. "Flipping is illegal" is a common urban myth that gets passed around the community until everyone takes it as faith.

You should make it a point when someone says "that's illegal" to retort "what law is being broken?" More often than not, you'll get a blank stare as a response. Most people who work in the real estate field accept things as gospel from their bosses or others who are more experienced. If you are told something is illegal or a scam, do some research and find out the truth. Question authority and get more than one opinion on the matter.

Bill's Advice: Know the Difference Between Law and Custom

It's common to confuse what is the law and what is customary practice. For example, I know many title companies that will not close a deal if the buyer is using a power of attorney to sign for the seller. Is any law being broken by a buyer signing on both sides of a transaction at closing? Of course not, but I can understand why a title company won't allow it as a matter of practice because a seller can come back later and claim not to have authorized the transaction.

Likewise, there may be dozens of customary practices that are done that way for one reason or another, even though there's no law requiring it. Know the difference so you can, when required, break the custom and get people to do things a different way when it works to your advantage.

Don't Involve Yourself in a Scam

There are hundreds if not thousands of laws that come into play when investing in real estate at both the state and federal level. This is particularly true when it comes to borrowing money. Even if they don't realize it, many people are probably breaking a number of laws in their business on a regular basis. Does this mean they are going to jail? Probably not, because more than likely their violation is not substantial, willful, or significant enough to catch the attention of a prosecutor, and, in many cases, the "powers that be" aren't likely to go after someone who is innocently walking over a few rules without bad intentions. If you do and you're caught, you're likely to get off with a warning.

Nevertheless, just because you aren't likely to get caught doesn't mean you should operate with complete disregard for the rules. More than once, you'll be asked to bend a rule, do things "under the table," or stretch the truth. Everyone walks near that fine line at one time or another in his or her own business. People often justify such behavior by saying "everyone does it" or "who's going to find out?" People often lie on a loan application, get away with it, then do it again, particularly when it comes to their income. The problem is that all it takes is once to get caught, and you'll face criminal prosecution. Remember, just because you are "stating" your income on a loan without submitting proof, this does not mean you have carte blanche to lie. A lender can check your tax returns after closing to see if the income you have stated on your application is consistent with your tax returns. If a seller, a buyer, a mortgage broker, or real estate broker asks you to lie, "fudge," or conceal substantial facts on a transaction, walk away from the deal.

Avoid doing business with people who operate in this fashion. Even if you play a minor part in a scam, you can be unwittingly dragged into a big mess and have your name ruined by a criminal or civil investigation. Long-term survival in real estate or any other field means keeping your business free from practices, associations, or ties with people who disregard the rules and engage in suspect practices.

Key Points to Remember

Defensive investors should avoid scams and borderline investments that sound like "easy money." There's no shortcut to success and anyone who tries to sell you one is suspect. When it comes to investing in other people's projects, it's "buyer beware."

The most important concepts addressed in this chapter are:

- If a deal sounds too good to be true, it probably is.
- Do your own research on market value... don't trust an appraisal.
- A real estate investor group can be a good or bad resource for deals, depending on the group and how you use it.
- Always do your own due diligence.
- Avoid bending the rules or associating with those who do.

CHAPTER

10

Treat Real Estate Investing as a Business

"Success in business requires training and discipline and hard work. But if you're not frightened by these things, the opportunities are just as great today as they ever were."

—David Rockefeller

Many real estate gurus make it sound as though getting rich is easy and can be done in your "spare time." (When's the last time you met someone with spare time?) Investing in real estate isn't like traditional investments in which you put up money and wait for something to happen. It's a hands-on endeavor that should be run more like a business than an investment, with proper planning and time management. Of course, this is often easier for those who are able to devote themselves to investing on a full-time basis. For the part-time investor, it may be tougher to get in the professional frame of mind while also juggling a full-time job. Our tenth principle is treating your investments as a business.

Being defensive means you must be different from the crowd, and the bulk of the real estate investing crowd takes their investing too casually. By treating your real estate investments as a business you plan things better, you think things out, and have a plan. Most people don't think about their investments beyond writing a check.

Should You Invest Full Time?

Obviously, devoting your energies to investing full time is an ideal way to gain valuable skills and experience in the shortest amount of time. Unfortunately, most people don't have the time or financial cushion necessary to invest on a full-time basis at the start.

At some point, entering the real estate investing business on a full-time basis offers several advantages over part-time investing. For one thing, as a full-time investor, you'll have more time and energy to focus on learning the necessary skills and techniques, which can often be challenging and time consuming to master.

In addition, success in real estate requires flexibility. You may quickly discover that you must be prepared to take calls at any time of the day or night. When you can offer more accessibility and availability to buyers and sellers, this increases your chances of a successful career.

As a full-time investor, you'll have the freedom to work your own hours. You can devote as many (or as few) hours to the business as you wish and can arrange your schedule to accommodate the needs of buyers or sellers.

In addition, some people simply like the idea of being self-employed. For those who hate having to answer to a boss, enjoy their independence, and want to have sole responsibility for their success, full-time investing may be a good choice. It's important to realize the downsides to self-employment, though. These include dealing with your own taxes, paying for your own health insurance, and not having any sick days or paid vacations.

By contrast, those who initially begin investing while maintaining a full-time "day job" will have less financial pressure because they'll have the security of a steady, reliable income. As a part-time investor, you enjoy the benefits that your employer provides, such as paid medical insurance or a retirement plan (although real estate can certainly be viewed as a retirement plan for those who continue to work at their profession for regular income).

Act Professionally and Look the Part

Whether you choose to invest in real estate as a part-time or full-time business, make it a priority to have a professional appearance. If you expect other people to take you seriously, you must first take yourself seriously. Get in the habit of establishing a strict schedule with regular working hours and be disciplined about this. You don't want to give people the impression that real estate investing is something you take lightly.

Many investors find that it's easier to get in the proper mindset if they look the part. Never underestimate the powerful effect clothing has on one's attitude. Many people find that they automatically feel more capable and motivated simply by putting on business attire.

Tools of the Trade

Once you've attained the proper professional mindset, also invest in the necessary equipment and tools to run a professional business. Following is our list of basics. You may need to expand on this list, depending on the type of investing you'll do and how much you'll travel.

Set Up a Professional Office

To establish a proper working environment first set up an office that will meet your needs. Financial and practical concerns will play a major role in dictating what type and size of office you can realistically maintain.

For some investors, a home office might make the most sense—or it may be necessary due to budgetary limitations. This can be fine, provided you're able to view this as a "real" office, not just an extra family room. In addition, when meeting with sellers, buyers, brokers, tenants, partners, and contractors, having a professional place of business is essential. Some people prefer "branch offices" like Starbucks and Denny's, but we recommend meeting in a more professional atmosphere. Consider leasing an executive office where a receptionist answers your phone and you can rent conference rooms by the hour.

Business Cards Are a Must

You'll find it tough to be taken seriously if you don't have a supply of high-quality business cards. Homemade business cards won't suffice; avoid these if at all possible. Always carry an adequate supply of your cards, as the business world thrives on networking and you can never predict when you might make a valuable connection. Color business cards are surprisingly affordable, and you can use a two-sided card as a billboard for both buying and selling properties.

Office Essentials

When you first establish an office, start by acquiring all the important office essentials. This usually, at the least, entails a computer, printer, decent digital camera (to take pictures of properties of interest), cell phone, and reliable answering system. A fax machine is also essential, although services such as **www.efax.com** provide a dedicated local number to accept faxes and email them to your computer.

Take Advantage of High-Tech Tools

You must be accessible to clients, brokers, and colleagues at any time, no matter where they may be. This will require you to have a cell phone and a professional email address. Avoid free email addresses like Yahoo! or Hotmail because these look amateurish. Instead, get a domain address such as **you@yourcompany.com** (available from Yahoo Small Business at **http://smallbusiness.yahoo.com/email**). If you plan to conduct a lot of business on the road, a laptop or PDA may be necessary to access property information Web sites. A navigation system will save you countless hours driving around looking for properties. If your car doesn't come with one, find the latest and greatest recommendations at **www.cnet.com**. Many wireless phone providers offer phones with built-in navigation systems.

Set Up a Reliable Message Retrieval System

One of your first investments should be a reliable voicemail system. You'll sorely regret missing out on good opportunities simply because you didn't have an efficient way to get your messages. You may even consider enlisting the help of an answering service (e.g., **www.patlive.com**) to field calls when you're unavailable. In addition, sophisticated, Web-based "follow me" forwarding numbers can be great if you're out and about a lot during the day (e.g., **www.ringcentral.com** or **www.virtualpbx.com**).

Bill's Advice: Don't Go Hog Wild!

Although it can be exciting to buy new electronic gadgets and other toys necessary to establish a business, remember that most businesses don't become profitable for at least a year or two after they launch. If you're a new investor, be fully prepared for the cash flow issues that come with real estate investing. For office furniture and equipment, consider leasing programs to conserve your cash.

Create a Web Site

Seriously consider having your own business Web site, even if it's simple and basic. In today's high-tech world, people automatically go online to research professionals' credentials and backgrounds. After meeting an investor, many people will immediately search for his or her Web site to ascertain if they're dealing with a serious professional.

A Web site is an effective way to establish a professional identity. In fact, it's impossible today to maintain a successful career in the business world without having an online presence. Furthermore, your Web site can also be a smart way to update clients and colleagues about the types of properties you currently want to buy or sell. Many providers will allow you to create an impressive Web site quickly and easily, even if you have absolutely no programming skills.

Here are a few recommended sites that are easy and affordable:

- **www.inetusa.com**
- **www.investorpro.com**
- **www.invest-o-matic.com**

Assessing Your Strengths and Weaknesses

Before embarking into real estate investing, take time to assess your strengths and weaknesses. Be honest with yourself and improve on your weak points or hire help to cover the patchy spots. (More on this will be covered later in the chapter.)

Here's our top-three list of strengths and weaknesses to assess:

1. How much credit do you have?
2. How much cash do you have?
3. What types of investments align with your strengths?

Where Do You Stand on Credit?

In today's world of easy-to-access money, if you have a good credit score, you can get financing from almost any lender. Remember, "money makes the world go 'round." Before you start investing full time, get as many lines of credit as you can while you have a regular full-time job. Lenders love to lend money when you don't need it, but when you need money it gets more difficult to borrow.

We suggest getting lines of credit on your home and any rentals you may already own. Increase your credit line on your credit cards. Don't use these credit cards frivolously, but they may come in handy if you need to purchase a home and rely on your credit cards for making a down payment or repairs. Remember that if you have a good credit score (700 or better), it will decrease as you use your credit, so get your credit score as high as you can.

What hurts your credit? In addition to the obvious—making late payments—certain activities generally hurt your credit score. They include:

- Going over your credit limit on any credit line, or even exceeding 50 percent of your credit line at any given time.
- If you take a lavish vacation or make a large purchase, split the expenses between two or more cards.
- Applying for too much credit in a short period of time.
- Having too many revolving accounts; stay away from department store credit cards, even if they offer you a discount on your purchase for applying for the account.
- Engaging in too many unnecessary transactions requiring someone to run your credit report (e.g., cell phone accounts, department store credit cards, etc.).

A fast and easy way to improve your credit quickly is to have a friend or relative add you as an authorized user on his or her credit card. This will improve your credit for the shared used of the account. In addition, dispute or remove old accounts or particularly negative information with the credit bureaus and this may improve your credit score. Sign up for an account at **www.myfico.com** or **www.freecreditreport.com** and you can check your FICO score, monitor your credit on a regular basis, and learn how to improve your score.

Bill's Advice: Don't Trust the "System"

The system is that you wait for your creditors to send you a bill each month and you send them a check, assuming they get it and cash it. The fact is, mail gets lost and systems break down. What should you do?

Pull your own credit report and look up every account that you have. Make a list of every creditor, when your account cycle runs, and when each bill is due. Make a system in your physical or electronic calendar to pay the bills each month on time, allowing for the mail to be late. Take advantage of online systems that mortgage companies use so you can pay online and verify receipt, or mail your checks using a two-day Federal Express or UPS carrier so you have proof of receipt and a signature from your creditors. Always verify that your creditor cashed the check on time by checking your bank statements each month. For that matter, don't even wait that long; sign up for online banking and log on to your bank's system to verify that your check was cashed. Because having good credit is so important and can be damaged by late payments, it's imperative that you keep on top of your payments and don't trust the "system."

How Much Cash Can You Apply to Your Investing Business?

Most people don't have a few hundred thousand dollars to invest. If you want to be a serious investor, it may be time to sell some of your toys such as a sports car or boat. Many investors have used money from the sale of jewelry that helped finance their first rental and they now have enough money to buy any amount of jewelry they desire. If you get serious about investing, make the sacrifice and envision the future.

You may also consider borrowing against a retirement plan or liquidating it for cash. Although there may be taxable penalties for doing so, a good real estate deal may be a better investment in the long run. Again, make sure it's a good deal; you don't want to exchange your hard-earned savings for a "lesson learned."

Gary's Advice: Leveraging Money in Your IRA or SEP

If you have substantial cash in your IRA or SEP, you can use this money in creative ways to purchase properties directly without incurring a penalty. You must have a self-directed IRA using a custodian (as opposed to a 401(k) plan with your current employer). While you can't generally borrow from your own IRA without penalty, you can lend money to others for deals secured by real estate at much higher rates than you can get with most traditional investments.

Make sure you discuss the ramifications of IRA investing with a reputable source; there is much advice floating around the Internet that is incorrect or borderline. Try **www.trustec.com** and **www.theentrustgroup.com**.

Cash is King—But So Are Great Deals

One of the biggest mistakes novice investors make is to put all their cash into their first deal. Remember, having a cash reserve can be just as important, if not more important, than building cash flow on a deal. Your real estate business, like any business, must be cash rich. Instead of spending your money on your first deal, spend it on marketing to find motivated sellers. Keep in mind that $50,000 will go a lot further toward advertising to find great deals than it will as a down payment on one house or condo.

Remember, also, this rule of thumb: *Find good deals and the money will find you*. If you don't have cash or good credit, the deals you bring to the table are the best collateral for credit. If you place a great deal under contract with substantial equity, you'll have an easier time finding financing options. If you don't have good credit, you can go to another investor and use his or her credit to get a loan and share the profits. If the deal is marginal and no one will lend you money, you'll have a difficult time finding partners.

In some sense, having too much cash and credit encourages you to take on risky deals simply because you can. If you have to pitch a deal to a partner, this is the ultimate litmus test because a third party looking at the deal may see things less optimistically than you do. In fact, if no one will partner with you on the deal, it may be a sign that you shouldn't do the deal at all!

Focus on Types of Investments That Align with Your Strengths

Decide what to do as an investor and realize that you can't do it all. Do you want to be a short-term investor and rehab properties or do want to be a long-term investor? Have heart-to-heart talks with people who know you well. They could be your spouse or significant other, accountant, banker, and best friend. Ask them to be honest with you and openly discuss your strengths and weaknesses.

It's easy to believe you can do everything yourself, but remember, real estate investing is a business. If you're currently working at a full-time job, are you doing everything at this company? You need to know your strengths and hire the experts in areas where you're weak.

Owning your own business isn't for everyone. If you've always worked for someone else, being your own boss sounds attractive. In some respects, this isn't quite the truth. Being your own boss means being an accountant, bookkeeper, stock clerk, receptionist, and office manager all in one. You have to deal with tax returns, payroll, office supplies, customer service, bills, and all the other hassles that come with a business.

Does it sound like fun? We think it is—once you learn how to manage your time and run your business. Being the master of your own life and career is well worth the other hassles of dealing with your own business.

Setting Goals

There are thousands of books about how to set goals, yet few people actually do it. In fact, most people spend more time planning their vacations than the next fiscal year in their business. People avoid setting goals because they think it's a daunting task. Goal setting is actually a simple process using the four Ps: purpose, planning, prioritizing, and persistence.

Purpose

The real success behind goal setting is the why? Without a purpose, a passion, or dream, the money goals aren't enough to drive most people. Let's face it, unless you have a massive ego like one famous developer with a bad haircut, the idea of simply amassing houses isn't all that exciting. Real estate isn't particularly fun, but it's the life opportunities it provides that will drive you.

Instead of planning how many houses you want to own, think about what you want for your life and how you can make real estate investing do that for you. Maybe your goal is to retire by age 60 and be a fishing guide in Montana, or maybe you want to quit your job within three years. For some people, it's having enough income to send their kids to the best colleges and universities. With these purposes in mind, goal setting becomes much more exciting.

Planning

Once you know what you desire, then you need to figure out how much income, cash, or equity you need to get there. Work the numbers backwards and you'll determine how many houses you need to buy, keep, flip, or partner in a year.

Gary's Advice: Follow My Simple Formula to Become Wealthy

I often tell people that a simple way to get wealthy in real estate is to buy one solid house a year for ten years. At the end of ten years, you can have millions of dollars in real estate. Then, depending on how old you are, spend the next ten to 20 years paying off these properties. If you're older or more ambitious, buy two or three houses a year for five years and then focus on paying them off. When retirement comes, sell off the properties that don't work and keep the good rentals for residual income. If you need cash to pay your kids' college expenses or take a vacation around the world with your spouse, you can borrow against the increased equity. I've helped several people over the past 30 years become millionaires with this simple formula—and it will work for you.

Prioritizing

How you spend your time in pursuit of your goals is important in attaining those goals. You need to plan your month, your week, and your day carefully to make sure you're on track. If you only write down goals and don't track your progress, you'll end up like most people who make New Year's resolutions.

The practice of "chunking" or breaking down your big goals into mini-goals makes larger tasks seem less daunting. For example, if you want to buy a house in 90 days, you may need to make 50 offers to get a real quality deal. Before you make 50 offers, you may need to view 200 houses. Before you view 200 houses, you may need to make 1,000 phone calls to sellers, real estate brokers, and banks. This sounds daunting, but when you break it down, you only have to make about 11 calls per day. Are you up to the task?

Bill's Advice: Use Software to Help You Plan

A good computer program can help you plan your goals, your workweek, and your appointments. We recommend:

- Microsoft Outlook
- ACT!
- GoldMine
- FranklinCovey Plan Plus

All of these programs allow you to electronically plan your daily, weekly, monthly, and yearly goals, breaking them down into manageable parts that you can achieve. Most of them will also synchronize to a handheld device such as a PDA or smartphone.

Always weigh efficiency versus effectiveness. Decide which tasks produce the most results—results that lead to monetary success in your real estate business. Too many people spin their wheels all day, are exhausted, and realize they really didn't complete the important things. They're being efficient. They call back people just because they called , file papers, sort their mail, return e-mails, and so on. However, *effectiveness* is when you actually do very little, but you're doing the *right* things that make the difference. So focus on the effective tasks and delegate the efficiency tasks to employees or independent contractors.

Persistence

If you want to get wealthy, real estate investing is definitely a longevity game. It isn't glamorous and it isn't easy on a day-to-day basis when your tenants walk out, your loan is declined, a hot water heater explodes, a roof leaks, and anything that can go wrong does. However, if you keep your eyes on the big picture, you'll succeed. The only thing we can control is our attitude. If you have a good attitude and think long term, you'll succeed in this business.

Enlisting Your Team

If you're a novice, you have a lot to learn before engaging in real estate transactions. You'll need several players on your team who can give you some practical advice based on their experiences with other investors.

Real Estate Attorney

Finding a good attorney is difficult because most attorneys are not investors or aren't familiar with creative real estate transactions. Most attorneys give you just enough advice to keep them from getting sued, but not enough advice to show you how to make more money out of a deal.

A good real estate attorney advises you of the risks, suggests alternative ways of handling a transaction, and charges a reasonable fee. A bad real estate attorney either says nothing, points out problems without offering solutions, or systematically kills deals.

Ask other investors and real estate brokers in your area who they use for legal counsel. Make an appointment with these attorneys to speak with them in person. Get a feel for their experience and personalities. Having a good attorney on your side is worth his or her weight in gold.

Title or Escrow Company

A competent title or escrow company can make closings run smoothly for you. Avoid using big-name companies. Find a small, local company that caters to investors. Make sure they understand creative closings such as "flips." You can usually obtain a good recommendation on a title or escrow company from other investors when you join a real estate investment group. In some states, only attorneys perform closings, which can be a blessing or a nightmare, depending on the attorney's experience and personality type.

Tax Advisor

In our experience, most CPAs and accountants are rank amateurs regarding real estate transactions. Most firms hire clerical help during the tax season so less-experienced personnel might even prepare your return. Tax return preparation is the easy part of doing taxes; the difficult (and more important) part is good planning and using aggressive strategies. Voraciously read information on how to save money on taxes. We recommend the *Real Estate Investor's Tax Guide* by Vernon Hoven (4th ed., Kaplan Publishing 2005) and *Tax Secrets of Millionaire Real Estate Investors* by Richard T. Williamson (Kaplan Publishing 2004).

Good Contractor or Handyman

A capable all-around contractor/handyman is essential to your success, especially if you don't have extensive rehab knowledge. You can find contractors by looking in the services directory of your newspaper or online at **craigslist.org**. Interview several people to find someone who'll give you free estimates and knows how to cut corners in all the right places. Ask other local investors for their recommendations.

Keep in mind that a handyman or contractor must not only know how to fix things, but how to fix things within a budget. More often than not, you will have a difficult time finding a contractor who can do a cheaper job than a better job!

Mortgage Broker

Mortgage brokers are a dime a dozen so be careful to find one who is savvy and creative, and has experience working with investors. Here's the problem with most mortgage brokers: They offer new loan programs that are untested so by the time you get halfway through the loan process, the qualifications have changed or are different from what they first represented.

Gary's Advice:
Ask Questions about Mortgage Brokers' Loan Programs

Before you use mortgage brokers who promise you the sun and moon, at a minimum, ask these five questions about their loan programs:

1. How many investors have done this program?
2. Can I have names and numbers for references?

3. How long have you been in the mortgage business?
4. How long have you been dealing with the particular company offering the loan program?
5. Can you give me all the details of the program and qualifications in writing?

Partner and/or Mentor

The less experience you have, the more you need to have partners and mentors to work with on your deals. Every situation is unique and the more you can tap into other people's knowledge and experience, the fewer mistakes you'll make.

There's an old expression about partnerships that goes like this: *A partnership starts between a person with experience and a person with money; in the end, the person with the experience walks away with the money and the person with the money walks away with experience.* Forming a partnership with another party for long-term investing can be a risky move. Partnerships are inherently risky and have a high failure rate. Investors who enter into partnerships assume a lot of risk because they become responsible for all of the actions and mistakes of the partner. If the partner does something foolish—or worse, illegal—the investor can be held legally responsible.

However, it's fairly common for investors to have a temporary "partner"—meaning someone who is enlisted for help (generally, financial help) as part of an isolated deal involving a specific property. In this case, consider drafting a joint venture agreement. A joint venture is essentially a partnership created for one specific purpose or project.

If you start out as a part-time investor, you can probably find a partner to be involved in your projects. For rehabs, you can team up with a contractor or another investor to help with a property you find. Either way, you can look at your first projects as an apprenticeship that will allow you to "earn while you learn."

You can also look for a knowledgeable and trustworthy mentor. The investment business should be approached with integrity and most of the people who succeed do business in an ethical way. Don't be a leech for information. Respect other people's time and be willing to pay for it.

Hire Employees to Increase Your Effectiveness

As soon as you are financially able, seriously consider outsourcing tasks or hiring employees. At the very least, a part-time secretary or assistant is helpful to field calls, show properties, and handle the clerical duties that would occupy a considerable portion of your time. Hiring office staff involves a monetary investment. However, if you find good employees, they'll prove to be well worth the investment because they'll allow you the time to be more effective and productive.

By the same token, though, a bad employee can cause considerable harm to your business, professional image, and reputation. Diligently screen all potential employees. This is especially important for employees who'll have contact with your clients, business associates, or the general public. You don't want the person who answers your business phone to sound unprofessional—or, worse, to be rude or unhelpful to people who contact you.

Of course, it's also important to do thorough background checks on potential hires to avoid hiring an employee who has a criminal record or other blemishes in their background. Web sites such as **www.trak-1.com** can help you do credit and background checks, but make sure you get a prospective employee's permission before running their credit report.

The best resource for finding an assistant is a person you know or who was referred by someone you know. You could hire an apprentice who wants to learn your business, but this often results in someone stealing your best secrets and then becoming your competition. Web sites like **www.craigslist.org** are a great resource for finding good part-time help.

Of course, if you have employees, you're required to attend to important legal details, such as collecting and paying withholding taxes, maintaining workmen's compensation insurance, and other necessities. This can be time consuming and challenging so it may be worthwhile to enlist the help of a payroll/accounting service such as **www.paycycle.com** to take care of these issues.

Learn Your Local Rules

As discussed in Chapter 8, it's wise to take the time and learn what is customary versus what is the law in your area when it comes to real estate investing. Too many people just "wing it" without learning the laws and the customary practices in their business. Such an attitude can lead to lost profits, failed businesses, and unnecessary lawsuits.

Here's the list of local rules you need to learn if you want to be defensive in your investing approach:

Landlord-Tenant Rules

If you plan to be a landlord, learn the local landlord tenant practices, including the required disclosures, the commonly used leases, and the required duties of a landlord. You also need to know what notices are required to be served before proceeding with an eviction.

Learn the regulations concerning security deposits. Many investors mistakenly assume they can keep a deposit if a tenant breaks his or her lease or does damage to a rental unit. However, virtually every state requires that the landlord give the tenant notice of his or her intent to keep the deposit in writing, as well as provide a written breakdown of what amount he or she is keeping and for what reason. In addition, many investors mistakenly assume that security deposits must be segregated in a separate bank account for each tenant. Most states exempt single-family or small apartment buildings from this regulation. You can find more information on state rental laws and security deposit rules at **www.rhol.com** and **www.mrlandlord.com**.

Real Estate Brokers

The "standard" real estate commission is often set by local custom, but this is completely negotiable. In fact, setting a standard commission between brokers in the community is considered illegal price-fixing. Take time to learn what the "standard" listing agreement looks like and what terms work against you. For example, the standard listing contract requires you to pay a commission even if you find a buyer. Negotiate this out of your contract if you plan on marketing your property in addition to listing it on the MLS, or negotiate that you pay the broker a smaller fee if you find the buyer. Most brokers tell you they can't take anything less than a 90-day listing because that's "the way we do things." That's untrue—everything is negotiable, so commit to a shorter time period if you can.

Contracts

In most parts of the country, there's a "standard" contract that brokers use to draft deals. As brokers, they're often required by law to use this contract when drafting a deal for someone else. However, a principal in the transaction is free to use any contract he or she chooses. Brokers often tell you that you must use the "official contract" form, which is nonsense. You are free to submit an offer in any manner you choose. As a matter of practice, however, brokers insist you redraft your offer on the official form.

Choice of Closing Agent

It is customary in most states that the seller chooses the title company, escrow company, attorney, or other person who closes the transaction. However, this does not mean that you, the buyer, can't request that your own attorney or favorite title company close the deal. The seller's real estate broker may balk or demand that the seller has the right to choose, but you can make your purchase agreement contingent on using a closing agent of your choice.

Inspections

Customarily, an inspection of the property is done after the property is under contract. This effectively gives buyers a way to "weasel out" of the deal if they change their minds by simply objecting to something that comes up during the inspection. If you are the seller, you can insist on buyers inspecting the property before making an offer, or limiting their inspection and right to object to property conditions. This curtails them from simply objecting to minor items and potentially wasting your time while tying up your property for weeks on end.

Recording Requirements

Virtually every transaction affecting a real estate deal (e.g., deeds, mortgages, etc.) is recorded at a county office, usually called the "County Clerk." Take time to learn the recording rules such as fees, document sizes, deed transfer tax, and whether the document must be signed before a notary public before recording. Often local officials make up their own rules that aren't required by law but become customary practice that differs from county to county within your state.

Foreclosure Rules

Foreclosure procedures change drastically from state to state, so it's important that you learn the technical details before investing in foreclosure deals. Many novice investors get burned because they didn't understand the technical details of their state's foreclosure process. Many states are implementing laws designed to protect homeowners from scam artists, such as requiring a right of rescission on a sale involving a property in foreclosure. Failing to comply with the required disclosures can result in a transaction being voided and a loss of thousands of dollars. In some states, you can end up in jail for noncompliance, so make sure you review your real estate practices with a good local attorney who is familiar with the law. A good state summary can be found at **www.newforeclosurelaw.com**

Personal Traits of a Defensive Investor

We suggest striving for certain personal attributes if you want to become a defensive investor and enjoy success. These traits can't be inherited or gained through shortcuts, but must be earned through diligent effort and focus of mind. Several times a year, take a good look in the mirror or ask a friend to assess these qualities for you. Are they part of your character?

Patience

As discussed in Chapter 1, a defensive investor doesn't try to "get rich quick." Real estate investing is a slow wealth-building process. We see investors do one deal, often out of sheer luck, then immediately dive into five deals at a time, running out of cash and leaving the business with their tails between their legs. Build your business slowly, one or two deals at a time, and don't take on too many projects until you have the experience and business systems in place to handle multiple projects.

On the other hand, don't fall into the trap of only working on one deal from start to finish before taking on another good deal because you lack the ability to focus on more than one project. If you have several good deals to choose from, hire a staff, bring on a partner, or find other investors to "wholesale" deals to as described in Chapter 8. While you don't want to get in over your head, you also don't want to turn away good business. Learn to manage your time and your life so that you can handle a good balance without losing your focus.

Stay away from large, risky projects until you have the financial ability to risk losing some money. As a defensive investor, you should keep the low-risk deals as the staple of your portfolio, only tackling larger projects when you can risk losing a small amount of your portfolio. "Betting the farm" on a deal is never a good idea.

Work Ethic

Real estate investing, like many home-based businesses, is often billed as "easy money." It may be quite simple, but it's not easy, as nothing worthwhile is easy. It takes hard work, particularly in the beginning stages of your business. Most people don't want to hear this truth because they believe that real estate investing is supposed to make them money so they don't have to work hard anymore. Someday, this may be the case, but in the beginning phases of any business, it takes working hard. After a few years, things get easier and you'll set up a system for employees and other people to do the majority of the work. For the short term, be prepared to work hard!

Bill's Advice: Forget Saying "Don't Work Too Hard"

When people tell me not to work too hard, I hate it and generally respond by saying, "Excuse me, but I work my *$@! off and I never apologize for it." You may be too polite to say this out loud, but keep the thought in your head!

People Skills

Real estate involves sellers, buyers, tenants, lenders, brokers, appraisers, contractors, insurance agents, lawyers, partners, accountants, property managers—the list goes on. The only thing they all have in common is that they are all people. People appraise your house, people approve your loan, and people rent your houses. Therefore, you need to master your people skills if you want to succeed in real estate.

We suggest you apply the virtues explained in Dale Carnegie's famous book *How to Win Friends and Influence People*. Learn how to become a good salesperson, a good negotiator, and a good conflict resolution manager. The better you are at dealing with people, the more success you'll have in all aspects of your real estate business. If you aren't a "people person," then acquire the necessary skills or hire people to deal with the people in your business. Eventually, however, you must improve your people skills. The people who deal with people in your business will eventually have to deal with you!

Attention to Detail

Some people are detail people and have no vision; others are visionary and ignore details. Both live in the extremes, but given the two, a visionary can be better than a technician in this field. However, if you're a visionary, you must learn to pay attention to detail or hire others who do; otherwise technical people won't want to do business with you. A lender may require documentation, a partner may ask for figures, or a buyer may want to know specifics. In each case, if you gloss over details, the detail-oriented people will distrust you and turn the other way. Furthermore, when it comes to taxes and legal issues, ignoring details can eventually get you into trouble.

Positive Mental Attitude

The success rate is very low in real estate because it is often a "needle in a haystack" to find the right deals. Often, it requires making 100 offers to find ten qualified prospects willing to consider your lowball offer—and only one in ten of those will accept it. The 100-10-1 rule is what many commissioned salespeople live by; your real estate investing is essentially that—a commission business. You only get paid when you close, but you get paid big. A guaranteed wage for guaranteed work is fine, but you'll never get wealthy without taking some calculated risk into the unknown world of being your own boss.

The problem is that most people remain a wage-based employee because they don't believe they can succeed, or they don't have enough mental toughness to continue in spite of failing. Henry Ford once said, "Whether you think you can or you think you can't, you're right!"

You must believe that you will succeed, take massive action, and continue taking action in spite of your failures. Eventually, you *will* succeed and it will be worth it, but you can't give up after working a few weeks. Expect it to take months, even years, but the payoff will be so big that your average hourly wage will turn out to be tremendous! There are no guarantees in this business, or any other for that matter—a mental dilemma you have to accept, even if it means starving for months before making a deal. If you can't, you'll forever be a wage-based employee.

Humility

T. S. Eliot said, "Humility is the most difficult of all virtues to achieve, nothing dies harder than the desire to think well of oneself." A big ego often gets the best of investors who start small and then lose patience or focus on their plan.

Don't get into the ego trap; there are already enough big egos in real estate. Being humble means being willing to accept that it takes patience, hard work, and a good mental attitude to succeed. It means accepting the fact that you may be required to do things you don't like or work hours that you don't want do. It means passing on big deals that you could brag about and accepting the fact that the risk is not worth the potential payoff.

Undoubtedly, you will make mistakes, which become learning experiences that prepare you for future business endeavors. However, there's no reason to make big mistakes when you can learn from the mistakes of others!

Being humble means admitting "I don't know" or "I need help" and taking the time to learn from other people who have "been there and done that." A lot of people love to offer advice, often when it's unsolicited. Not all the advice you get will be valuable. However, if you ask the right people for advice, make sure you listen carefully and take the advice they offer.

We are humble enough to admit that we don't know it all, but we share our experiences in this book. We hope that you are humble enough to take these lessons to heart and apply what you've learned.

Key Points to Remember

The successful investor treats investments as a business instead of an investment. An investment is something you put money into; a business is something that pays you back!

The most important concepts addressed in this chapter are:

- Treat real estate investing like a business and it will pay off like one.
- Write down your goals and set regular plans of action.
- Get the help you need through partners, mentors, or employees.
- Learn the local laws, rules, and customs of your business

CHAPTER

Summary

The Ten Principles of Defensive Investing

1. Don't try to get rich quick.
2. You can profit in any market, but you must know your market.
3. Learn how to valuate a property.
4. Determine your profit before you buy.
5. Always invest in "safe" deals.
6. Manage your cash flow.
7. Have multiple exit strategies.
8. You've earned it, now learn how to keep it.
9. Avoid common investment scams.
10. Treat real estate investing as a business.

APPENDIX 1: Internet Resources for Market Data

Realtor.com
www.realtor.org/research

Realty Times
www.realtytimes.com

National Association of Home Builders
www.nahb.org

Signil Wealth Network
www.signil.com

Apartment Index
www.aptindex.com

Foreclosures.com
www.foreclosures.com

Inman Real Estate News Service
www.inman.com

Real Estate Journal Online
www.realestatejournal.com

Hoovers (a Dunn & Bradstreet Company)
www.hoovers.com/free

White House Economic Statistics Briefing Room
www.whitehouse.gov/fsbr/employment.html

Real Estate ABC
www.realestateabc.com/outlook.htm

Globe Street
www.globest.com

Local Market Monitor
www.localmarketmonitor.com

U.S. Census Bureau
www.census.gov/hhes/www/housing.html

U.S. Department of Labor Statistics (for information on inflation)
www.bls.gov

APPENDIX 2: Sample Residential Appraisal Report

FROM:

Telephone Number: Fax Number:

INVOICE

INVOICE NUMBER

DATE

REFERENCE

Internal Order #:
Lender Case #:
Client File #:
Main File # on form:
Other File # on form:
Federal Tax ID:
Employer ID:

TO:

Telephone Number: Fax Number:
Alternate Number: E-Mail:

WE APPRECIATE YOUR BUSINESS!

DESCRIPTION

Lender: Client:
Purchaser/Borrower:
Property Address:
City:
County: State: Zip:
Legal Description:

FEES	AMOUNT
SUBTOTAL	350.00

PAYMENTS	AMOUNT
Check #: Date: Description:	
Check #: Date: Description:	
Check #: Date: Description:	
SUBTOTAL	
Thank You TOTAL DUE	$ 350.00

ROUGET REAL ESTATE APPRAISALS

APPRAISAL OF REAL PROPERTY

LOCATED AT:

FOR:

AS OF:

BY:

Uniform Residential Appraisal Report

File # MC16243Oxf

The purpose of this summary appraisal report is to provide the lender/client with an accurate, and adequately supported, opinion of the market value of the subject property.

SUBJECT

Property Address | City | State | Zip Code
Borrower | Owner of Public Record | County
Legal Description
Assessor's Parcel # | Tax Year 2005 | R.E. Taxes $ 1,128.00
Neighborhood Name Mission Viejo | Map Reference 2080 | Census Tract 0070.71
Occupant ☐ Owner ☐ Tenant ☒ Vacant | Special Assessments $ 0.00 | ☐ PUD HOA $ ☐ per year ☐ per month
Property Rights Appraised ☒ Fee Simple ☐ Leasehold ☐ Other (describe)
Assignment Type ☐ Purchase Transaction ☒ Refinance Transaction ☐ Other (describe)
Lender/Client Meridias Capital | Address
Is the subject property currently offered for sale or has it been offered for sale in the twelve months prior to the effective date of this appraisal? ☒ Yes ☐ No
Report data source(s) used, offering price(s), and date(s). MLS#406188, Offering Price of $150,000, Sold Price $145,525, Sold Date 10/31/2006

CONTRACT

I ☐ did ☐ did not analyze the contract for sale for the subject purchase transaction. Explain the results of the analysis of the contract for sale or why the analysis was not performed. N/A

Contract Price $ N/A | Date of Contract N/A | Is the property seller the owner of public record? ☐ Yes ☐ No Data Source(s) N/A
Is there any financial assistance (loan charges, sale concessions, gift or downpayment assistance, etc.) to be paid by any party on behalf of the borrower? ☐ Yes ☐ No
If Yes, report the total dollar amount and describe the items to be paid. N/A N/A

NEIGHBORHOOD

Note: Race and the racial composition of the neighborhood are not appraisal factors.

Neighborhood Characteristics				One-Unit Housing Trends				One-Unit Housing				Present Land Use %	
Location	☐ Urban	☒ Suburban	☐ Rural	Property Values	☐ Increasing	☒ Stable	☐ Declining	PRICE		AGE		One-Unit	90 %
Built-Up	☐ Over 75%	☒ 25-75%	☐ Under 25%	Demand/Supply	☐ Shortage	☒ In Balance	☐ Over Supply	$ (000)		(yrs)		2-4 Unit	3 %
Growth	☐ Rapid	☒ Stable	☐ Slow	Marketing Time	☒ Under 3 mths	☐ 3-6 mths	☐ Over 6 mths	126	Low	15		Multi-Family	3 %
								310	High	32		Commercial	2 %
								190	Pred.	26		Other	2 %

Neighborhood Boundaries The subject's area is bounded on the North by Hampden Avenue, on the East by Buckley Road, on the South by Quincy Avenue and on the West by Chambers Road.
Neighborhood Description See Attached Supplemental Addenda

Market Conditions (including support for the above conclusions) See Attached Supplemental Addenda

SITE

Dimensions Survey not provided | Area 7,187 SF | Shape Irregular | View Resid/Avg
Specific Zoning Classification R1 | Zoning Description Single Family Detached Residential
Zoning Compliance ☒ Legal ☐ Legal Nonconforming (Grandfathered Use) ☐ No Zoning ☐ Illegal (describe)
Is the highest and best use of subject property as improved (or as proposed per plans and specifications) the present use? ☒ Yes ☐ No If No, describe

Utilities	Public	Other (describe)		Public	Other (describe)	Off-site Improvements - Type	Public	Private
Electricity	☒	☐ Xcel Energy	Water	☒	☐	Street Asphalt	☒	☐
Gas	☒	☐ Xcel Energy	Sanitary Sewer	☒	☐	Alley None	☐	☐

FEMA Special Flood Hazard Area ☐ Yes ☒ No | FEMA Flood Zone X | FEMA Map # 0800020195E | FEMA Map Date 8/16/1995
Are the utilities and off-site improvements typical for the market area? ☒ Yes ☐ No If No, describe
Are there any adverse site conditions or external factors (easements, encroachments, environmental conditions, land uses, etc.)? ☐ Yes ☒ No If Yes, describe
Site is encumbered by normal utility and easements of records.

IMPROVEMENTS

General Description		Foundation		Exterior Description	materials/condition	Interior	materials/condition
Units ☒ One ☐ One with Accessory Unit		☐ Concrete Slab	☐ Crawl Space	Foundation Walls	Concrete	Floors	Carpet/Tile/New
# of Stories	One	☒ Full Basement	☐ Partial Basement	Exterior Walls	Frame	Walls	Drywall/New Paint
Type ☒ Det. ☐ Att. ☐ S-Det./End Unit		Basement Area	912 sq.ft.	Roof Surface	Asphalt Shingles	Trim/Finish	Wood/Good
☒ Existing ☐ Proposed ☐ Under Const.		Basement Finish	90 %	Gutters & Downspouts	Metal	Bath Floor	Tile/New
Design (Style)	Ranch	☐ Outside Entry/Exit	☐ Sump Pump	Window Type	Double Windows	Bath Wainscot	Tile/New
Year Built	1981	Evidence of ☐ Infestation		Storm Sash/Insulated	Yes/Yes	Car Storage	☐ None
Effective Age (Yrs)	5	☐ Dampness	☐ Settlement	Screens	Yes	☒ Driveway	# of Cars 4
Attic	☐ None	Heating ☒ FWA ☐ HWBB	☐ Radiant	Amenities	☐ Woodstove(s) #	Driveway Surface	Concrete
☐ Drop Stair	☐ Stairs	☐ Other	Fuel Gas	☒ Fireplace(s) # 1	☒ Fence Privacy	☒ Garage	# of Cars 2
☐ Floor	☒ Scuttle	Cooling ☐ Central Air Conditioning		☒ Patio/Deck Open	☒ Porch Covered	☐ Carport	# of Cars
☐ Finished	☐ Heated	☐ Individual	☐ Other	☐ Pool	☐ Other	☒ Att. ☐ Det.	☐ Built-in

Appliances P Refrigerator ☒ Range/Oven ☒ Dishwasher ☒ Disposal ☐ Microwave P Washer/Dryer ☐ Other (describe)
Finished area above grade contains: 5 Rooms 2 Bedrooms 1 Bath(s) 912 Square Feet of Gross Living Area Above Grade
Additional features (special energy efficient items, etc.). This property features double pane windows.

Describe the condition of the property (including needed repairs, deterioration, renovations, remodeling, etc.). The property is in good condition. The property recently received the following updating and remodeling: Remodeled kitchen with new tile flooring, new cabinets, new countertops, new fixtures and appliances, remodeled bathroom with new tile flooring, new cabinets and fixtures, new interior paint and new doors throughout, new carpet, newly finished basement with 1 family room, 2 bedrooms and 1 bathroom. No repairs necessary per inspection.

Are there any physical deficiencies or adverse conditions that affect the livability, soundness, or structural integrity of the property? ☐ Yes ☒ No If Yes, describe
No physical deficiencies or adverse conditions were noted during the inspection

Does the property generally conform to the neighborhood (functional utility, style, condition, use, construction, etc.)? ☒ Yes ☐ No If No, describe
The property does conform in general to the neighborhood in terms of functional utility, style, condition, use and type of construction.

Uniform Residential Appraisal Report

File # MC16243Oxf

There are 3 comparable properties currently offered for sale in the subject neighborhood ranging in price from $ 185,000 to $ 199,900 .

There are 9 comparable sales in the subject neighborhood within the past twelve months ranging in sale price from $ 185,000 to $ 195,000 .

FEATURE	SUBJECT	COMPARABLE SALE # 1		COMPARABLE SALE # 2		COMPARABLE SALE # 3	
Address	16243 East Oxford Drive Aurora CO	3657 South Norfolk Way Aurora, CO 80013		3869 South Ouray Way Aurora, CO 80013		15563 East Princeton Avenue Aurora, CO 80013	
Proximity to Subject		0.6 miles NE		0.47 miles NE		0.41 miles SW	
Sale Price	$ N/A		$ 185,000		$ 188,000		$ 195,000
Sale Price/Gross Liv. Area	$ sq.ft.	$ 202.85 sq.ft.		$ 206.14 sq.ft.		$ 213.82 sq.ft.	
Data Source(s)		County Records/Deed data		County Records/Deed data		County Records/Deed data	
Verification Source(s)		MLS#348603		MLS#380917		MLS#410168	
VALUE ADJUSTMENTS	DESCRIPTION	DESCRIPTION	+(-) $ Adjustment	DESCRIPTION	+(-) $ Adjustment	DESCRIPTION	+(-) $ Adjustment
Sales or Financing Concessions		Conventional None Noted		FHA $4,700	-4,700	Conventional None Noted	
Date of Sale/Time		06/16/2006		09/21/2006		10/24/2006	
Location	Aurora South	Mission Viejo		Mission Viejo		Mission Viejo	
Leasehold/Fee Simple	Fee Simple	Fee Simple		Fee Simple		Fee Simple	
Site	7,187 SF	5,880 SF		5,357 SF		5,227 SF	
View	Resid/Avg	Resid/Avg		Resid/Avg		Resid/Avg	
Design (Style)	Ranch	Ranch		Ranch		Ranch	
Quality of Construction	Frame	Frame		Frame		Frame	
Actual Age	25 Years	27 Years		26 Years		29 Years	
Condition	Good	Good		Good		Good	
Above Grade Room Count (Total / Bdrms. / Baths)	5 / 2 / 1	5 / 2 / 1		5 / 2 / 1		5 / 2 / 1	
Gross Living Area	912 sq.ft.	912 sq.ft.		912 sq.ft.		912 sq.ft.	
Basement & Finished Rooms Below Grade	912 Sq.Ft. 821 SF Fin	912 SF 912 SF Fin		912 SF 866 SF Fin		912 SF 820 SF Fin	
Functional Utility	Average	Average		Average		Average	
Heating/Cooling	GFA/None	GFA/EC	-1,000	GFA/None		GFA/EC	-1,000
Energy Efficient Items	Double Pan Win	Double Pan Win		Double Pan Win		Double Pan Win	
Garage/Carport	2 Car Garage	2 Car Garage		2 Car Garage		2 Car Garage	
Porch/Patio/Deck	PorchDeck	Porch	+2,000	PorchPatio		PorchPatio	
Outdoor Amenities/Features	Fence	Fence		Fence		Fence	
Updating	Good	Good		Inferior	+8,000	Good	
Net Adjustment (Total)		☒ + ☐ -	$ 1,000	☒ + ☐ -	$ 3,300	☐ + ☒ -	$ -1,000
Adjusted Sale Price of Comparables		Net Adj. % Gross Adj. %	$ 186,000	Net Adj. % Gross Adj. %	$ 191,300	Net Adj. % Gross Adj. %	$ 194,000

SALES COMPARISON APPROACH

I ☒ did ☐ did not research the sale or transfer history of the subject property and comparable sales. If not, explain

My research ☒ did ☐ did not reveal any prior sales or transfers of the subject property for the three years prior to the effective date of this appraisal.

Data Source(s) County Records/Deed Data

My research ☒ did ☐ did not reveal any prior sales or transfers of the comparable sales for the year prior to the date of sale of the comparable sale.

Data Source(s) County Records/Deed Data

Report the results of the research and analysis of the prior sale or transfer history of the subject property and comparable sales (report additional prior sales on page 3).

ITEM	SUBJECT	COMPARABLE SALE #1	COMPARABLE SALE #2	COMPARABLE SALE #3
Date of Prior Sale/Transfer	10/31/2006	No prior sale in	No prior sale in	No prior sale in
Price of Prior Sale/Transfer	$145,525	the past 12 months	the past 12 months	the past 12 months
Data Source(s)	County records	County records	County records	County records
Effective Date of Data Source(s)	11/30/2006	11/30/2006	11/30/2006	11/30/2006

Analysis of prior sale or transfer history of the subject property and comparable sales The subject sold in October 2006 for $145,525. This prior sale was a typical arm's-length transaction and the property was in fix up condition. It has been since remodeled. Comparable#5 sold in February 2006 for $158,200. This prior sale was a typical arm's-length transaction and the property was in fix up condition. It has been since remodeled and has sold in July 2006 for $189,000. Other comparables do not have any prior sales history in the past 12 months.

Summary of Sales Comparison Approach All of the comparables and the subject are located in the subdivision of Mission Viejo and are the most similar comparables available in terms of style, size, appeal and marketability. Comparables #1 - #7 are closed sales from within the past five months. Comparable #8 is currently listed for sale. All comparables are considered good indicators of the subject's current market value.

Indicated Value by Sales Comparison Approach $ 190,000

RECONCILIATION

Indicated Value by: Sales Comparison Approach $ 190,000 **Cost Approach (if developed) $** 191,436 **Income Approach (if developed) $**

The Sales Comparison Approach was given primary consideration as it most closely represents the motivations of the typical buyer. The lack of sufficient rental data prohibits the application of the Income Approach to Value.

This appraisal is made ☒ "as is", ☐ subject to completion per plans and specifications on the basis of a hypothetical condition that the improvements have been completed, ☐ subject to the following repairs or alterations on the basis of a hypothetical condition that the repairs or alterations have been completed, or ☐ subject to the following required inspection based on the extraordinary assumption that the condition or deficiency does not require alteration or repair: See attached addenda.

Based on a complete visual inspection of the interior and exterior areas of the subject property, defined scope of work, statement of assumptions and limiting conditions, and appraiser's certification, my (our) opinion of the market value, as defined, of the real property that is the subject of this report is $ 190,000 **, as of** 11/29/2006 **, which is the date of inspection and the effective date of this appraisal.**

Freddie Mac Form 70 March 2005 Page 2 of 6 Fannie Mae Form 1004 March 2005

Uniform Residential Appraisal Report

File # MC16243Oxf

SALES COMPARISON APPROACH

FEATURE	SUBJECT	COMPARABLE SALE # 4		COMPARABLE SALE # 5		COMPARABLE SALE # 6	
Address	16243 East Oxford Drive Aurora CO	16652 East Mansfield Circle Aurora, CO 80013		4266 South Naples Way Aurora, CO 80013		4211 South Nucla Way Aurora, CO 80013	
Proximity to Subject		0.38 miles NE		0.32 miles SE		0.33 miles SE	
Sale Price	$ N/A		$ 190,000		$ 189,000		$ 194,450
Sale Price/Gross Liv. Area	$ sq.ft.	$ 208.33 sq.ft.		$ 207.24 sq.ft.		$ 213.21 sq.ft.	
Data Source(s)		County Records/Deed data		County Records/Deed data		County Records/Deed data	
Verification Source(s)		MLS#414422		MLS#323245		MLS#337463	
VALUE ADJUSTMENTS	DESCRIPTION	DESCRIPTION	+(-) $ Adjustment	DESCRIPTION	+(-) $ Adjustment	DESCRIPTION	+(-) $ Adjustment
Sales or Financing Concessions		Conventional None Noted		Conventional $6,000	-6,000	Conventional $5,300	-5,300
Date of Sale/Time		09/14/2006		07/07/2006		06/28/2006	
Location	Aurora South	Mission Viejo		Mission Viejo		Mission Viejo	
Leasehold/Fee Simple	Fee Simple	Fee Simple		Fee Simple		Fee Simple	
Site	7,187 SF	6,054 SF		5,270 SF		5,226 SF	
View	Resid/Avg	Resid/Avg		Resid/Avg		Resid/Avg	
Design (Style)	Ranch	Tri-Level		Ranch		Ranch	
Quality of Construction	Frame	Frame		Frame		Frame	
Actual Age	25 Years	26 Years		26 Years		26 Years	
Condition	Good	Good		Good		Good	
Above Grade Room Count	Total 5 / Bdrms. 2 / Baths 1	Total 5 / Bdrms. 2 / Baths 1		Total 5 / Bdrms. 2 / Baths 1		Total 5 / Bdrms. 2 / Baths 1	
Gross Living Area	912 sq.ft.	912 sq.ft.		912 sq.ft.		912 sq.ft.	
Basement & Finished Rooms Below Grade	912 Sq.Ft. 821 SF Fin	912 SF 696 SF Fin	+1,200	912 SF 912 SF Fin		912 SF 866 SF Fin	
Functional Utility	Average	Average		Average		Average	
Heating/Cooling	GFA/None	GFA/AC	-2,000	GFA/AC	-2,000	GFA/AC	-2,000
Energy Efficient Items	Double Pan Win	Double Pan Win		Double Pan Win		Double Pan Win	
Garage/Carport	2 Car Garage	2 Car Garage		2 Car Garage		2 Car Garage	
Porch/Patio/Deck	PorchDeck	PorchPatio		PorchDeck		PorchPatio	
Outdoor Amenities/Features	Fence	Fence		Fence		Fence	
Updating	Good	Good		Inferior	+8,000	Good	
Net Adjustment (Total)		☐ + ☒ -	$ -800	☐ + ☐ -	$	☐ + ☒ -	$ -7,300
Adjusted Sale Price of Comparables		Net Adj. % Gross Adj. %	$ 189,200	Net Adj. % Gross Adj. %	$ 189,000	Net Adj. % Gross Adj. %	$ 187,150

SALE HISTORY

Report the results of the research and analysis of the prior sale or transfer history of the subject property and comparable sales (report additional prior sales on page 3).

ITEM	SUBJECT	COMPARABLE SALE # 4	COMPARABLE SALE # 5	COMPARABLE SALE # 6
Date of Prior Sale/Transfer	10/31/2006	No prior sale in	02/06/2006	No prior sale in
Price of Prior Sale/Transfer	$145,525	the past 12 months	$158,200	the past 12 months
Data Source(s)	County records	County records	County records	County records
Effective Date of Data Source(s)	11/30/2006	11/30/2006	11/30/2006	11/30/2006

Analysis of prior sale or transfer history of the subject property and comparable sales The subject sold in October 2006 for $145,525. This prior sale was a typical arm's-length transaction and the property was in fix up condition. It has been since remodeled. Comparable#5 sold in February 2006 for $158,200. This prior sale was a typical arm's-length transaction and the property was in fix up condition. It has been since remodeled and has sold in July 2006 for $189,000. Other comparables do not have any prior sales history in the past 12 months.

ANALYSIS / COMMENTS

Analysis/Comments

Sales Concessions was adjusted downward at $1/dollar amount of concession received.

Finished basement difference was adjusted at $10/SF.

Central Air Conditioning was adjusted at $2,000. Evaporative Cooler was adjusted at $1,000.

Porch, Patio and Deck difference were adjusted at $2,000.

Comparables #2, #5 and #7 have been adjusted accordingly for inferior updating. These adjustments have been made in accordance with realtor's comments reported on the comparables MLS sheet.

Comparable#9 is an active listing. This comparable received a downward adjustment of 2.3% of its listed price which correspond to the the average list to sold price difference in the past 12 months for properties located within the subject market area.

All the above adjustments are made to reflect the market reaction for these differences, using the appraiser's personal research, analysis and opinion.

Uniform Residential Appraisal Report

File # MC16243Oxf

SALES COMPARISON APPROACH

FEATURE	SUBJECT	COMPARABLE SALE #7		COMPARABLE SALE #8		COMPARABLE SALE #9	
Address	16243 East Oxford Drive Aurora CO	3511 South Lewiston Way Aurora, CO 80013		4292 South Nucla Way Aurora, CO 80013			
Proximity to Subject		0.68 miles N		0.36 miles SE			
Sale Price	$ N/A		$ 190,000		$ 199,900		$
Sale Price/Gross Liv. Area	$ sq.ft.	$ 208.33 sq.ft.		$ 219.19 sq.ft.		$ sq.ft.	
Data Source(s)		County Records/Deed data		County Records/Deed data			
Verification Source(s)		MLS#259653		MLS#411731			
VALUE ADJUSTMENTS	DESCRIPTION	DESCRIPTION	+(-) $ Adjustment	DESCRIPTION	+(-) $ Adjustment	DESCRIPTION	+(-) $ Adjustment
Sales or Financing Concessions		Conventional $9,052	-9,052	Active (-2.3%) Active Listing	-4,600		
Date of Sale/Time		06/30/2006		Unknown			
Location	Aurora South	Mission Viejo		Mission Viejo			
Leasehold/Fee Simple	Fee Simple	Fee Simple		Fee Simple			
Site	7,187 SF	4,791 SF		7,361 SF			
View	Resid/Avg	Resid/Avg		Resid/Avg			
Design (Style)	Ranch	Ranch		Ranch			
Quality of Construction	Frame	Frame		Frame			
Actual Age	25 Years	27 Years		26 Years			
Condition	Good	Good		Good			
Above Grade Room Count	Total 5 / Bdrms. 2 / Baths 1	Total 5 / Bdrms. 2 / Baths 1		Total 5 / Bdrms. 2 / Baths 1		Total / Bdrms. / Baths	
Gross Living Area	912 sq.ft.	912 sq.ft.		912 sq.ft.		sq.ft.	
Basement & Finished Rooms Below Grade	912 Sq.Ft. 821 SF Fin	912 SF 456 SF Fin	+3,700	912 SF 866 SF Fin			
Functional Utility	Average	Average		Average			
Heating/Cooling	GFA/None	GFA/None		GFA/AC	-2,000		
Energy Efficient Items	Double Pan Win	Double Pan Win		Double Pan Win			
Garage/Carport	2 Car Garage	2 Car Garage		2 Car Garage			
Porch/Patio/Deck	PorchDeck	Porch	+2,000	PorchPatio			
Outdoor Amenities/Features	Fence	Fence		Fence			
Updating	Good	Above Average	+3,000	Good			
Net Adjustment (Total)		☐ + ☒ -	$ -352	☐ + ☒ -	$ -6,600	☐ + ☐ -	$
Adjusted Sale Price of Comparables		Net Adj. % Gross Adj. %	$ 189,648	Net Adj. % Gross Adj. %	$ 193,300	Net Adj. % Gross Adj. %	$

SALE HISTORY

Report the results of the research and analysis of the prior sale or transfer history of the subject property and comparable sales (report additional prior sales on page 3).

ITEM	SUBJECT	COMPARABLE SALE #7	COMPARABLE SALE #8	COMPARABLE SALE #9
Date of Prior Sale/Transfer	10/31/2006	No prior sale in	No prior sale in	
Price of Prior Sale/Transfer	$145,525	the past 12 months	the past 12 months	
Data Source(s)	County records	County records	County records	
Effective Date of Data Source(s)	11/30/2006	11/30/2006	11/30/2006	

Analysis of prior sale or transfer history of the subject property and comparable sales The subject sold in October 2006 for $145,525. This prior sale was a typical arm's-length transaction and the property was in fix up condition. It has been since remodeled. Comparable#5 sold in February 2006 for $158,200. This prior sale was a typical arm's-length transaction and the property was in fix up condition. It has been since remodeled and has sold in July 2006 for $189,000. Other comparables do not have any prior sales history in the past 12 months.

ANALYSIS / COMMENTS

Analysis/Comments

Freddie Mac Form 70 March 2005 Fannie Mae Form 1004 March 2005

Uniform Residential Appraisal Report

File # MC16243Oxf

ADDITIONAL COMMENTS

Unless otherwise specifically noted in the body of this report, it is assumed: that the existing improvements on the property or properties being appraised are structurally sound, seismically safe and code conforming; that all building components (mechanical systems, plumbing, etc.) are in good working order with no major deferred maintenance or repair required; that the roof and exterior are in good condition and free from intrusion by the elements; that the property or properties have been engineered in such a manner that the improvements, as currently constituted, conform to all applicable local and state building codes.

The appraiser is not an engineer and is not competent to judge matters of an engineering nature. The appraiser has not retained independent structural, mechanical, electrical, or civil engineers in connection with this appraisal and, therefore, makes no representations relative to the condition of improvements; and the appraiser was not furnished any engineering studies by the owners or by the party requesting this appraisal. If questions in these areas are critical to the decision process of the reader, the advice of competent engineering consultants should be obtained and relied upon. It is specifically assumed that any knowledgeable and prudent purchaser would, as a precondition to closing a sale, obtain a satisfactory engineering report relative to the structural integrity of the property and the integrity of homes construction components.

Structural problems may not be visually detectable. If engineering consultants retained should report negative factors of a material nature, or if such are later discovered, relative to the condition of improvements, such information could have a substantial negative impact on the conclusions reported in this appraisal. Accordingly, if negative findings are reported by engineering consultants, the appraiser reserves the right to amend the appraisal conclusions reported herein.

Unless otherwise stated in this report, the existence of hazardous material, which may or may not be present on the property was not observed by the appraiser. The appraiser has no knowledge of the existence of such materials on or in the property. The appraiser, however, is not qualified to detect such substances. The presence of substances such as asbestos, urea formaldehyde foam insulation, contaminated ground water, or other potentially hazardous material on or in the property that would cause a loss in value. No responsibility is assumed for any such conditions, or for any expertise or engineering knowledge required to discover them. The client is urged to retain an expert in this field, if desired. In its present condition the subject property is assumed to be safe according to the standards established by the Environmental Protection Agency.

The appraiser uses an electronic signature when e-mailing appraisal reports. The signature is controlled by an personal identification number and the appraiser has sole personalized control of applying the digital signature as defined by Uniform Standards of Professional Appraisal Practice (USPAP).

All the comparables data reported in the sales comparison analysis is taken from the MLS and/or County Records which describes each comparables characteristics at the time of their purchase or listing. All pictures of the comparables are taken from the MLS which best represents each comparable at the time of their purchase or listing.

COST APPROACH TO VALUE (not required by Fannie Mae)

Provide adequate information for the lender/client to replicate the below cost figures and calculations.

Support for the opinion of site value (summary of comparable land sales or other methods for estimating site value) Land value estimates were derived through allocation and reflects only contributory value towards the subject's improvements.

ESTIMATED ☐ REPRODUCTION OR ☒ REPLACEMENT COST NEW	OPINION OF SITE VALUE	=$	26,000
Source of cost data Means	DWELLING 912 Sq.Ft. @ $ 90.00	=$	82,080
Quality rating from cost service Average Effective date of cost data 2006 Guide	912 Sq.Ft. @ $ 40.00	=$	36,480
Comments on Cost Approach (gross living area calculations, depreciation, etc.)	Kitch-bath equip, Fixtures, Features, Amenities	=$	40,000
Cost approach estimates were derived through Means cost manual and	Garage/Carport 440 Sq.Ft. @ $ 25.00	=$	11,000
adjusted for the local market. The actual may vary from this estimate.	Total Estimate of Cost-New	=$	169,560
Estimated remaining economic life is 55 years.	Less Physical / Functional / External		
	Depreciation 14,124	=$(	14,124)
	Depreciated Cost of Improvements	=$	155,436
	"As-is" Value of Site Improvements	=$	10,000
Estimated Remaining Economic Life (HUD and VA only) 55 Years	INDICATED VALUE BY COST APPROACH	=$	191,436

INCOME APPROACH TO VALUE (not required by Fannie Mae)

Estimated Monthly Market Rent $ N/A X Gross Rent Multiplier 0.00 = $ Indicated Value by Income Approach

Summary of Income Approach (including support for market rent and GRM)

PROJECT INFORMATION FOR PUDs (if applicable)

Is the developer/builder in control of the Homeowners' Association (HOA)? ☐ Yes ☐ No Unit type(s) ☐ Detached ☐ Attached

Provide the following information for PUDs ONLY if the developer/builder is in control of the HOA and the subject property is an attached dwelling unit.

Legal Name of Project

Total number of phases Total number of units Total number of units sold

Total number of units rented Total number of units for sale Data source(s)

Was the project created by the conversion of existing building(s) into a PUD? ☐ Yes ☐ No If Yes, date of conversion.

Does the project contain any multi-dwelling units? ☐ Yes ☐ No Data Source

Are the units, common elements, and recreation facilities complete? ☐ Yes ☐ No If No, describe the status of completion.

Are the common elements leased to or by the Homeowners' Association? ☐ Yes ☐ No If Yes, describe the rental terms and options.

Describe common elements and recreational facilities.

Freddie Mac Form 70 March 2005 Page 3 of 6 Fannie Mae Form 1004 March 2005

Uniform Residential Appraisal Report

File # MC16243Oxf

This report form is designed to report an appraisal of a one-unit property or a one-unit property with an accessory unit; including a unit in a planned unit development (PUD). This report form is not designed to report an appraisal of a manufactured home or a unit in a condominium or cooperative project.

This appraisal report is subject to the following scope of work, intended use, intended user, definition of market value, statement of assumptions and limiting conditions, and certifications. Modifications, additions, or deletions to the intended use, intended user, definition of market value, or assumptions and limiting conditions are not permitted. The appraiser may expand the scope of work to include any additional research or analysis necessary based on the complexity of this appraisal assignment. Modifications or deletions to the certifications are also not permitted. However, additional certifications that do not constitute material alterations to this appraisal report, such as those required by law or those related to the appraiser's continuing education or membership in an appraisal organization, are permitted.

SCOPE OF WORK: The scope of work for this appraisal is defined by the complexity of this appraisal assignment and the reporting requirements of this appraisal report form, including the following definition of market value, statement of assumptions and limiting conditions, and certifications. The appraiser must, at a minimum: (1) perform a complete visual inspection of the interior and exterior areas of the subject property, (2) inspect the neighborhood, (3) inspect each of the comparable sales from at least the street, (4) research, verify, and analyze data from reliable public and/or private sources, and (5) report his or her analysis, opinions, and conclusions in this appraisal report.

INTENDED USE: The intended use of this appraisal report is for the lender/client to evaluate the property that is the subject of this appraisal for a mortgage finance transaction.

INTENDED USER: The intended user of this appraisal report is the lender/client.

DEFINITION OF MARKET VALUE: The most probable price which a property should bring in a competitive and open market under all conditions requisite to a fair sale, the buyer and seller, each acting prudently, knowledgeably and assuming the price is not affected by undue stimulus. Implicit in this definition is the consummation of a sale as of a specified date and the passing of title from seller to buyer under conditions whereby: (1) buyer and seller are typically motivated; (2) both parties are well informed or well advised, and each acting in what he or she considers his or her own best interest; (3) a reasonable time is allowed for exposure in the open market; (4) payment is made in terms of cash in U. S. dollars or in terms of financial arrangements comparable thereto; and (5) the price represents the normal consideration for the property sold unaffected by special or creative financing or sales concessions* granted by anyone associated with the sale.

*Adjustments to the comparables must be made for special or creative financing or sales concessions. No adjustments are necessary for those costs which are normally paid by sellers as a result of tradition or law in a market area; these costs are readily identifiable since the seller pays these costs in virtually all sales transactions. Special or creative financing adjustments can be made to the comparable property by comparisons to financing terms offered by a third party institutional lender that is not already involved in the property or transaction. Any adjustment should not be calculated on a mechanical dollar for dollar cost of the financing or concession but the dollar amount of any adjustment should approximate the market's reaction to the financing or concessions based on the appraiser's judgment.

STATEMENT OF ASSUMPTIONS AND LIMITING CONDITIONS: The appraiser's certification in this report is subject to the following assumptions and limiting conditions:

1. The appraiser will not be responsible for matters of a legal nature that affect either the property being appraised or the title to it, except for information that he or she became aware of during the research involved in performing this appraisal. The appraiser assumes that the title is good and marketable and will not render any opinions about the title.

2. The appraiser has provided a sketch in this appraisal report to show the approximate dimensions of the improvements. The sketch is included only to assist the reader in visualizing the property and understanding the appraiser's determination of its size.

3. The appraiser has examined the available flood maps that are provided by the Federal Emergency Management Agency (or other data sources) and has noted in this appraisal report whether any portion of the subject site is located in an identified Special Flood Hazard Area. Because the appraiser is not a surveyor, he or she makes no guarantees, express or implied, regarding this determination.

4. The appraiser will not give testimony or appear in court because he or she made an appraisal of the property in question, unless specific arrangements to do so have been made beforehand, or as otherwise required by law.

5. The appraiser has noted in this appraisal report any adverse conditions (such as needed repairs, deterioration, the presence of hazardous wastes, toxic substances, etc.) observed during the inspection of the subject property or that he or she became aware of during the research involved in performing the appraisal. Unless otherwise stated in this appraisal report, the appraiser has no knowledge of any hidden or unapparent physical deficiencies or adverse conditions of the property (such as, but not limited to, needed repairs, deterioration, the presence of hazardous wastes, toxic substances, adverse environmental conditions, etc.) that would make the property less valuable, and has assumed that there are no such conditions and makes no guarantees or warranties, express or implied. The appraiser will not be responsible for any such conditions that do exist or for any engineering or testing that might be required to discover whether such conditions exist. Because the appraiser is not an expert in the field of environmental hazards, this appraisal report must not be considered as an environmental assessment of the property.

6. The appraiser has based his or her appraisal report and valuation conclusion for an appraisal that is subject to satisfactory completion, repairs, or alterations on the assumption that the completion, repairs, or alterations of the subject property will be performed in a professional manner.

Uniform Residential Appraisal Report

File # MC16243Oxf

APPRAISER'S CERTIFICATION: The Appraiser certifies and agrees that:

1. I have, at a minimum, developed and reported this appraisal in accordance with the scope of work requirements stated in this appraisal report.

2. I performed a complete visual inspection of the interior and exterior areas of the subject property. I reported the condition of the improvements in factual, specific terms. I identified and reported the physical deficiencies that could affect the livability, soundness, or structural integrity of the property.

3. I performed this appraisal in accordance with the requirements of the Uniform Standards of Professional Appraisal Practice that were adopted and promulgated by the Appraisal Standards Board of The Appraisal Foundation and that were in place at the time this appraisal report was prepared.

4. I developed my opinion of the market value of the real property that is the subject of this report based on the sales comparison approach to value. I have adequate comparable market data to develop a reliable sales comparison approach for this appraisal assignment. I further certify that I considered the cost and income approaches to value but did not develop them, unless otherwise indicated in this report.

5. I researched, verified, analyzed, and reported on any current agreement for sale for the subject property, any offering for sale of the subject property in the twelve months prior to the effective date of this appraisal, and the prior sales of the subject property for a minimum of three years prior to the effective date of this appraisal, unless otherwise indicated in this report.

6. I researched, verified, analyzed, and reported on the prior sales of the comparable sales for a minimum of one year prior to the date of sale of the comparable sale, unless otherwise indicated in this report.

7. I selected and used comparable sales that are locationally, physically, and functionally the most similar to the subject property.

8. I have not used comparable sales that were the result of combining a land sale with the contract purchase price of a home that has been built or will be built on the land.

9. I have reported adjustments to the comparable sales that reflect the market's reaction to the differences between the subject property and the comparable sales.

10. I verified, from a disinterested source, all information in this report that was provided by parties who have a financial interest in the sale or financing of the subject property.

11. I have knowledge and experience in appraising this type of property in this market area.

12. I am aware of, and have access to, the necessary and appropriate public and private data sources, such as multiple listing services, tax assessment records, public land records and other such data sources for the area in which the property is located.

13. I obtained the information, estimates, and opinions furnished by other parties and expressed in this appraisal report from reliable sources that I believe to be true and correct.

14. I have taken into consideration the factors that have an impact on value with respect to the subject neighborhood, subject property, and the proximity of the subject property to adverse influences in the development of my opinion of market value. I have noted in this appraisal report any adverse conditions (such as, but not limited to, needed repairs, deterioration, the presence of hazardous wastes, toxic substances, adverse environmental conditions, etc.) observed during the inspection of the subject property or that I became aware of during the research involved in performing this appraisal. I have considered these adverse conditions in my analysis of the property value, and have reported on the effect of the conditions on the value and marketability of the subject property.

15. I have not knowingly withheld any significant information from this appraisal report and, to the best of my knowledge, all statements and information in this appraisal report are true and correct.

16. I stated in this appraisal report my own personal, unbiased, and professional analysis, opinions, and conclusions, which are subject only to the assumptions and limiting conditions in this appraisal report.

17. I have no present or prospective interest in the property that is the subject of this report, and I have no present or prospective personal interest or bias with respect to the participants in the transaction. I did not base, either partially or completely, my analysis and/or opinion of market value in this appraisal report on the race, color, religion, sex, age, marital status, handicap, familial status, or national origin of either the prospective owners or occupants of the subject property or of the present owners or occupants of the properties in the vicinity of the subject property or on any other basis prohibited by law.

18. My employment and/or compensation for performing this appraisal or any future or anticipated appraisals was not conditioned on any agreement or understanding, written or otherwise, that I would report (or present analysis supporting) a predetermined specific value, a predetermined minimum value, a range or direction in value, a value that favors the cause of any party, or the attainment of a specific result or occurrence of a specific subsequent event (such as approval of a pending mortgage loan application).

19. I personally prepared all conclusions and opinions about the real estate that were set forth in this appraisal report. If I relied on significant real property appraisal assistance from any individual or individuals in the performance of this appraisal or the preparation of this appraisal report, I have named such individual(s) and disclosed the specific tasks performed in this appraisal report. I certify that any individual so named is qualified to perform the tasks. I have not authorized anyone to make a change to any item in this appraisal report; therefore, any change made to this appraisal is unauthorized and I will take no responsibility for it.

20. I identified the lender/client in this appraisal report who is the individual, organization, or agent for the organization that ordered and will receive this appraisal report.

Uniform Residential Appraisal Report

File # MC16243Oxf

21. The lender/client may disclose or distribute this appraisal report to: the borrower; another lender at the request of the borrower; the mortgagee or its successors and assigns; mortgage insurers; government sponsored enterprises; other secondary market participants; data collection or reporting services; professional appraisal organizations; any department, agency, or instrumentality of the United States; and any state, the District of Columbia, or other jurisdictions; without having to obtain the appraiser's or supervisory appraiser's (if applicable) consent. Such consent must be obtained before this appraisal report may be disclosed or distributed to any other party (including, but not limited to, the public through advertising, public relations, news, sales, or other media).

22. I am aware that any disclosure or distribution of this appraisal report by me or the lender/client may be subject to certain laws and regulations. Further, I am also subject to the provisions of the Uniform Standards of Professional Appraisal Practice that pertain to disclosure or distribution by me.

23. The borrower, another lender at the request of the borrower, the mortgagee or its successors and assigns, mortgage insurers, government sponsored enterprises, and other secondary market participants may rely on this appraisal report as part of any mortgage finance transaction that involves any one or more of these parties.

24. If this appraisal report was transmitted as an "electronic record" containing my "electronic signature," as those terms are defined in applicable federal and/or state laws (excluding audio and video recordings), or a facsimile transmission of this appraisal report containing a copy or representation of my signature, the appraisal report shall be as effective, enforceable and valid as if a paper version of this appraisal report were delivered containing my original hand written signature.

25. Any intentional or negligent misrepresentation(s) contained in this appraisal report may result in civil liability and/or criminal penalties including, but not limited to, fine or imprisonment or both under the provisions of Title 18, United States Code, Section 1001, et seq., or similar state laws.

SUPERVISORY APPRAISER'S CERTIFICATION: The Supervisory Appraiser certifies and agrees that:

1. I directly supervised the appraiser for this appraisal assignment, have read the appraisal report, and agree with the appraiser's analysis, opinions, statements, conclusions, and the appraiser's certification.

2. I accept full responsibility for the contents of this appraisal report including, but not limited to, the appraiser's analysis, opinions, statements, conclusions, and the appraiser's certification.

3. The appraiser identified in this appraisal report is either a sub-contractor or an employee of the supervisory appraiser (or the appraisal firm), is qualified to perform this appraisal, and is acceptable to perform this appraisal under the applicable state law.

4. This appraisal report complies with the Uniform Standards of Professional Appraisal Practice that were adopted and promulgated by the Appraisal Standards Board of The Appraisal Foundation and that were in place at the time this appraisal report was prepared.

5. If this appraisal report was transmitted as an "electronic record" containing my "electronic signature," as those terms are defined in applicable federal and/or state laws (excluding audio and video recordings), or a facsimile transmission of this appraisal report containing a copy or representation of my signature, the appraisal report shall be as effective, enforceable and valid as if a paper version of this appraisal report were delivered containing my original hand written signature.

APPRAISER

Signature ____________
Name ____________
Company Name ____________
Company Address ____________
____
Telephone Number ____________
Email Address ____________
Date of Signature and Report ____________
Effective Date of Appraisal ____________
State Certification # ____________
or State License # ____________
or Other (describe) ____________ State # ____________
State ____________
Expiration Date of Certification or License ____________

ADDRESS OF PROPERTY APPRAISED
____
____

APPRAISED VALUE OF SUBJECT PROPERTY $ ____________

LENDER/CLIENT
Name ____________
Company Name ____________
Company Address ____________
____
Email Address ____________

SUPERVISORY APPRAISER (ONLY IF REQUIRED)

Signature ____________
Name ____________
Company Name ____________
Company Address ____________
____
Telephone Number ____________
Email Address ____________
Date of Signature ____________
State Certification # ____________
or State License # ____________
State ____________
Expiration Date of Certification or License ____________

SUBJECT PROPERTY

☐ Did not inspect subject property
☐ Did inspect exterior of subject property from street
Date of Inspection ____________
☐ Did inspect interior and exterior of subject property
Date of Inspection ____________

COMPARABLE SALES

☐ Did not inspect exterior of comparable sales from street
☐ Did inspect exterior of comparable sales from street
Date of Inspection ____________

Supplemental Addendum File No. MC16243Oxf

Borrower/Client			
Property Address			
City	County	State	Zip Code
Lender			

SUPPLEMENTAL ADDENDA

Neighborhood Description:

There are no apparent adverse factors which would affect the subject's marketability.

Access to all residential support facilities is considered average for the area:
Access to bus lines, Denver's Central Business District (19 miles away from Denver Downtown)
Commuter feeder freeways (within 2 mile from I-225)
Local parks(Mission Viejo Park, Cherry Creek State Park, Cherry Creek Lake are located within a mile/Meadow Hills Golf Course is located within a mile)
Schools (Mission Viejo Elementary School- Laredo Junior High School - Smoky Hill Senior High School are all nearby)
Hospitals (Centennial Medical Plaza is located within 5 miles)
Shopping (Park Meadows Shopping Center is located 6.5 miles)

Market Conditions:

The general market can best be described as stable and the trend is for stable real estate values.
(No significant value increase within the past 18 months was found when using statistical tool for properties located in the subdivision of Mission Viejo. The analysis of a similar 6-month period from year-to-year is reported below)

May 01, 2005 to Nov. 30, 2005:
Average Sold Price: $203,816
Median Sold Price: $195,500
Mode Sold Price: $190,000
List to Sold Price Difference Ratio: 97.65%

May 01, 2006 to Nov. 30, 2006:
Average Sold Price: $206,894
Median Sold Price: $195,000
Mode Sold Price: $190,000
List to Sold Price Difference Ratio: 97.72%

A paired sales analysis has been developped to reinforced the appraiser's opinion that real estate values have been stable in the subdivision of Mission Viejo:
- Property located on 15695 East Princeton Avenue in the subject's subdivision sold October 24th 2005 for $197,000 with seller's concessions.
- Property located on 15563 East Princeton Avenue in the subject's subdivision sold October 24th 2006 for $195,000 with no seller's concessions.

Both of these property are the same model (912SF ranch with full finished basement), are located on the same street, have similar view amenity, same site size, same age, same 2-car garage, similar condition and level of updating. These purchases are not flip transactions and the properties were in similar condition at the time of both sale. This paired sales analysis shows no value increase within the past 12 months which is in line with the numbers found earlier using statistical tools.

Marketing time in the subject area is generally less than 90 days.
Today Average Days on Market is 81 Days

Seller concessions in the form of loan discount points are common.

This analysis has been completed using all information from all comparables property similar to the subject available within the subject's market area. These data have been obtained using MLS statiscal tools.

Supplemental Addendum File No. MC16243Oxf

Borrower/Client			
Property Address			
City	County	State	Zip Code
Lender			

GENERAL ADDENDA

General Comments:

This appraisal report was prepared by Frederic Rouget at the request of and for the exclusive use of following designated client and user, Meridias Capital, and no others. This appraisal report is intended for the sole purpose of estimating the market value of the subject property. The function is to assist the client in evaluating the subject property for lending purposes. The information and opinions contained in this report set forth is the appraiser's best judgement in light of the information available at the time of preparation of this report.

Scope of the Appraisal:

The subject property has been physically inspected on the exterior and interior in order to determine the physical characteristics of the property. Measurements and pictures of the subject property have been taken at the time of the inspection and are reported in this appraisal with a sketch and exterior/interior photos. The physical inspection accomplishmed is cursory in nature which is considered sufficient for an appraisal inspection based on USPAP guidelines. It is hereby noted that the appraiser is not a certified home inspector.

Comparable properties have been researched and those presented herein are considered to be the best indicators of value.
A thourough subject's market area analysis has been completed using statiscal data as well as paired sales analysis.
Access and distance to all residential support facilities have been researched for the subject property.
In the sales comparison analysis, adjustments have been made to all value influencing factors and have been market derived using the appraiser's research and analysis.
The most accurate market value is developped during the reconciliation, using the sales comparison analysis as a primary approach to valuation.

Data gathered during the inspection as well as information derived from the appraiser's research and anlysis are presented in this report, using Fannie Mae and USPAP Guidelines.

SINGLE FAMILY COMPARABLE RENT SCHEDULE

File No. MC16243Oxf Page #13

This form is intended to provide the appraiser with a familiar format to estimate the market rent of the subject property. Adjustments should be made only for items of significant difference between the comparables and the subject property.

ITEM	SUBJECT		COMPARABLE NO. 1		COMPARABLE NO. 2		COMPARABLE NO. 3	
Address	16243 East Oxford Drive Aurora CO		3162 South Norfolk Street Aurora CO		15538 East Nassau Drive Aurora CO		2634 South Norfolk Street Aurora CO	
Proximity to Subject			1.16 miles NE		0.4 miles W		1.85 miles N	
Date Lease Begins Date Lease Expires								
Monthly Rental	If Currently Rented: $		$ 1,450		$ 1,195		$ 1,500	
Less: Utilities Furniture	$		$		$		$	
Adjusted Monthly Rent	$		$ 1,450		$ 1,195		$ 1,500	
Data Source	County Records/Deed Inspection		County Records rentclicks.com		County Records rentclicks.com		County Records rentclicks.com	
RENT ADJUSTMENTS	DESCRIPTION		DESCRIPTION	+(–)$ Adjust.	DESCRIPTION	+(–)$ Adjust.	DESCRIPTION	+(–)$ Adjust.
Rent Concessions			None Known None Known		None Known None Known		None Known None Known	
Location/View	Aurora South Resid/Avg		Aurora South Resid/Avg		Aurora South Resid/Avg		Aurora South Resid/Avg	
Design and Appeal	Ranch Average		Bi Level Average		Ranch Average		Bi Level Average	
Age/Condition	25 Years Good		32 Years Good		32 Years Inferior	+50	32 Years Good	
Above Grade Room Count (Total / Bdrms / Baths)	5 / 2 / 1		5 / 2 / 1		5 / 2 / 1		5 / 2 / 1	
Gross Living Area	912 Sq. Ft.		1,160 Sq. Ft.	-50	960 Sq. Ft.		1,007 Sq. Ft.	
Other (e.g., basement, etc.)	912 Sq.Ft. 821 SF Fin		888 Sq.Ft. 888 SF Fin		499 Sq.Ft. 349 SF Fin	+20 +50	816 Sq.Ft. 816 SF Fin	
Other:	Fence Good		2 Car Garage Updating/Good		2 Car Garage Updating/Inf	+50	2 Car Garage Updating/Good	
Net Adj. (total)			☐ + ☒ – $	-50	☒ + ☐ – $	170	☐ + ☐ – $	
Indicated Monthly Market Rent				$ 1,400		$ 1,365		$ 1,500

Comments on market data, including the range of rents for single family properties, an estimate of vacancy for single family rental properties, the general trend of rents and vacancy, and support for the above adjustments. (Rent concessions should be adjusted to the market, not to the subject property.) The market rent data range is from $1,200 to $1,500. The general trend of rents and vacancy (5%) is stable along with the economy. Gross living area SF were adjusted at $25/100SF, unfinished basement SF were adjusted at $5/100SF, finished basement were adjusted $10/100SF. Comparable#2 was adjusted for inferior condition and inferior updating.

Final Reconciliation of Market Rent: The market data rent is $1,400.00

I (WE) ESTIMATE THE MONTHLY MARKET RENT OF THE SUBJECT AS OF 12/18/2006 20__ TO BE $ ________

Appraiser(s) SIGNATURE ________ Review Appraiser (If applicable) SIGNATURE ________

NAME ________ NAME ________

Freddie Mac Form 1000 (8/88) [Y2K] Fannie Mae Form 1007 (8/88)

Real Estate Evaluations

Form RSL — "WinTOTAL" appraisal software by a la mode, inc. — 1-800-ALAMODE

Operating Income Statement

MC16243Oxf

One- to Four-Family Investment Property and Two- to Four-Family Owner-Occupied Property

Property Address

Street City State Zip Code

General Instructions: This form is to be prepared jointly by the loan applicant, the appraiser, and the lender's underwriter. The applicant must complete the following schedule indicating each unit's rental status, lease expiration date, current rent, market rent, and the responsibility for utility expenses. Rental figures must be based on the rent for an "unfurnished" unit.

	Currently Rented	Expiration Date	Current Rent Per Month	Market Rent Per Month	Utility Expense	Paid By Owner	Paid By Tenant
Unit No. 1	Yes ☐ No ☒		$	$ 1,400	Electricity	☐	☐
Unit No. 2	Yes ☐ No ☐		$	$	Gas	☐	☐
Unit No. 3	Yes ☐ No ☐		$	$	Fuel Oil	☐	☐
Unit No. 4	Yes ☐ No ☐		$	$	Fuel (Other)	☐	☐
Total			$	$ 1,400	Water/Sewer	☐	☐
					Trash Removal	☐	☐

The applicant should complete all of the income and expense projections and for existing properties provide actual year-end operating statements for the past two years *(for new properties the applicant's projected income and expenses must be provided).* This Operating Income Statement and any previous operating statements the applicant provides must then be sent to the appraiser for review, comment, and/or adjustments next to the applicant's figures *(e.g. Applicant/Appraiser 288/300).* If the appraiser is retained to complete the form instead of the applicant, the lender must provide to the appraiser the aforementioned operating statements, mortgage insurance premium, HOA dues, leasehold payments, subordinate financing, and/or any other relevant information as to the income and expenses of the subject property received from the applicant to substantiate the projections. The underwriter should carefully review the applicant's/appraiser's projections and the appraiser's comments concerning those projections. The underwriter should make any final adjustments that are necessary to more accurately reflect any income or expense items that appear unreasonable for the market. *(Real estate taxes and insurance on these types of properties are included in PITI and not calculated as an annual expense item)* Income should be based on the current rents, but should not exceed market rents. When there are no current rents because the property is proposed, new, or currently vacant, market rents should be used.

Annual Income and Expense Projection for Next 12 months

Income *(Do not include income for owner-occupied units)*	By Applicant/Appraiser	Adjustments by Lender's Underwriter
Gross Annual Rental *(from unit(s) to be rented)* (Market)	$ 16,800	$
Other Income *(include sources)*	+	+
Total	$ 16,800	$
Less Vacancy/Rent Loss	− 840 (5 %)	− (%)
Effective Gross Income	$ 15,960	$

Expenses *(Do not include expenses for owner-occupied units)*		
Electricity		
Gas		
Fuel Oil		
Fuel (Type -)		
Water/Sewer		
Trash Removal		
Pest Control		
Other Taxes or Licenses		
Casual Labor This includes the costs for public area cleaning, snow removal, etc., even though the applicant may not elect to contract for such services.		
Interior Paint/Decorating This includes the costs of contract labor and materials that are required to maintain the interiors of the living unit.		
General Repairs/Maintenance This includes the costs of contract labor and materials that are required to maintain the public corridors, stairways, roofs, mechanical systems, grounds, etc.		
Management Expenses These are the customer expenses that a professional management company would charge to manage the property.		
Supplies This includes the costs of items like light bulbs, janitorial supplies, etc.		
Total Replacement Reserves - See Schedule on Pg. 2	233	
Miscellaneous		
Total Operating Expenses	$ 233	$

Freddie Mac
Form 998 Aug 88

This Form Must Be Reproduced By Seller
Page 1 of 2

Fannie Mae
Form 216 Aug 88

Replacement Reserve Schedule

Adequate replacement reserves must be calculated regardless of whether actual reserves are provided for on the owner's operating statements or are customary in the local market. This represents the total average yearly reserves. Generally, all equipment and components that have a remaining life of more than one year - such as refrigerators, stoves, clothes washers/dryers, trash compactors, furnaces, roofs, and carpeting, etc. - should be expensed on a replacement cost basis.

Equipment	Replacement Cost		Remaining Life			By Applicant/ Appraiser	Lender Adjustments
Stoves/Ranges	@ $ 450	ea. ÷	15 Yrs. x	1	Units =	$ 30	$
Refrigerators	@ $ 300	ea. ÷	20 Yrs. x	1	Units =	$ 15	$
Dishwashers	@ $ 300	ea. ÷	20 Yrs. x	1	Units =	$ 15	$
A/C Units	@ $	ea. ÷	Yrs. x		Units =	$	$
C. Washer/Dryers	@ $	ea. ÷	Yrs. x		Units =	$	$
HW Heaters	@ $	ea. ÷	Yrs. x		Units =	$	$
Furnace(s)	@ $ 1,500	ea. ÷	20 Yrs. x	1	Units =	$ 75	$
(Other)	@ $	ea. ÷	Yrs. x		Units =	$	$
Roof	@ $ 1,200	÷	20 Yrs. x	One Bldg. =		$ 60	$

Carpeting (Wall to Wall)

	Total Sq. Yds.	Per Sq. Yd.	Remaining Life	By Applicant/ Appraiser	Lender Adjustments
(Units)	50 Total Sq. Yds. @	$ 15 Per Sq. Yd. ÷	20 Yrs. =	$ 38	$
(Public Areas)	Total Sq. Yds. @	$ Per Sq. Yd. ÷	Yrs. =	$	$
Total Replacement Reserves. (Enter on Pg. 1)				$ 233	$

Operating Income Reconciliation

$ 15,960 (Effective Gross Income) − $ 233 (Total Operating Expenses) = $ 15,727 (Operating Income) ÷ 12 = $ 1,311 (Monthly Operating Income)

$ $ 1,311 (Monthly Operating Income) − $ (Monthly Housing Expense) = $ (Net Cash Flow)

(Note: Monthly Housing Expense includes principal and interest on the mortgage, hazard insurance premiums, real estate taxes, mortgage insurance premiums, HOA dues, leasehold payments, and subordinate financing payments.)

Underwriter's instructions for 2-4 Family Owner-Occupied Properties

- If Monthly Operating Income is a positive number, enter as "Net Rental Income" in the "Gross Monthly Income" section of Freddie Mac Form 65/Fannie Mae Form 1003. If Monthly Operating Income is a negative number, it must be included as a liability for qualification purposes.
- The borrower's monthly housing expense-to-income ratio must be calculated by comparing the total Monthly Housing Expense for the **subject property** to the borrower's stable monthly income.

Underwriter's instructions for 1-4 Family Investment Properties

- If Net Cash Flow is a positive number, enter as "Net Rental Income" in the "Gross Monthly Income" section of Freddie Mac Form 65/Fannie Mae Form 1003. If Net Cash Flow is a negative number, it must be included as a liability for qualification purposes.
- The borrower's monthly housing expense-to-income ratio must be calculated by comparing the total monthly housing expense for the borrower's **primary residence** to the borrower's stable monthly income.

Appraiser's Comments *(including sources for data and rationale for the projections)*
The owner has not rented the property yet and the appraiser is using market rent derived from market rent survey. Per market analysis and typical practice/market condition, it is typical for tenants to pay all utilities expense. All maintenance and general repairs have been performed recently and no other expense are foreseen in a near future.

Appraiser Name | Appraiser Signature | Date

Underwriter's Comments and Rationale for Adjustments

Underwriter Name | Underwriter Signature | Date

Location Map

Borrower/Client			
Property Address			
City	County	State	Zip Code
Lender			

Building Sketch

Borrower/Client			
Property Address			
City	County	State	Zip Code
Lender			

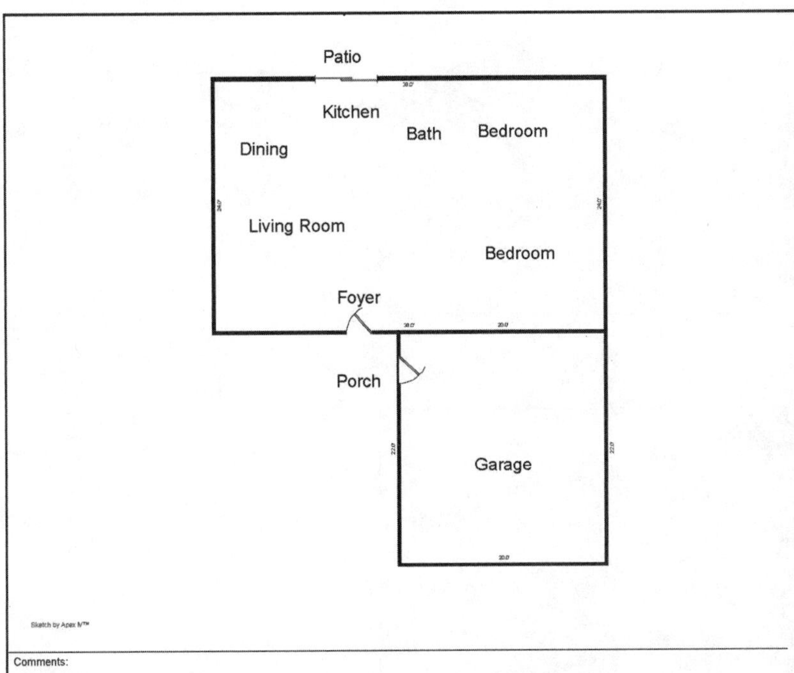

Sketch by Apex IV™

Comments:

AREA CALCULATIONS SUMMARY			
Code	Description	Net Size	Net Totals
GLA1	First Floor	912.0	912.0
GAR	Garage	440.0	440.0
	Net LIVABLE Area	(Rounded)	912

LIVING AREA BREAKDOWN	
Breakdown	Subtotals
First Floor 24.0 x 38.0	912.0
1 Item (Rounded)	912

Subject Photo Page

Borrower/Client			
Property Address			
City	County	State	Zip Code
Lender			

Subject Front

16243 East Oxford Drive

Sales Price	N/A
Gross Living Area	912
Total Rooms	5
Total Bedrooms	2
Total Bathrooms	1
Location	Aurora South
View	Resid/Avg
Site	7,187 SF
Quality	Frame
Age	25 Years

Subject Rear

Subject Street

Subject Photo Page

Borrower/Client			
Property Address			
City	County	State	Zip Code
Lender			

Subject Living Room

Sales Price	N/A
Gross Living Area	912
Total Rooms	5
Total Bedrooms	2
Total Bathrooms	1
Location	
View	Resid/Avg
Site	7,187 SF
Quality	Frame
Age	25 Years

Subject Kitchen

Subject Bathroom

Subject Photo Page

Borrower/Client			
Property Address			
City	County	State	Zip Code
Lender			

Subject Bedroom

Sales Price	N/A
Gross Living Area	912
Total Rooms	5
Total Bedrooms	2
Total Bathrooms	1
Location	Aurora South
View	Resid/Avg
Site	7,187 SF
Quality	Frame
Age	25 Years

Subject Basement

Subject Street

Comparable Photo Page

Borrower/Client			
Property Address			
City	County	State	Zip Code
Lender			

Comparable 1

Prox. to Subject	0.6 miles NE
Sale Price	185,000
Gross Living Area	912
Total Rooms	5
Total Bedrooms	2
Total Bathrooms	1
Location	Mission Viejo
View	Resid/Avg
Site	5,880 SF
Quality	Frame
Age	27 Years

Comparable 2

Prox. to Subject	0.47 miles NE
Sale Price	188,000
Gross Living Area	912
Total Rooms	5
Total Bedrooms	2
Total Bathrooms	1
Location	Mission Viejo
View	Resid/Avg
Site	5,357 SF
Quality	Frame
Age	26 Years

Comparable 3

Prox. to Subject	0.41 miles SW
Sale Price	195,000
Gross Living Area	912
Total Rooms	5
Total Bedrooms	2
Total Bathrooms	1
Location	Mission Viejo
View	Resid/Avg
Site	5,227 SF
Quality	Frame
Age	29 Years

Comparable Photo Page

Borrower/Client			
Property Address			
City	County	State	Zip Code
Lender			

Comparable 4

Prox. to Subject	0.38 miles NE
Sale Price	190,000
Gross Living Area	912
Total Rooms	5
Total Bedrooms	2
Total Bathrooms	1
Location	Mission Viejo
View	Resid/Avg
Site	6,054 SF
Quality	Frame
Age	26 Years

Comparable 5

Prox. to Subject	0.32 miles SE
Sale Price	189,000
Gross Living Area	912
Total Rooms	5
Total Bedrooms	2
Total Bathrooms	1
Location	Mission Viejo
View	Resid/Avg
Site	5,270 SF
Quality	Frame
Age	26 Years

Comparable 6

Prox. to Subject	0.33 miles SE
Sale Price	194,450
Gross Living Area	912
Total Rooms	5
Total Bedrooms	2
Total Bathrooms	1
Location	Mission Viejo
View	Resid/Avg
Site	5,226 SF
Quality	Frame
Age	26 Years

Comparable Photo Page

Borrower/Client			
Property Address			
City	County	State	Zip Code
Lender			

Comparable 7

Prox. to Subject	0.68 miles N
Sales Price	190,000
Gross Living Area	912
Total Rooms	5
Total Bedrooms	2
Total Bathrooms	1
Location	Mission Viejo
View	Resid/Avg
Site	4,791 SF
Quality	Frame
Age	27 Years

Comparable 8

Prox. to Subject	0.36 miles SE
Sales Price	199,900
Gross Living Area	912
Total Rooms	5
Total Bedrooms	2
Total Bathrooms	1
Location	Mission Viejo
View	Resid/Avg
Site	7,361 SF
Quality	Frame
Age	26 Years

Comparable 9

Prox. to Subject	
Sales Price	
Gross Living Area	
Total Rooms	
Total Bedrooms	
Total Bathrooms	
Location	
View	
Site	
Quality	
Age	

APPENDIX 3: Recommended Reading

Investing

Bronchick, William and Dahlstrom, Robert. *Financing Secrets of a Millionaire Real Estate Investor*. Kaplan Publishing (2003).

Bronchick, William and Dahlstrom, Robert. *Flipping Properties: Generate Instant Cash Profits in Real Estate*, 2nd ed. Kaplan Publishing (2006).

Bronchick, William. *Wealth Protection Secrets of a Millionaire Real Estate Investor*. Kaplan Publishing (2003).

Evans, Blanche. *Bubbles, Booms, and Busts: Make Money in ANY Real Estate Market*. McGraw Hill (2007).

Gallinelli, Frank. *What Every Real Estate Investor Needs to Know about Cash Flow...And 36 Other Key Financial Measures*. McGraw Hill (2003).

McLean, Andrew James and Eldred, Gary W. *Investing in Real Estate*, 5th ed. John Wiley & Sons, Inc. (2005).

Reilly, John. *The Language of Real Estate*. Kaplan Publishing (2006).

Shemin, Robert. *Secrets of a Millionaire Real Estate Investor*. Kaplan Publishing (2000).

Strauss, Spencer and Stone, Martin. *The Unofficial Guide to Real Estate Investing*. John Wiley & Sons, Inc. (2003).

Whitney, Russ. *Millionaire Real Estate Mentor: Investing in Real Estate: A Comprehensive and Detailed Guide to Financial Freedom for Everyone*. Kaplan Publishing (2003).

Landlording

Goodwin, Daniel et al. *The Landlord's Handbook*, 3rd ed. Kaplan Publishing (2003).

Robinson, Leigh. Landlording: *A Handymanual for Scrupulous Landlords and Landladies Who Do It Themselves*, 10th ed., Express Publishing (2006).

Taylor, Jeffrey. *The Landlord's Kit: A Complete Set of Ready-To-Use Forms, Letters, and Notices to Increase Profits, Take Control, and Eliminate the Hassle*. Kaplan Publishing (2002).

Personal Growth

Carnegie, Dale. *How to Win Friends and Influence People*, rev. ed. Pocket Books (1981).

Clason, George S. *The Richest Man in Babylon*. Signet (1988).

Hill, Napoleon. *Think and Grow Rich*. Aventine Press, Inc. (2004).

APPENDIX 4: Resources for Tenant Screening

Thorough tenant screening is a critical aspect of being a landlord. Don't shortcut this vital step. Use the following resources to check candidate tenants thoroughly:

- **www.mrlandlord.com**
- **www.tenantscreening.com**
- **www.intelius.com**
- **www.trak-1.com**
- **www.amerusa.net**
- **www.ussearch.com**
- **www.e-renter.com**
- **www.tenantchk.com**
- **www.tenantcheckusa.com**
- **www.citicredit.net**

APPENDIX 5: Sample Property Cash Flow Analysis

Here is an example of how a property cash flow analysis form is used.

Property Address:	4434 Main Street, Anywhere, USA
Property Type:	8 Units Residential
Property Value:	$600,000
Purchase Price:	$500,000
Loan:	$400,000—interest only* payments of 7.5%
Monthly Payments:	$2,796.86
Down Payment:	$100,000

ANNUAL GROSS OPERATING INCOME				
	Rents	65,000		
	Vending	2,000		
	Garages	2,000		
			Total GOI	$69,000
ANNUAL VACANCY				
	10%	6,900		
			Total NOI	$62,910
ANNUAL OPERATING EXPENSES				
	Repairs	5,000		
	Cleaning	1,000		
	Management	5,000		
	Property taxes	5,000		
	Insurance	2,000		
	Utilities	2,000		
	Maintenance	1,500		
	Association dues	N/A		
	Rental tax	N/A		
	Evictions	1,000		
	Legal	1,000		
	Water/sewer	3,000		
	Trash	1,200		
	Vending	300		
	Accounting	900		
	Advertising	800		
	Banking	200		
			Total OE	$24,900
ANNUALNET OPERATING INCOME				$38,010
ANNUAL CAP RATE				6.3%
ANNUAL DEBT SERVICE				$30,000
NET INCOME BEFORE TAXES*				$ 8,010
ANNUAL CASH ON CASH RETURN				8%

* *Note that interest-only payments are used for this example. A fully amortized loan will be mostly interest in the first few years, and mostly principal payments in the latter years. Principal payments are not deductible, but will affect your cash flow.*

Download this and other forms for FREE at *www.DefensiveRealEstateInvesting.com*

APPENDIX 6: Sample Property Disclosure Form

SELLER'S PROPERTY DISCLOSURE

Seller states that the information contained in this Disclosure is correct to the best of Seller's CURRENT ACTUAL KNOWLEDGE as of this Date. Broker may deliver a copy of this Disclosure to prospective buyers.

Date: ______________________________

Property Address: ______________________________

Seller: ______________________________

		IN WORKING CONDITION					
A.	**APPLIANCES**	**Not Included**	**Yes**	**No**	**Do Not Know**	**Age If Known**	**COMMENTS**
1	Built-in Vacuum Sys. & Accessories						
2	Clothes Dryer						
3	Clothes Washer						
4	Dishwasher						
5	Disposal						
6	Freezer						
7	Gas Grill						
8	Hood						
9	Microwave Oven						
10	Oven						
11	Range						
12	Refrigerator						
13	Room Air Conditioner						
14	T.V. Antenna ☐ Owned ☐ Leased						
15	Satellite System or DSS Dish ☐ Owned ☐ Leased						
16	Trash Compactor						
17							
18							

		IN WORKING CONDITION					
B.	**ELECTRICAL SYSTEM**	**Not Included**	**Yes**	**No**	**Do Not Know**	**Age If Known**	**COMMENTS**
1	Air Purifier						
2	Security System ☐ Owned ☐ Leased						
3	Ceiling Fan(s) #________						
4	Garage Door Opener						
5	Garage Door Control(s) #______						
6	Inside Telephone Wiring and Blocks/Jacks						
7	Intercom						
8	In-wall Speakers						
9	Smoke/Fire Detector(s)						
10	Light Fixtures						
11	Switches & Outlets						
12	Interior 110 Volt Aluminum Wiring ☐ Yes ☐ No ☐ Do Not Know						
13	Vent Fan(s)						
14	Sauna						
15	220 Volt Service ☐ Yes ☐ No ☐ Do Not Know						
16							
17							

Download this and other forms for free at www.defensiverealestateinvesting.com

		IN WORKING CONDITION					
C.	**HEATING AND COOLING**	**Not Included**	**Yes**	**No**	**Do Not Know**	**Age If Known**	**COMMENTS**
1	Attic/Whole House Fan						
2	Central Air Conditioning						
3	Evaporative Cooler						
4	Heating System: Type(s) ____________ Fuel(s) ____________						
5	Fireplace: Fuel(s) ____________						
6	Fireplace Insert						
7	Stove: Fuel(s) ____________						
8	When was fireplace/wood stove, chimney/flue last cleaned: Date ________ ☐ Do Not Know						
9	Humidifier						
10	Propane Tank ☐ Owned ☐ Leased						
11	Radiant Heating System ☐ Interior ☐ Exterior Hose Type ____________						
12							
13							
D.	**WATER SYSTEMS**						
1	Type of Water Supply: ☐ Public ☐ Community ☐ Well ☐ Shared Well ☐ Cistern ☐ None ☐ Other If the Property is served by a well, supply to Buyer a copy of the well permit. Well Permit # ____________ Water Company Name: ____________						
2	Other Water Rights included: ☐ Yes ☐ No						
3	Type of Sanitary Sewer Service: ☐ Public ☐ Community ☐ Septic System ☐ None ☐ Other If the Property is served by an on site septic system, supply to Buyer a copy of the permit. ☐ Tank ☐ Leach ☐ Lagoon						
		IN WORKING CONDITION					
		Not Included	**Yes**	**No**	**Do Not Know**	**Age If Known**	**COMMENTS**
4	Water Heater: Fuel Type ____________						
5	Hot Tub or Spa						
6	Plumbing						
7	Polybutylene Pipe ☐ Yes ☐ No ☐ Do Not Know						
8	Galvanized Pipe ☐ Yes ☐ No ☐ Do Not Know						
9	Pool						
10	Sump Pump						
11	Underground Sprinkler System						
12	Fire Sprinkler System						
13	Water Purifier						
14	Water Softener ☐ Owned ☐ Leased						
15							
16							

E.	ROOF Age, if known: _______ years	Yes	No	Do Not Know	COMMENTS
1	Roof leak				
	Past				
	Present				
2	Damage to the roof				
	Past				
	Present				
3	Roof under warranty ☐ Yes ☐ No ☐ Do Not Know				
4	Warranty transferable ☐ Yes ☐ No ☐ Do Not Know				
5	Expiration date of warranty: ________________				
6	Roof material: ________________________				
7					
8					
F.	**ENVIRONMENTAL CONDITIONS** To Seller's current actual knowledge, do any of the following conditions **now exist or have they ever existed:**	**Yes**	**No**	**Do Not Know**	**COMMENTS**
1	Methane Gas				
2	Radon Gas (EPA encourages all buyers to test for radon.)				
3	Radioactive Materials				
4	Toxic Materials				
5	Urea Formaldehyde Foam Insulation (UFFI)				
6	Asbestos: Type ________________________ Location ______________________				
7	Underground or above ground Storage Tank(s)				
8	Underground Transmission Lines				
9	Pets kept on the Property				
10	Dead, diseased or infected trees or shrubs				
11	Governmentally designated Noxious Weeds (within the last 3 years only)				
12	Property used as, situated on, or adjacent to, a dump, land fill, or municipal solid waste land fill				
13	Mine shafts, tunnels or abandoned wells on the Property				
14	Within governmentally designated Flood Plain area				
15	Sliding, settling, upheaval, movement or instability of earth, or expansive soil of the Property				
16	Governmentally designated geological hazard or sensitive area				
17	Received any notice that a portion of the Property is a governmentally designated wetland area				
18	Sewage problems				
19					
20					
G.	**STRUCTURAL CONDITIONS** To Seller's current actual knowledge, do any of the following conditions **now exist or have they ever existed:**	**Yes**	**No**	**Do Not Know**	**COMMENTS**
1	Structural problems				
2	Moisture and/or water problems				
3	Damage due to termites, other insects or rodents				
4	Damage due to wind, fire or flood				
5					
6					

Download this and other forms for free at www.defensiverealestateinvesting.com

H.	OTHER DISCLOSURES To Seller's current actual knowledge, do any of the following conditions **now exist:**	Yes	No	Do Not Know	COMMENTS
1	Encroachments, boundary disputes, unrecorded easements				
2	Shared or common areas with adjoining properties				
3	Zoning violations, variances, conditional use or non-conforming use				
4	Building Code violations				
5	Violation of restrictive covenants or owners' association rules or regulations				
6	Non-conforming use				
7	Notice of any adverse conditions about the Property from any governmental or quasi-governmental agency which have not been resolved				
8	Other legal action related to the Property				
9	Notice or threat of condemnation proceedings				
10	Property is part of an owners' association				
11	Special assessments or increases in regular assessments approved by the owners' association, but not yet implemented				
12	Governmental special improvements approved but not yet installed, which may become a lien against the Property				
13	Exterior Artificial Stucco				
14	Any additions or alterations made without a required building permit				
15					
16					

The information contained in this Disclosure has been furnished by Seller, who certifies to the truth thereof based on Seller's CURRENT ACTUAL KNOWLEDGE. Any changes will be disclosed by Seller to Buyer promptly after discovery. Seller hereby receipts for a copy of this Disclosure.

______________________________ ______________________________

Seller Seller

Date of Seller's Signature: __________________ Date of Seller's Signature: __________________

- Buyer acknowledges that Seller's indication that an item is "working" is not to be construed as a warranty of its continued operability or as a representation or warranty that such item is fit for Buyer's intended purposes or use of the Property. Buyer hereby receipts for a copy of this Disclosure. Even though Seller has answered the above questions to the best of Seller's current actual knowledge, Buyer should obtain expert assistance to accurately and fully evaluate the Property regarding use and access, water, sewer, other utilities, environmental and geological conditions, noxious weeds and other matters which may affect Buyer's use of the Property. Valuable information may be obtained from various local/state/federal agencies, and other experts may perform more specific evaluations of the Property.

______________________________ ______________________________

Buyer Buyer

Date of Buyer's Signature: __________________ Date of Buyer's Signature: __________________

Download this and other forms for free at www.defensiverealestateinvesting.com

APPENDIX 7: Sample Independent Contractor Agreement

INDEPENDENT CONTRACTOR AGREEMENT

AGREEMENT made this _______ day of ________________, 20___ by and between ______________________________ (hereinafter "Corporation") whose address is ______________________________ and ______________________________, whose address is ______________________________ (hereinafter "Contractor").

SERVICES TO BE PERFORMED

Contractor agrees to perform the following services for Corporation:

____

____

____

____

____

PLACE OF PERFORMANCE

The work described above shall be performed at:______________________________

____

TIME PERIOD

Contractor agrees to commence work as soon as practical and complete all work by____________________, 20____. Contractor agrees to subtract $________ per day for each day the work is not completed as liquidated damages and not as a penalty from the total bill of services performed.

PAYMENT FOR SERVICES

Contractor shall be paid not by the hour or the day, but upon complete of certain repairs as follows: ______________________________

____

SUPERVISION

Corporation shall not supervise or directly control the work of Contractor. Corporation does reserve the right, from time to time, to inspect the work being performed to determine whether it is being performed in a good and "workmanlike" manner. Contractor shall have the ultimate authority to determine the hours of work, the length of workdays, the means and methods of performance of the work, and Corporation shall not interfere in this regard.

MATERIALS

Contractor will obtain and provide all necessary materials for the services described above at his or her own expense.

INVOICES

Contractor agrees to provide Corporation with written invoices for all work performed.

SUBCONTRACTORS OR ASSISTANTS

Contractor may, in his or her discretion and at his or her own expense, employ such assistants or subcontractors as may be necessary for the performance of work. Contractor agrees to pay any wages, taxes, unemployment insurance, withholding taxes, and workers' compensation insurance required by law for assistants or subcontractors. Said assistants or subcontractors will not be paid or supervised by Corporation.

EQUIPMENT

Contractor agrees to provide his or her own equipment or tools for the work to be performed.

INSURANCE

Contractor agrees to provide his or her own liability insurance for work performed, naming Corporation as additional insured. In the event that Contractor does not maintain insurance, he or she shall defend and indemnify Corporation for all lawsuits, accidents, or claims arising out of his work or the work of his assistants or subcontractors.

INDEPENDENT CONTRACTOR

Contractor agrees that he or she is completely independent from Corporation and is not an employee of Corporation. Contractor warrants that he or she may and in fact does work for other individuals and/or entities.

______________________________ ______________________________

Contractor Corporation

APPENDIX 8: Sample Joint Venture Agreement

JOINT VENTURE AGREEMENT

THIS JOINT VENTURE AGREEMENT (the "Agreement") made and entered into as of this ________________day of __________________, 20____ by and between ____________________________ and ____________________________________.

1. BUSINESS PURPOSE:

The business of the Joint Venture shall be to purchase certain real estate located at ____ in the County of ____________________________, State of ____________________ for the purpose of renovation and sale for profit.

2. TERM OF THE AGREEMENT:

This Joint Venture shall commence on the date first above written and shall continue in existence until terminated, liquidated, or dissolved by law or as hereinafter provided.

3. OBLIGATIONS OF THE JOINT VENTURERS:

[Set forth in detail the obligations of the parties, for example, who will contribute cash, property, and other services; who will pay workers; who will supervise the project; and who will contribute money for cost overruns.]

4. PROFITS AND LOSSES:

Upon the sale of the property and receipt of all proceeds therefrom, the parties will be reimbursed their actual, out-of-pocket expenses directly related to the Venture. After all expenses, debts, and costs related to the Venture and the property, the parties agree to split the Net Proceeds as follows:

____________________________ shall receive _______%

____________________________ shall receive _______%

5. INDEMNIFICATION OF THE JOINT VENTURERS:

The parties to this Agreement shall have no liability to the other for any loss suffered which arises out of any action or inaction if, in good faith, it is determined that such course of conduct was in the best interests of the Joint Venture and such course of conduct did not constitute negligence or misconduct. The parties to this Agreement shall each be indemnified by the other against losses, judgments, liabilities, expenses, and amounts paid in settlement of any claims sustained by it in connection with the Joint Venture.

6. DISSOLUTION:

The Joint Venture shall be dissolved upon the happening of any of the following events:

(a) The adjudication of bankruptcy, filing of a petition pursuant to a Chapter of the Federal Bankruptcy Act, withdrawal, removal, or insolvency of either of the parties.

(b) The sale or other disposition, not including an exchange of all, or substantially all, of the Joint Venture assets.

(c) Mutual agreement of the parties.

7. COMPLETE AGREEMENT:

This Agreement constitutes the full and complete understanding and agreement of the parties hereto with respect to the subject matter hereof and there are no agreements, understandings, restrictions, or warranties among the parties other than those set forth herein provided for.

8. UNIFORM PARTNERSHIP ACT

Anything not specifically set forth herein shall be governed by the applicable rules of the Uniform Partnership Act of the State of ______________________.

IN WITNESS WHEREOF, the parties hereto have executed this Agreement as of the day and year first above written. Signed, sealed, and delivered in the presence of:

______________________________ ______________________________

Joint Venturer Joint Venturer

APPENDIX 9: Sample General Release of Liability Form

GENERAL RELEASE OF LIABILITY

TO ALL TO WHOM THESE PRESENTS SHALL COME OR MAY CONCERN, KNOW THAT

_________________________ residing at_____________________, as RELEASOR, in consideration of $____ and other good and valuable consideration received from ______________________________, as RELEASEE, receipt whereof is hereby acknowledged, releases and discharges the RELEASEE, RELEASEE'S heirs, executors, administrators, successors, and assigns from all actions, causes of action, suits, debts, dues, sums of money, accounts, reckonings, bonds, bills, specialties, covenants, contracts, controversies, agreements, promises, variances, trespasses, damages, judgments, extents, executions, claims, and demands whatsoever, in law, admiralty, or equity, which against the RELEASEE, the RELEASOR, RELEASOR'S successors and assigns ever had, now have, or hereafter can, shall or may have, for, upon, or by reason of any matter, cause, or omission whatsoever.

Whenever the text hereof requires, the use of singular number shall include the appropriate plural number as the text of the within instrument may require.

This RELEASE may not be changed orally.

IN WITNESS WHEREOF, the RELEASOR has caused this RELEASE to be executed and duly witnessed in the presence of [specify name of witness].

____________________________ ____________________________

Signature of RELEASOR Signature of Witness

STATE OF)
) ss:
COUNTY OF)

On__________ 20 _____, before me personally came ______________________, to me known, who, by me duly sworn, did depose and say that deponent executed the foregoing RELEASE in my presence and that deponent signed deponent's name by like order.

____

NOTARY

APPENDIX 10: IRS Publication 537

Department of the Treasury

Internal Revenue Service

Publication 537
Cat. No. 15067V

Installment Sales

For use in preparing

1998 Returns

Get forms and other information faster and easier by:
COMPUTER
• World Wide Web • www.irs.ustreas.gov
• FTP • ftp.irs.ustreas.gov
• IRIS at FedWorld • (703) 321-8020
FAX
• From your FAX machine, dial • (703) 368-9694
See *How To Get More Information* in this publication.

Contents

Introduction

An installment sale is a sale of property where you receive at least one payment after the close of the tax year of the sale. If you dispose of property in an installment sale, you report part of your gain or profit when you receive each installment payment. You cannot use the installment method to report a loss.

This publication discusses the general rules that apply to all installment sales. It also discusses more complex rules that apply only when certain conditions exist or certain types of property are sold. There are two examples of reporting installment sales on Form 6252 at the end of the publication.

If you sold your home or other nonbusiness property under an installment plan, you will need to read only the *General Rules*. If you sold business or rental property or had a like-kind exchange or other complex situation, see the appropriate discussion under *Other Rules*.

If you sold your entire interest in a passive activity, special rules apply to the treatment of passive activity losses. Generally, you are in a passive activity if you have a trade or business activity in which you do not materially participate or have a rental activity. See Publication 925 for information on this topic.

Useful Items

You may want to see:

Publication

- ☐ **523** Selling Your Home
- ☐ **541** Partnerships
- ☐ **544** Sales and Other Dispositions of Assets
- ☐ **550** Investment Income and Expenses
- ☐ **551** Basis of Assets
- ☐ **925** Passive Activity and At-Risk Rules

Form (and Instructions)

☐ **6252** Installment Sale Income

See *How To Get More Information* near the end of this publication for information about getting these publications and the form.

What Is an Installment Sale?

An installment sale is a sale of property where you receive at least one payment after the close of the tax year of the sale. The installment sale rules do not apply to the regular sale of inventory. See *Sale of a Business* under *Other Rules.*

If a sale qualifies as an installment sale, you must report the gain on the sale under the installment method unless you elect to recognize gain under your regular method of accounting. Under the installment method, you report prorated gain on the sale only as payments are received. It does not matter whether you use the cash or accrual method of accounting. For information on recognizing the entire gain in the year of sale, see *Electing Out of Installment Method* under *Other Rules,* later.

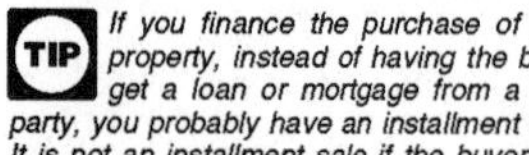

If you finance the purchase of your property, instead of having the buyer get a loan or mortgage from a third party, you probably have an installment sale. It is not an installment sale if the buyer borrows the money from a third party and then pays you the total selling price.

General Rules

The buyer's "installment obligation" to make future payments to you can be in the form of a deed of trust, note, land contract, mortgage, or other evidence of the buyer's debt to you. The rules discussed in this publication generally apply regardless of the form of the installment obligation.

Stock or securities. You cannot use the installment method to report gain from the sale of stock or securities traded on an established securities market. You must report the entire gain on the sale in the year in which the trade date falls.

Dealer sales. Sales of personal property by a person who regularly sells or otherwise disposes of the same type of property on the installment plan cannot be reported under the installment method. This also applies to real property held for sale to customers in the ordinary course of a trade or business. However, this does not apply to an installment sale of property used or produced in farming.

Special rule. Dealers of timeshares and residential lots can report certain sales on the installment method if they elect to pay a special interest charge. For more information, see section 453(l) of the Internal Revenue Code.

Sale at a loss. If your sale results in a loss, you cannot use the installment method. If the loss is on an installment sale of business assets, you can deduct it only in the tax year of sale. You cannot deduct a loss on the sale of property owned for personal use.

Unstated interest. If your sale calls for payments in a later year and the sales contract provides for little or no interest, you may have to figure unstated interest, even if you have a loss. See *Unstated Interest,* later.

Figuring Installment Income

Each payment on an installment sale usually consists of the following three parts.

1) Interest income.
2) Return of your adjusted basis in the property.
3) Gain on the sale.

In each year you receive a payment, you must include the interest part in income, as well as the part that is your gain on the sale. You do not include in income the part that is the return of your basis in the property.

Interest income. You must report interest as ordinary income. Interest is generally not included in a down payment. However, you may have to treat part of each later payment as interest, even if it is not called interest in your agreement with the buyer. See *Unstated Interest,* later.

Return of basis and gain on sale. The rest of each payment is treated as if it were made up of two parts. One part is a tax-free return of your adjusted basis in the property. The other part is your gain.

Figuring gain part of payment. To figure what part of any payment is gain, multiply the payment (less interest) by the gross profit percentage. Use the following worksheet to figure the gross profit percentage.

1) Selling price .... ______
2) Installment sale basis:
   Adjusted basis of property ... ______
   Selling expenses .... ______
   Depreciation recapture .... ______ ______
3) Gross profit (line 1 – line 2) .... ______
4) Contract price .... ______
5) Gross profit percentage (line 3 ÷ line 4) . ______

Selling price. The selling price is the total cost of the property to the buyer. It includes any money and the fair market value of any property you are to receive. Fair market value (FMV) is discussed later under *Payment of property.* It also includes any debt the buyer pays, assumes, or takes, to which the property is subject. The debt could be a note, mortgage, or any other liability, such as a lien, accrued interest, or taxes you owe on the property. If the buyer pays any of your selling expenses for you, that amount is also included in the selling price. The selling price does not include interest, whether stated or unstated.

Installment sale basis. This publication refers to the adjusted basis plus selling expenses and depreciation recapture income (see *Other Rules)* as the installment sale basis.

Adjusted basis. Basis is a way of measuring your investment in the property you are selling. The way you figure basis depends on how you first acquired the property. The basis of property you bought is generally its cost. The basis of property you inherited, received as a gift, built yourself, or received in a tax-free exchange is figured differently.

While you own personal-use property, various events may change your original basis in the property. Some events, such as adding rooms or making permanent improvements, increase basis. Others, such as deductible casualty losses or depreciation previously allowed or allowable, decrease basis. The result is adjusted basis.

For more information on how to figure basis and adjusted basis, see Publication 551.

Selling expenses. Selling expenses are any expenses that relate to the sale of the property. They include commissions, attorney fees, and any other expenses paid on the sale. Selling expenses are added to the basis of the sold property.

Depreciation recapture. If you took depreciation deductions on the asset, part of the gain on the sale of the asset may be recaptured as ordinary income. See the discussion of depreciation recapture under *Other Rules,* later.

Gross profit. For an installment sale, gross profit is the total gain you report on the installment method.

To figure your gross profit, subtract your installment sale basis from the selling price. If the property you sold was your home, subtract from the gross profit any gain you can exclude. See *Sale of your home,* later, under *Reporting Installment Income.*

Contract price. The contract price is the total of all principal payments you are to receive on the installment sale. It includes payments you are considered to receive, even though you are not paid anything directly. See *Payments Received,* later.

If part of the selling price is paid in cash and you hold a mortgage payable from the buyer to you for the remainder, then the contract price equals the selling price.

Gross profit percentage. A certain percentage of each payment (after subtracting interest) is reported as gain from the sale. It is called the "gross profit percentage" and is figured by dividing your gross profit from the sale by the contract price.

The gross profit percentage generally remains the same for each payment you receive. However, see the example under *Selling price reduced,* later, for a situation where the gross profit percentage changes.

Example. You sell property at a contract price of $2,000 and your gross profit is $500. Your gross profit percentage is 25% ($500 ÷ $2,000). After subtracting interest, you report as gain from the sale, 25% of each payment, including the down payment, for the tax year you receive the payment.

Amount to include in income. Each year you receive a payment on the installment sale, multiply the payment (less interest) by the gross profit percentage to determine the amount you must include in income for the tax year. In certain circumstances, you may be considered to have received a payment, even though you received nothing directly. In addition to cash, a receipt of property or the assumption of your mortgage on the property sold may be considered a payment. For a detailed discussion, see *Payments Received* under *Other Rules,* later.

Selling price reduced. If the selling price is reduced at a later date, the gross profit on the sale will also change. You must then refigure your gross profit percentage for the remaining payments. Refigure your gross profit using the reduced sale price and then subtract the gain already reported. Spread the remaining gain over the remaining installments. You cannot go back and refigure the gain you reported in earlier years.

Example. In 1996, you sold land with a basis of $40,000 for $100,000. Your gross profit was $60,000. You received a $20,000 down payment and the buyer's note for $80,000. The note provides for four annual payments of $20,000 each, plus 12% interest, beginning in 1997. Your gross profit percentage is 60%. You reported a gain of $12,000 on each payment received in 1996 and 1997.

In 1998, you and the buyer agreed to reduce the purchase price to $85,000 and payments during 1998, 1999, and 2000 are reduced to $15,000 for each year.

The new gross profit percentage, 46.67%, is figured as follows.

1) Reduced selling price		$85,000
2) Minus: Basis		40,000
3) Adjusted gross profit		$45,000
4) Minus: Gain reported in 1996 & 1997		24,000
5) Gain to be reported		$21,000
6) Selling price to be received:		
Reduced selling price	$85,000	
Minus: Payments received in 1996 and 1997	40,000	$45,000
7) New gross profit percentage (line 5 ÷ line 6)		46.67%

You will report a gain of $7,000 (46.67% of $15,000) on each of the $15,000 installments due in 1998, 1999, and 2000.

Reporting Installment Income

Form 6252. You must use Form 6252 to report a sale of property as an installment sale. Use the form to report the sale in the year it takes place and to report payments received in later years. Attach it to your tax return for each year.

Form 6252 will help you determine the gross profit, contract price, gross profit percentage, and how much of each payment received during the tax year to include in income.

Form 6252 is divided into the following parts.

1) Part I, *Gross Profit and Contract Price,* is completed for the year of sale.
2) Part II, *Installment Sale Income,* is completed for the year of sale and for any year you receive a payment or are considered to have received a payment.
3) Part III, *Related Party Installment Sale Income,* is completed if you sold the property to a related person, as discussed later under *Sale to Related Person.*

Year of sale. Answer the questions at the beginning of the form and complete Part I and Part II. Question 3 asks whether you sold the property to a related party. If you answer "Yes," answer question 4 and complete Part III.

Later years. Answer the questions at the beginning of the form and complete Part II for each year in which you receive a payment on the sale. If you sold the property to a related person, you may have to complete Part III also.

Schedule D (Form 1040). Enter the gain figured on Form 6252 for personal-use property (capital assets) on Schedule D (Form 1040), *Capital Gains and Losses.* If your gain from the installment sale qualifies for long-term capital gain treatment in the year of sale, it will continue to qualify in later tax years. Your gain is long-term if you owned the property for more than one year when you sold it.

Form 4797. An installment sale of property used in your business or that earns rent or royalty income may result in a capital gain, an ordinary gain, or both. All or part of any gain from its disposition may be ordinary gain from depreciation recapture. Use Form 4797 to report these transactions and to determine the ordinary or capital gain or loss.

Sale of your home. If you sell your home, you may be able to exclude all or part of the gain on the sale. See Publication 523 for information about excluding the gain. If the sale is an installment sale, any gain you exclude is not included in gross profit when figuring your gross profit percentage.

Seller-financed mortgage. Special reporting procedures apply if you finance the sale of your home to an individual.

When you report interest income received from a buyer who uses the property as a personal residence, write the buyer's name, address, and social security number (SSN) on line 1 of Schedule B (Form 1040) or Schedule 1 (Form 1040A).

When deducting the mortgage interest, the buyer must write your name, address, and SSN on line 11 of Schedule A (Form 1040).

If either person fails to include the other person's SSN, a $50 penalty may apply.

Other Rules

The rules discussed in this part of the publication apply only in certain circumstances or to certain types of property. The rules cover the following topics.

1) Electing out of the installment method.
2) Payments received, including those considered received.
3) An escrow account.
4) Depreciation recapture income.
5) A sale to a related person.
6) A like-kind exchange.
7) A contingent payment sale.
8) A single sale of several assets.
9) The sale of a business.
10) Unstated interest.
11) Disposition of an installment obligation.
12) A repossession.

Electing Out of Installment Method

You must use the installment method to report an installment sale unless you elect not to use that method. If you make the election, you generally report the entire gain in the year of sale, even though you will not be paid all of the selling price in that year.

To figure the gain to report, use the FMV of the buyer's installment obligation. Notes, mortgages, and land contracts are examples of obligations that are included at FMV.

You must figure the FMV of the buyer's installment obligation, whether or not you would actually be able to sell it. If you use the cash method of accounting, the FMV of the obligation will never be considered less than the FMV of the property sold (minus any other consideration received). If you use an accrual method of accounting, you must always use the full face value of the installment obligation as its FMV.

Example. You sold a parcel of land for $50,000. You received a $10,000 down payment and will receive the balance over the next 10 years at $4,000 a year, plus 8% interest. The buyer gave you a note for $40,000. The note had an FMV of $40,000. You paid a commission of 6%, or $3,000, to a broker for negotiating the sale. The land cost $25,000 and you owned it for more than one year. You decide to elect out of the installment method and report the entire gain in the year of sale.

Gain realized:		
Selling price		$50,000
Minus: Property's adj. basis	$25,000	
Commission	3,000	28,000
Gain realized		$22,000
Gain recognized in year of sale:		
Cash		$10,000
Market value of note		40,000
Total realized in year of sale		$50,000
Minus: Property's adj. basis	$25,000	
Commission	3,000	28,000
Gain recognized		$22,000

The recognized gain of $22,000 is long-term capital gain. Since you include the entire gain in income in the year of sale, you do not include in income any principal payments you receive in later tax years. The interest on the note is ordinary income and is reported as interest income each year.

How to elect out. To make this election, do not report your sale on Form 6252. Instead, report it on Schedule D (Form 1040) or Form 4797, whichever applies.

When to elect out. Make this election by the due date, including extensions, for filing your tax return for the year the sale takes place. Once made, the election generally cannot be revoked. However, you can apply to the IRS to revoke the election not to use the installment method. You will not be allowed to revoke the election if either of the following situations applies.

1) One of the purposes is to avoid federal income tax.
2) The tax year in which any payment was received has closed.

You may qualify for an automatic extension of six months from the due date of the return, ***excluding extensions,*** to make this election. See Regulations sections 301.9100–2(b) and (d) for more information. You can read the full text of these provisions at some IRS offices and public libraries.

Payments Received

Including Payments Considered Received

You must figure your gain each year on the payments you receive, or are treated as receiving, from an installment sale. These payments include the down payment and each later payment of principal on the buyer's debt to you.

In certain situations, you are considered to have received a payment, even though the buyer does not pay you directly. These situations arise if the buyer assumes or pays any of your debts, such as a loan, or pays any of your expenses, such as a sales commission.

Buyer pays seller's expenses. If the buyer pays any of your expenses related to the sale of your property, it is considered a payment to you in the year of sale. Include these expenses in the selling and contract prices when figuring the gross profit percentage.

Buyer assumes mortgage. If the buyer assumes or pays off your mortgage, or otherwise takes the property subject to the mortgage, the following rules apply.

Mortgage less than basis. If the buyer assumes a mortgage that is less than your installment sale basis in the property, it is not considered a payment to you. The contract price equals the selling price minus the mortgage. This difference is all that you will directly collect from the buyer.

Example. You sell property with an adjusted basis of $19,000. You have selling expenses of $1,000. The buyer assumes your existing mortgage of $15,000 and agrees to pay you $10,000 (a cash down payment of $2,000 and $2,000 (plus 8% interest) in each of the next 4 years).

The selling price is $25,000 ($15,000 + $10,000). Your gross profit is $5,000 ($25,000 – $20,000 installment sale basis). The contract price is $10,000 ($25,000 – $15,000 mortgage). Your gross profit percentage is 50% ($5,000 ÷ $10,000). You report half of each $2,000 payment received as gain from the sale. You also report all interest you receive as ordinary income.

Mortgage more than basis. If the buyer assumes a mortgage that is more than your installment sale basis in the property, you recover your entire basis. You are also relieved of the obligation to repay the amount borrowed. The part of the mortgage greater than your basis is treated as a payment received in the year of sale. This is in addition to the buyer's other payments.

To figure the contract price, subtract the mortgage from the selling price. This is the total you will actually receive from the buyer. Add to this amount the "payment" you are considered to receive (the difference between the mortgage and your installment sale basis). The contract price is then the same as your gross profit from the sale.

If the mortgage the buyer assumes is equal to or more than your installment sale basis in the property, the gross profit percentage will always be 100%.

Example. The selling price for your property is $9,000. The buyer will pay you $1,000 annually (plus 8% interest) over the next 3 years and assume an existing mortgage of $6,000. Your adjusted basis in the property is $4,400. You have selling expenses of $600, for a total installment sale basis of $5,000. The part of the mortgage that is more than your installment sale basis is $1,000 ($6,000 – $5,000). This amount is included in the contract price and treated as a payment received in the year of sale. The contract price is $4,000:

Selling price		$9,000
Minus: Mortgage		(6,000)
Amount actually received		$3,000
Add difference:		
Mortgage	$6,000	
Less: Installment sale basis	5,000	1,000
Contract price		$4,000

Your gross profit on the sale is also $4,000:

Selling price	$9,000
Minus: Installment sale basis	(5,000)
Gross profit	$4,000

Your gross profit percentage is 100%. Report 100% of each payment as gain from the sale. Treat the $1,000 difference between the mortgage and your installment sale basis as a payment and report 100% of it as gain in the year of sale.

Mortgage canceled. If the buyer of your property is the person who holds the mortgage on it, your debt is canceled, not assumed. You are considered to receive a payment equal to the outstanding canceled debt.

Example. Mary Jones loaned you $4,500 in 1994 in exchange for a note mortgaging a tract of land you owned. On April 4, 1998, she bought the land for $7,000. At that time, $3,000 of her loan to you was outstanding. She agreed to forgive this $3,000 debt and to pay you $2,000 (plus interest) on August 1, 1998, and August 1, 1999. She did not assume an existing mortgage. She canceled the $3,000 debt you owed her. You are considered to have received a $3,000 payment at the time of the sale.

Buyer assumes other debts. If the buyer assumes your other debts, such as a loan or back taxes, it may be considered a payment to you in the year of sale.

If the buyer assumes the debt instead of paying it off, only part of it may have to be treated as a payment. Compare the debt to your installment sale basis in the property being sold. If the debt is less than your installment sale basis, none of it is treated as a payment. If it is more, only the difference is treated as a payment. If the buyer assumes more than one debt, any part of the total that is more than your installment sale basis is considered a payment. These rules are the same as the rules discussed earlier under *Buyer assumes mortgage.* However, they apply to only the following two types of debts the buyer assumes.

1) Those acquired from ownership of the property you are selling, such as a mortgage, lien, overdue interest, or back taxes.
2) Those acquired in the ordinary course of your business, such as a balance due for inventory you purchased.

If the buyer assumes any other type of debt, such as a personal loan, it is treated as if the buyer had paid off the debt at the time of the sale. The value of the assumed debt is then considered a payment to you in the year of sale.

Payment of property. If you receive property rather than money from the buyer, it is still considered a payment. However, see *Like-Kind Exchange,* later. The value of the payment is the property's FMV on the date you receive it.

Fair market value (FMV). This is the price at which property would change hands between a buyer and a seller, neither being required to buy or sell, and both having a reasonable knowledge of all necessary facts. If your installment sale fits this description, the value assigned to property in your agreement with the buyer is good evidence of its FMV.

Third-party note. If the property the buyer gives you is a third-party note (or other obligation of a third party), you are considered to have received a payment equal to the note's FMV. Because the note is itself a payment on your installment sale, any payments you later receive from the third party are not considered payments on your sale.

Example. You sold real estate in an installment sale. As part of the down payment, the buyer assigned to you a $5,000, 8% note of a third party. The FMV of the third-party note at the time of your sale was $3,000. This amount, not $5,000, is a payment to you in the year of sale. Because the third-party note had an FMV equal to 60% of its face value ($3,000 ÷ $5,000), 60% of each payment of principal you receive on this note is a return of capital. The remaining 40% is ordinary income. Report the interest you receive in full as ordinary income.

Bond. A bond or other evidence of debt you receive from the buyer that is payable on demand is treated as a payment in the year you receive it. If you receive a government or corporate bond that has interest coupons attached or that can be readily traded in an established securities market, you are considered to have received payment equal to the bond's FMV. Accrual basis taxpayers should see Regulations section 15A.453–1(e)(2).

Buyer's note. The buyer's note (unless payable on demand) is not considered payment on the sale. Its full face value is included when figuring the selling price and the contract price. Payments you receive on the note are used to figure your gain in the year you receive them.

Guarantee. If a third party or government agency guarantees the buyer's payments to you on an installment obligation, the guarantee itself is not considered payment.

Installment obligation used as security (pledge rule). If you use an installment obligation to secure any debt, the net proceeds from the debt may be treated as a payment on the installment obligation. This is known as the pledge rule and it applies if the selling price of the property was over $150,000. It does not apply to the following dispositions.

1) Sales of property used or produced in farming.
2) Sales of personal-use property.
3) Qualifying sales of timeshares and residential lots.

The net debt proceeds are the gross debt minus the direct expenses of getting the debt. The amount treated as a payment is considered received on the later of either of the following dates.

1) The date the debt becomes secured.

2) The date you receive the debt proceeds.

A debt is secured by an installment obligation to the extent that payment of principal or interest on the debt is directly secured (under the terms of the loan or any underlying arrangement) by any interest in the installment obligation.

Limit. The net debt proceeds treated as a payment on the pledged installment obligation cannot be more than the excess of the amount in item 1 over the amount in item 2, below.

1) The total contract price on the installment sale.

2) Any payments received on the installment obligation before the date the net debt proceeds are treated as a payment.

Installment payments. The pledge rule accelerates the reporting of the installment obligation payments. Do not report payments received on the obligation after it has been pledged until the payments received are more than the amount reported under the pledge rule.

Exception. The pledge rule does not apply to debt incurred after December 17, 1987, to refinance a debt under the following circumstances.

1) The debt was outstanding on December 17, 1987.

2) The debt was secured by that installment sale obligation on that date and at all times thereafter until the refinancing occurred.

A refinancing as a result of the creditor's calling of the debt is treated as a continuation of the original debt if a person other than the creditor or a person related to the creditor provides the refinancing.

This exception applies only to the refinancing that does not exceed the principal of the original debt immediately before the refinancing. Any excess is treated as a payment on the installment obligation.

Escrow Account

In some cases, the sales agreement, or a later agreement, may call for the buyer to establish an irrevocable escrow account from which the remaining installment payments (including interest) are to be made. Generally, these sales cannot be reported on the installment method. The buyer's obligation is paid in full when the balance of the purchase price is deposited into the escrow account. When an escrow account is established, you no longer rely on the buyer for the rest of the payments, but on the escrow arrangement.

Example. You sell property for $10,000. The sales agreement calls for a down payment of $1,000 and payment of $1,500 in each of the next 6 years to be made from an irrevocable escrow account containing the balance of the purchase price plus interest. You cannot report the sale on the installment method because the full purchase price is considered received in the year of sale. You must report the entire gain in the year of sale.

Escrow established in a later year. If you make an installment sale and in a later year an irrevocable escrow account is established to pay the remaining installments plus interest, the amount placed in the escrow account represents payment of the balance of the installment obligation. Therefore, you cannot use the installment method to report any payments you receive from the escrow account.

Substantial restriction. If an escrow arrangement imposes a substantial restriction on your right to receive the sale proceeds, the sale can be reported on the installment method, provided it otherwise qualifies. For an escrow arrangement to impose a substantial restriction, it must serve a bona fide purpose of the buyer, that is, a real and definite restriction placed on the seller or a specific economic benefit conferred on the buyer.

Depreciation Recapture Income

If you sell property for which you claimed depreciation deductions, report any depreciation recapture income in the year of sale, whether or not an installment payment was received that year. Figure your depreciation recapture income (including the section 179 deduction and the section 179A deduction recapture) in Part III of **Form 4797.** Report the recapture income in Part II of Form 4797 as ordinary income in the year of sale. The recapture income is also included in Part I of Form 6252. However, the gain equal to the recapture income is not reported on the installment method. Report any gain greater than the recapture income on the installment method. For more information on depreciation recapture, see chapter 3 in Publication 544.

The ordinary recapture income reported in the year of sale is included in your installment sale basis in determining your gross profit on the installment sale. See the discussion under *General Rules,* earlier.

Sale to Related Person

Two special rules apply to an installment sale between related persons. Test your sale against Rule 1 first. If Rule 1 does not apply, test your sale against Rule 2. For purposes of these rules, spouses, children, grandchildren, brothers, sisters, and parents are all considered related persons. A partnership or corporation in which you have an interest, or an estate or trust with which you have a connection, can also be considered a related person.

For more information on these kinds of sales, see section 453 of the Internal Revenue Code.

Rule 1—Sale of Depreciable Property

If you sell depreciable property to certain related persons, you cannot report the sale using the installment method. Instead, all payments to be received are considered received in the year of sale. Depreciable property for this rule is any property that the purchaser can depreciate.

Payments to be received include the total of all noncontingent payments and the FMV of any payment contingent as to amount.

In the case of contingent payments for which the FMV cannot be reasonably determined, the basis is recovered ratably. The purchaser cannot increase the basis of any property acquired in the sale by any amount before the seller includes the amount in income.

Exceptions to Rule 1. Rule 1 will not apply if no significant tax deferral benefit will be derived from the sale. It does not apply if you can show to the satisfaction of IRS that avoidance of federal income tax was not one of the principal purposes of the sale.

Rule 2—Sale and Resale

Generally, a special rule applies if you (an installment seller) make a first disposition (sale or exchange) to a related person who then makes a second disposition (sale, exchange, or gift) under the following circumstances.

1) The related person makes the second disposition before making all payments on the first disposition.

2) The related person makes the second disposition within 2 years of the first disposition.

Under this rule, you treat part or all of the amount the related person realizes (or the FMV if the disposed property is not sold or exchanged) from the second disposition as if you received it from the first disposition at the time of the second disposition.

Example 1. In 1997, Harvey Green sold farm land to his son Bob for $500,000, which was to be paid in five equal payments over 5 years, plus adequate stated interest on the balance due. His installment sale basis for the farm land was $250,000 and the property was not subject to any outstanding liens or mortgages. His gross profit percentage is 50% (gross profit of $250,000 ÷ contract price of $500,000). He received $100,000 in 1997 and included $50,000 in income for that year ($100,000 × 0.50). Bob made no improvements to the property and sold it to Alfalfa Inc. in 1998 for $600,000 after making the payment for that year. The amount realized from the second disposition is $600,000. Harvey figures his installment sale income for 1998 as follows:

Lesser of: 1) Amount realized on second disposition, or 2) Contract price on first disposition	$500,000
Subtract: Sum of payments from Bob in 1997 and 1998	− 200,000
Amount treated as payment because of second disposition	$300,000
Add: Payment from Bob in 1998	+ 100,000
Total payments received and treated as received for 1998	$400,000
Multiply by gross profit %	× .50
Installment sale income for 1998	$200,000

Harvey will not include in his installment sale income any principal payments he receives on the installment obligation for 1999, 2000, and 2001 because he has already reported the total payments of $500,000 from the first disposition ($100,000 in 1997 and $400,000 in 1998).

Example 2. Assume the facts are the same as *Example 1* except that Bob sells the property for only $400,000. The gain for 1998 is figured as follows:

Lesser of: 1) Amount realized on second disposition, or 2) Contract price on first disposition	$400,000
Subtract: Sum of payments from Bob in 1997 and 1998	– 200,000
Amount treated as payment because of second disposition	$200,000
Add: Payment from Bob in 1998	+ 100,000
Total payments received and treated as received for 1998	$300,000
Multiply by gross profit %	× .50
Installment sale income for 1998	$150,000

Harvey receives a $100,000 payment in 1999 and another in 2000. They are not taxed because he treated the $200,000 from the disposition in 1998 as a payment received and paid tax on the gain. In 2001, he receives the final $100,000 payment. He figures the gain he must recognize in 2001 as follows:

Total payments from the first disposition received by the end of 2001		$500,000
Minus the sum of:		
Payment from 1997	$100,000	
Payment from 1998	100,000	
Amount treated as payment in 1998	200,000	
Total on which gain was previously recognized		– 400,000
Payment on which gain is recognized for 2001		$100,000
Multiply by gross profit %		× .50
Installment sale income for 2001		$50,000

Exceptions to Rule 2. These rules do not apply to a second disposition, and any later transfer, if you can show, to the satisfaction of the IRS, that neither the first disposition (to the related person) nor the second disposition had as one of its principal purposes the avoidance of federal income tax. Generally, an involuntary second disposition will qualify under the nontax avoidance exception, such as when a creditor of the related person forecloses on the property or the related person declares bankruptcy.

The nontax avoidance exception also applies to a second disposition that is also an installment sale if the terms of payment under the installment resale are substantially equal to or longer than those for the first installment sale. However, the exception does not apply if the resale terms permit significant deferral of recognition of gain from the first sale as, for example, if amounts from the resale are collected sooner.

In addition, any sale or exchange of stock to the issuing corporation is not treated as a first disposition. An involuntary conversion is not treated as a second disposition if the first disposition occurred before the threat of conversion. A transfer after the death of the person making the first disposition or the related person's death, whichever is earlier, is not treated as a second disposition.

Like-Kind Exchange

If you trade business or investment property for the same kind of property, you can postpone reporting part of the gain. These trades are known as "like-kind exchanges." The property you receive in a like-kind exchange is treated as if it were a continuation of the property you give up.

In a like-kind exchange, you do not have to report any part of your gain if you receive only like-kind property. However, if you also receive money or other property in the exchange, you must report your gain to the extent of the money and the FMV of the other property received.

For more information on like-kind exchanges, see *Like-Kind Exchanges* in chapter 1 of Publication 544.

Installment payments. If, in addition to like-kind property, you receive an installment obligation in the exchange, the following rules apply.

1) The contract price is reduced by the FMV of the like-kind property received in the trade.

2) The gross profit is reduced by any gain on the trade that can be postponed.

3) Like-kind property received in the trade is not considered payment on the installment obligation.

Example. In 1998, George Brown trades personal property with an installment sale basis of $400,000 for like-kind property having an FMV of $200,000. He also receives an installment note for $800,000 in the trade. Under the terms of the note, he is to receive $100,000 (plus interest) in 1999 and the balance of $700,000 (plus interest) in 2000.

George's selling price is $1,000,000 ($800,000 installment note + $200,000 FMV of like-kind property received). His gross profit is $600,000 ($1,000,000 – $400,000 installment sale basis). The contract price is $800,000 ($1,000,000 – $200,000). The gross profit percentage is 75% ($600,000 ÷ $800,000). He reports no gain in 1998 because the like-kind property he receives is not treated as a payment for figuring gain. He reports $75,000 gain for 1999 (75% of $100,000 payment received) and $525,000 gain for 2000 (75% of $700,000 payment received).

Deferred exchanges. A deferred exchange is one in which you have transferred the property and are to receive like-kind property at a later date. Under this type of exchange, the person receiving your property may be required to place funds in an escrow account or trust. If certain rules are met, these funds will not be considered a payment until you have the right to receive the funds or, if earlier, the end of the exchange period. See Regulations section 1.1031(k)–1(j)(2) for these rules.

Contingent Payment Sale

For installment sales, a contingent payment sale is one whose total selling price cannot be determined by the end of the tax year in which the sale takes place.

If the selling price cannot be determined by the end of the tax year, the contract price and the gross profit percentage cannot be determined (using the same rules that apply to an installment sale with a fixed selling price). This happens, for example, if you sell your business and the selling price includes a percentage of its profits in future years.

For rules on using the installment method for a contingent payment sale or a contingent payment sale with unstated interest, see Regulations section 15A.453–1(c).

Single Sale of Several Assets

If you sell different types of assets in a single sale, you must identify each asset to determine whether you can use the installment method to report the sale of that asset. You also have to allocate part of the selling price to each asset. If you sell assets that constitute a trade or business, see *Sale of a Business,* next.

Unless an allocation of the selling price has been agreed to by both parties in an arm's-length transaction, you must allocate the selling price to an asset based on its FMV. If the buyer assumes a debt, or takes the property subject to a debt, you must reduce the FMV by the debt. This is the net FMV.

A sale of separate and unrelated assets of the same type under a single contract is reported as one transaction for the installment method. However, if an asset is sold at a loss, its disposition cannot be reported on the installment method. It must be reported separately. The remaining assets sold at a gain are reported together.

Example. You sold three separate and unrelated parcels of real property (A, B, and C) under a single contract calling for a total selling price of $130,000. The total selling price consisted of a cash payment of $20,000, the buyer's assumption of a $30,000 mortgage on parcel B, and an installment obligation of $80,000 payable in eight annual installments, plus interest at 8% a year.

Your installment sale basis for each parcel was $15,000. Your net gain was $85,000 ($130,000 – $45,000). You report the gain on the installment method.

The sales contract did not allocate the selling price or the cash payment received in the year of sale among the individual parcels. The FMV of parcels A, B, and C were $60,000, $60,000, and $10,000, respectively.

Since the installment sale basis for parcel C was more than its FMV, it was sold at a loss and must be treated separately. You must allocate the total selling price and the amounts received in the year of sale between parcel C and the remaining parcels.

Of the total $130,000 selling price, you must allocate $120,000 to parcels A and B together and $10,000 to parcel C. You should allocate the cash payment of $20,000 received in the year of sale and the note receivable on the basis of the proportionate net FMV. The allocation is figured as follows:

	Parcels A and B	Parcel C
FMV	$120,000	$10,000
Minus: Mortgage assumed	30,000	-0-
Net FMV	$90,000	$10,000
Proportionate net FMV: Percentage of total	90%	10%
Payments in year of sale:		
$20,000 × 90%	$18,000	
$20,000 × 10%		$2,000
Excess of parcel B mortgage over installment sale basis	15,000	
Allocation of payments received (or considered received) in year of sale	$33,000	$2,000

You cannot report the sale of parcel C on the installment method because the sale results in a loss. You report this loss of $5,000 ($10,000 selling price – $15,000 installment sale basis) in the year of sale. However, if parcel C was held for personal use, the loss is not deductible.

You allocate the installment obligation of $80,000 to the properties sold based on their proportionate net FMVs (90% to parcels A and B, 10% to parcel C).

Sale of a Business

The installment sale of an entire business for one overall price under a single contract is not the sale of a single asset.

Allocation of selling price. The selling price must be allocated for each asset class for the following reasons.

1) The sale of a business generally includes real and personal property that can be reported on the installment method and inventory items that cannot.

2) Any depreciation recapture income from the sale of depreciable property cannot be reported on the installment method. It is reported in full in the year of the sale.

3) Assets sold at a loss cannot be reported on the installment method.

Inventory. If inventory items are included in an installment sale, you may have an agreement stating which payments are for inventory and which are for the other assets being sold. If you do not, each payment must be allocated between the inventory and the other assets sold.

The sale of inventory items cannot be reported on the installment method. All gain or loss on their sale must be reported in the year of sale, even if you are paid in later years.

Report the amount you receive (or will receive) on the sale of inventory items as ordinary business income. Use your basis in the items to figure the cost of goods sold and deduct the part of the selling expenses allocated to inventory as an ordinary business expense.

Residual method. Except for assets exchanged under the like-kind exchange rules, both the buyer and seller of a business must use the residual method to allocate the sale price to each business asset transferred. This method determines gain or loss from the transfer of each asset.

The residual method must be used for any transfer of a group of assets that constitutes a trade or business and for which the buyer's basis is determined only by the amount paid for the assets. This applies to both direct and indirect transfers, such as the sale of a business or the sale of a partnership interest in which the basis of the buyer's share of the partnership assets is adjusted for the amount paid. A group of assets constitutes a trade or business if goodwill or going concern value could, under any circumstances, attach to the assets.

The residual method provides for the sale price to first be reduced by cash, demand deposits, and similar accounts transferred by the seller. The sale price remaining after this reduction must be allocated among the various business assets in a specified order.

The allocation must be made among the following assets in proportion to (but not in excess of) their FMV on the purchase date in the following order.

1) Certificates of deposit, U.S. government securities, readily marketable stock or securities, and foreign currency.

2) All other assets except section 197 intangibles.

3) Section 197 intangibles, except intangible assets in the nature of goodwill and going concern value.

4) Section 197 intangibles in the nature of goodwill and going concern value.

More information. For more information, see *Sale of a Business* in chapter 2 of Publication 544. For more information on section 197 intangibles, see chapter 12 of Publication 535.

How to report the sale of a business. Both the seller and buyer must prepare and attach **Form 8594**, *Asset Acquisition Statement Under Section 1060,* to their income tax return for the year the sale occurred. If the amount allocated to any asset is increased or decreased after Form 8594 is filed, a supplemental statement in Part III of a new Form 8594 must be completed.

Sale of partnership interest. A partner who sells a partnership interest at a gain may be able to report the sale on the installment method. The sale of a partnership interest is treated as the sale of a single capital asset. However, the partner must allocate a portion of the proceeds to ordinary income if the partnership's assets included unrealized receivables and inventory items. (The term "unrealized receivables" includes depreciation recapture income, discussed earlier.)

The gain allocated to the unrealized receivables and the inventory cannot be reported under the installment method. The gain allocated to the other assets can be reported under the installment method.

For more information on the treatment of unrealized receivables and inventory, see Publication 541.

Example

On January 4, 1998, you sold the machine shop you operated since 1988. You received a $100,000 down payment and the buyer's note for $120,000. The note payments are $15,000 each, plus 10% interest, due every July 1 and January 1, beginning in 1999. The total selling price is $220,000. Your selling expenses are $11,000. The selling expenses are divided among all the assets sold, including inventory.

Your selling expense for each asset is 5% of the asset's selling price ($11,000 selling expense ÷ $220,000 total selling price).

The FMV, adjusted basis, and depreciation claimed on each asset sold are as follows:

Asset	FMV	Depreciation Claimed	Adjusted Basis
Inventory	$10,000	-0-	$8,000
Land	42,000	-0-	15,000
Building	48,000	$9,000	36,000
Machine A	71,000	27,200	63,800
Machine B	24,000	12,960	22,040
Truck	6,500	18,624	5,376
	201,500	67,784	150,216

Under the residual method, you allocate the selling price to each of the assets based on their FMV ($201,500). The remaining amount is allocated to your section 197 intangible, goodwill ($18,500).

The assets included in the sale, their selling prices based on their FMVs, the selling expense allocated to each asset, the adjusted basis, and the gain for each asset are shown in the following chart.

	Sale Price	Sale Exp.	Adj. Basis	Gain
Inventory	$10,000	$500	$8,000	$1,500
Land	42,000	2,100	15,000	24,900
Building	48,000	2,400	36,000	9,600
Mch. A	71,000	3,550	63,800	3,650
Mch. B	24,000	1,200	22,040	760
Truck	6,500	325	5,376	799
Goodwill	18,500	925	-0-	17,575
	$220,000	$11,000	$150,216	$58,784

The building was acquired in 1988, the year the business began, and it is section 1250 property. There is no depreciation recapture income because the building was depreciated using the straight line method.

All gain on the truck, machine A, and machine B is depreciation recapture income since it is the lesser of the depreciation claimed or the gain on the sale. Figure depreciation recapture in Part III of Form 4797.

The total depreciation recapture income reported in Part II of Form 4797 is $5,209. This consists of $3,650 on machine A, $799 on the truck, and $760 on machine B (the gain on each item since it was less than the depreciation claimed). These gains are reported in full in the year of sale and are not included in the installment sale computation.

Of the $220,000 total selling price, the $10,000 for inventory assets cannot be reported on the installment method. The selling prices of the truck and machines are also removed from the total selling price because gain on these items is reported in full in the year of sale.

The selling price equals the contract price for the installment sale ($108,500). The assets included in the installment sale, their selling price, and their installment sale basis are shown in the following chart.

	Selling Price	Installment Sale Basis	Gross Profit
Land	$42,000	$17,100	$24,900
Building	48,000	38,400	9,600
Goodwill	18,500	925	17,575
Total	$108,500	$56,425	$52,075

The ***gross profit percentage*** (gross profit ÷ contract price) for the installment sale is 48% ($52,075 ÷ $108,500). The gross profit percentage for each asset is figured as follows:

	Percentage
Land— $24,900 ÷ $108,500	22.95
Building— $9,600 ÷ $108,500	8.85
Goodwill— $17,575 ÷ $108,500	16.20
Total	48.00

Since the sale includes assets sold on the installment method and assets for which the gain is reported in full in the year of sale, payments must be allocated between the installment part of the sale and the part reported in the year of sale. The selling price for the installment sale is $108,500. This is 49.3% of the total selling price of $220,000 ($108,500 ÷ $220,000). The selling price of assets not reported on the installment method is $111,500. This is 50.7% ($111,500 ÷ $220,000) of the total selling price.

Multiply principal payments by 49.3% to determine the part of the payment for the installment sale. The balance, 50.7%, is for the part reported in the year of the sale.

The gain on the sale of the inventory, machines, and truck is reported in full in the year of sale. When you receive principal payments in later years, no part of the payment for the sale of these assets is included in gross income. Only the part for the installment sale (49.3%) is used in the installment sale computation.

The only payment received in 1998 is the down payment of $100,000. The part of the payment for the installment sale is $49,300 ($100,000 × 49.3%). This amount is used in the installment sale computation.

Installment income for 1998. Your installment income for each asset is the gross profit percentage for that asset times $49,300, the installment income received in 1998.

	Income
Land—22.95% of $49,300	$11,314
Building—8.85% of $49,300	4,363
Goodwill—16.2% of $49,300	7,987
Total installment income for 1998	$23,664

Installment income after 1998. You figure installment income for years after 1998 by applying the same gross profit percentages to 49.3% of the total payments you receive on the buyer's note during the year.

Unstated Interest

An installment sale contract generally provides that each deferred payment on the sale will include interest or that there will be an interest payment in addition to the principal payment. Interest provided in the contract is called ***stated interest.***

If an installment sale contract with some or all payments due more than one year after the date of sale does not provide for interest, part of each payment due more than 6 months after the date of sale may be treated as interest. The amount treated as interest is called ***unstated interest.***

When the stated interest rate in the contract is lower than the applicable federal rate (AFR), defined below, unstated interest is the difference between interest figured at the federal rate and any interest figured at the rate specified in the sales contract.

Generally, the unstated interest rules do not apply to a debt given in consideration for a sale or exchange of personal-use property. Personal-use property is any property in which substantially all of its use by the buyer is not in connection with a trade or business or an investment activity.

Applicable federal rate (AFR). The AFR depends on the month the binding contract for the sale or exchange of property is made and the term of the instrument. For an installment obligation, the term of the instrument is its weighted average maturity, as defined in Regulations section 1.1273–1(e)(3). The AFR for each term is shown below.

- For a term of 3 years or less, the AFR is the federal short-term rate.
- For a term of over 3 years, but not over 9 years, the AFR is the federal mid-term rate.
- For a term of over 9 years, the AFR is the federal long-term rate.

The applicable federal rates are published monthly in the Internal Revenue Bulletin. You can get this information by contacting an IRS office.

Effects of Unstated Interest

If the unstated interest rules apply, you and the buyer must treat part of the installment sale price as interest. The unstated interest rules require you to treat part of each payment as interest, even though it is not called interest in your agreement with the buyer. Unstated interest reduces the stated selling price of the property and increases your interest income. It also reduces the buyer's basis in the property and increases the buyer's interest expense.

If you do not use the installment method to report the sale, you report the entire gain in the year of sale. You must reduce the selling price by the total unstated interest before you can determine the gain.

You must report the unstated interest plus any interest specified under the contract on your tax return.

Figuring Unstated Interest

A debt instrument must provide for adequate stated interest. If not, unstated interest is figured on the debt. Generally, a debt instrument provides for adequate stated interest if it calls for interest at a rate no lower than the test rate of interest applicable to the debt instrument.

Test rate of interest. The test rate of interest for a debt instrument is the 3-month rate. The 3-month rate is the lower of either of the following AFRs.

1) The lowest AFR in effect during the 3-month period ending with the first month in which there is a binding written contract that substantially sets forth the terms under which the sale or exchange is ultimately consummated.
2) The lowest AFR in effect during the 3-month period ending with the month in which the sale or exchange occurs.

Special rules. For sales or exchanges of property (other than new section 38 property, which includes most tangible personal property) involving seller financing of $3,823,100 or less, the test rate of interest cannot be more than 9%, compounded semiannually. For seller financing over $3,823,100, and for all sales or exchanges of new section 38 property, the test rate of interest is 100% of the AFR.

For information on new section 38 property, see section 48(b) of the Internal Revenue Code, as in effect before the enactment of Public Law 101–508.

Relationship of Internal Revenue Code sections 1274 and 483. Unstated interest is imposed under section 1274 or 483 of the Code, depending on the characteristics (amount, kind of property, etc.) of the debt instrument and the sale or exchange for which it is given in consideration.

Section 1274 applies to any debt instrument issued for the sale or exchange of property if some or all payments due under the debt instrument are due more than 6 months after the date of sale or exchange. The AFR is determined under section 1274 and interest determined under that section is treated as original issue discount.

Section 483 applies to sales or exchanges of property not covered by the provisions of section 1274. Interest determined under section 483 is treated as unstated interest.

Section 483 rules. The section 483 rules apply to payments on the sale or exchange of property under a contract in which the following conditions exist.

1) Some or all payments are due more than one year after the date of sale or exchange.
2) There is total unstated interest (or inadequate stated interest).

Unstated interest is figured on any payment that meets the following conditions.

1) The payment constitutes all or part of the selling price.
2) The payment is due more than 6 months after the date of sale or exchange.

Total unstated interest. Total unstated interest is the amount equal to the excess of item 1 over item 2, listed next.

1) The sum of payments due under the contract.
2) The sum of the present values of the payments and the present values of any interest payments due under the contract.

Transactions to which section 483 rules apply. The section 483 rules apply to the following items.

1) Debt instruments from the transactions listed below.
   a) The sale or exchange of a farm for $1,000,000 or less by the following persons.
      i) An individual.
      ii) An estate.
      iii) A testamentary trust.
      iv) A small business corporation (defined in section 1244(c)(3) of the Internal Revenue Code).
      v) A domestic partnership that meets requirements similar to those of section 1244(c)(3).
   b) The sale or exchange of a main home by the owner.
   c) The sale or exchange of property with total payments (principal and interest) of $250,000 or less.
   d) Certain land transfers between related persons.
2) A cash method debt instrument.

Sale of a farm. The section 483 rules apply to the sale of a farm if the selling price cannot exceed $1,000,000. If the selling price can exceed $1,000,000, the section 1274 rules (discussed later) apply. For determining the selling price, all sales and exchanges that are part of the same transaction (or a series of transactions) are treated as one sale or exchange.

Sale with total payments of $250,000 or less. The section 483 rules apply if the sum of the following amounts does not exceed $250,000.

1) The total payments (interest and principal) due under the debt instrument and under all other debt instruments received as consideration for the sale or exchange.

2) The total of any other consideration to be received for the sale or exchange.

The section 1274 rules apply if the amount exceeds $250,000.

Any consideration (other than a debt instrument) is taken into account at its FMV. All sales and exchanges that are part of the same transaction (or series of related transactions) are treated as one sale or exchange.

Land sale between related persons. The section 483 rules apply to debt instruments issued in a land sale between related persons to the extent the sum of the following amounts does not exceed $500,000.

- The stated principal of the debt instrument issued in the sale or exchange.
- The total stated principal of any other debt instruments for prior land sales between these individuals during the calendar year.

The section 1274 rules, if otherwise applicable, apply to debt instruments issued in a sale of land to the extent the stated principal amount is in excess of $500,000, or if any party to the sale is a nonresident alien.

Related persons include an individual and the members of the individual's family and their spouses. Members of an individual's family include the individual's spouse, brother and sister (whether by whole or half blood), ancestors, and lineal descendants.

Cash method debt instrument. This is any debt instrument given as consideration for the sale or exchange of property (other than new section 38 property) with a stated principal of $2,730,800 or less if the following items apply.

1) The lender (holder) does not use an accrual method of accounting and is not a dealer in the type of property sold or exchanged.
2) Both the borrower (issuer) and the lender jointly elect to account for interest on the debt instrument under the cash method of accounting.
3) Section 1274 of the Internal Revenue Code would apply except for the election in (2) above.

Exceptions to section 483 rules. The unstated interest rules do not apply to the following types of transactions.

Sale price of $3,000 or less. If it can be determined at the time of sale or exchange of the property that the selling price will not exceed $3,000, the unstated interest rules do not apply to the sale or exchange.

Carrying charges. The buyer of personal property does not figure unstated interest if any part of the payment includes separately stated carrying charges.

Additional exceptions. See the discussion of the exceptions that apply to both sections 483 and 1274, later.

Section 1274 rules. The section 1274 rules apply to any debt instrument given in consideration for the sale or exchange of property under the following conditions in **both** 1) and 2).

1) The stated redemption price at maturity for the debt instrument exceeds the amount in either a) or b), below.
   a) The stated principal when there is adequate stated interest.
   b) The imputed principal in all other cases.
2) Some or all payments under the debt instrument are due more than 6 months after the date of the sale or exchange.

Imputed principal. There is adequate stated interest under section 1274 if the stated principal for a debt instrument is less than or equal to the imputed principal. The imputed principal of any debt instrument is equal to the sum of the present values of all payments under the debt instrument. The present value of any payment is determined by using the AFR for the date of sale or exchange. If a debt instrument has a single fixed interest rate paid or compounded at least annually, and the rate is equal to or greater than the test rate, there is adequate stated interest.

Issue price. In transactions to which section 1274 applies, the issue price of the debt instrument must be determined. Where there is adequate stated interest, the issue price is the stated principal. If the debt instrument does not provide for adequate stated interest, the issue price of the instrument is the imputed principal of the debt instrument. The issue price of a debt instrument is generally used to determine the sale price (in whole or in part) of any property acquired for the debt instrument.

Exceptions to imputed principal rules. The imputed principal rules do not apply to any of the debt instruments involved in transactions listed earlier under *Transactions to which section 483 rules apply.* (Also see *Exceptions to sections 483 and 1274,* below.)

Assumption of debt instrument. Do not apply the imputed principal rules to the assumption of a debt instrument or if property is taken subject to the debt instrument. However, these rules do apply if the terms or conditions of the debt instrument are modified or the nature of the transaction is changed.

Exceptions to sections 483 and 1274. The unstated interest and imputed principal rules do not apply in the following circumstances.

Publicly traded debt instruments or property. Transactions involving publicly traded debt instruments or any debt instrument issued in consideration for the sale or exchange of publicly traded property are not subject to these rules. A publicly traded instrument is one that is traded on an established securities market.

Patents. When all substantial rights to a patent, or an undivided interest in property that includes part of all substantial rights to a patent, are sold or exchanged, do not figure unstated interest or imputed principal on any amount contingent on the productivity, use, or disposition of the property transferred. This rule applies only if long-term capital gain or loss treatment applies to the sale (see Publication 544).

Annuities. Payments that depend in whole or in part on the life expectancy of any individual do not require the computation of unstated interest or imputed principal.

Personal-use property. Debt instruments issued in consideration for the sale or exchange of personal-use property where substantially all of its use by the buyer is for other than a trade or business or as income-producing property are not subject to the unstated interest or imputed principal rules.

More information. For information on figuring unstated interest and other special rules, see sections 483 and 1274 of the Internal Revenue Code and their regulations.

Disposition of Installment Obligation

A disposition generally includes a sale, exchange, cancellation, bequest, distribution, or transmission of an installment obligation. An "installment obligation" is the buyer's note, deed of trust, or other evidence the buyer will make future payments to you.

If you are using the installment method and you dispose of the installment obligation, you generally have a gain or loss to report. It is considered gain or loss on the sale of the property for which you received the installment obligation. If the original installment sale produced ordinary income, the disposition of the obligation will result in ordinary income or loss. If the original sale resulted in a capital gain, the disposition of the obligation will result in a capital gain or loss.

Use the following rules to figure your gain or loss from the disposition of an installment obligation.

1) If you ***sell or exchange the obligation,*** or if you accept less than face value in satisfaction of the obligation, the gain or loss is the difference between your basis in the obligation and the amount you realize.
2) If you ***dispose of the obligation in any other way,*** the gain or loss is the difference between your basis in the obligation and its FMV at the time of the disposition. This rule applies, for example, when you give the installment obligation to someone else or cancel the buyer's debt to you.

Basis. Figure your basis in an installment obligation by multiplying the unpaid balance on the obligation by your gross profit percentage. Subtract that amount from the unpaid balance. The result is your basis in the installment obligation.

Example. Several years ago, you sold property on the installment method. The buyer still owes you $10,000 of the sale price. This is the unpaid balance on the buyer's installment obligation to you. Because your gross profit percentage is 60%, $6,000 (60% x $10,000) is the profit owed you on the obligation. The rest of the unpaid balance, $4,000, is your basis in the obligation.

Transfer between spouses or former spouses. No gain or loss is recognized on the transfer of an installment obligation between a husband and wife or a former husband and wife if incident to a divorce. A transfer is incident to a divorce if it occurs within one year after the date on which the marriage ends or is related to the end of the marriage. The same tax treatment of the transferred obligation applies to the transferee spouse or former spouse as would have applied to the transferor spouse or former spouse. The basis of the obligation to the transferee spouse (or former spouse) is the adjusted basis of the transferor spouse.

The nonrecognition rule does not apply if the spouse or former spouse receiving the obligation is a nonresident alien.

Gift. A gift of an installment obligation is a disposition. The gain or loss is the difference between your basis in the obligation and its FMV at the time you make the gift.

For gifts between spouses or former spouses, see *Transfers between spouses or former spouses,* above.

Cancellation. If an installment obligation is canceled or otherwise becomes unenforceable, it is treated as a disposition other than a sale or exchange. Your gain or loss is the difference between your basis in the obligation and its FMV at the time you cancel it. If the parties are related, the FMV of the obligation is considered to be no less than its full face value.

Forgiving part of the buyer's debt. If you accept part payment on the balance of the buyer's installment debt to you and forgive the rest of the debt, you treat the settlement as a disposition of the installment obligation. The gain or loss is the difference between your basis in the obligation and the amount you realize on the settlement.

If you reduce the selling price but do not cancel the rest of the buyer's debt to you, it is not considered a disposition of the installment obligation. You must refigure the gross profit percentage and apply it to payments you receive after the reduction. See *Selling price reduced* under *General Rules,* earlier.

Assumption. If the buyer of your property sells it to someone else and you agree to let the new buyer assume the original buyer's installment obligation, you have not disposed of the installment obligation. It is not a disposition even if the new buyer pays you a higher rate of interest than the original buyer.

Transfer due to death. The transfer of an installment obligation (other than to a buyer) as a result of the death of the seller (or other holder of the obligation) is not a disposition. Any unreported gain from the installment obligation is not treated as gross income to the decedent. No income is reported on the decedent's return due to the transfer. This means whoever receives the installment obligation as a result of the seller's death is taxed on the installment payments the same as the seller would have been if the seller had lived to receive the payments.

However, if an installment obligation is canceled, becomes unenforceable, or is transferred to the buyer because of the death of the holder of the obligation, it is a disposition. The estate must figure its gain or loss on the disposition. If the holder and the buyer were related, the FMV of the installment obligation is considered to be no less than its full face value.

Repossession

If you repossess your property after making an installment sale, you must figure the following amounts.

1) Your gain (or loss) on the repossession.
2) Your basis in the repossessed property.

The rules for figuring these amounts depend on the kind of property you repossess. The rules for repossessions of personal property differ from those for real property. Special rules may apply if you repossess property that was your main home before the sale.

The repossession rules apply whether or not title to the property was ever transferred to the buyer. It does not matter how you repossess the property, whether you foreclose or the buyer voluntarily surrenders the property to you. However, it is not a repossession if the buyer puts the property up for sale and you repurchase it.

For the repossession rules to apply, the repossession must at least partially discharge (satisfy) the buyer's installment obligation to you. The discharged obligation must be secured by the property you repossess. This requirement is met if the property is auctioned off after you foreclose and you apply the installment obligation to your bid price at the auction.

Reporting the repossession. You report gain or loss from a repossession on the same form you used to report the original sale. If you reported the sale on Form 4797, use Form 4797 to report the gain or loss on the repossession.

Personal Property

If you repossess personal property, you may have a gain or a loss on the repossession. In some cases, you may also have a bad debt.

To figure your gain or loss, subtract the total of your basis in the installment obligation and any repossession expenses you have from the FMV of the property. If you receive anything from the buyer besides the repossessed property, it is added to the property's FMV before making this calculation.

How you figure your basis in the installment obligation depends on whether or not you reported the original sale on the installment method. The method you used to report the original sale also affects the character of your gain or loss on the repossession.

For sales not reported on the installment method: (see *Electing Out of Installment Method,* earlier.)

Basis in installment obligation. Your basis is figured on its full face value or its FMV at the time of the original sale, whichever you used to figure your gain or loss in the year of sale. From this amount, subtract all payments of principal you have received on the obligation. The result is your basis in the installment obligation. If only part of the obligation is discharged by the repossession, figure your basis in only that part.

Gain or loss. To your basis in the obligation, add any repossession costs. If the FMV of the property you repossess is more than this total, you have a gain. Because it is gain on the installment obligation, it is all ordinary income. If the FMV of the repossessed property is less than the total of your basis plus repossession costs, you have a loss. Because you included the full gain in income in the year of sale, the loss is a bad debt. How you deduct the bad debt depends on whether you sold business or nonbusiness property in the original sale. See Publication 550 for information on nonbusiness bad debts and chapter 14 of Publication 535 for information on business bad debts.

For sales reported on the installment method:

Basis in installment obligation. Multiply the unpaid balance of your installment obligation by your gross profit percentage. Subtract that amount from the unpaid balance. The result is your basis in the installment obligation.

Gain or loss. If the FMV of the repossessed property is more than the total of your basis in the obligation plus any repossession costs, you have a gain. If the FMV is less, you have a loss. Your gain or loss on the repossession is the same character (capital or ordinary) as your gain on the original sale.

Use the following worksheet to determine the taxable gain or loss on a repossession of personal property reported on the installment method.

1) FMV of property repossessed		____
2) Unpaid balance of installment obligation	____	
3) Unrealized profit (line 2 × gross profit %)	____	
4) Basis of obligation (line 2 – line 3)	____	
5) Plus: Repossession costs	____	____
6) Gain or loss on repossession (line 1 – line 5)		____

Example. You sold your piano for $1,500 in December 1997 for $300 down and $100 a month (plus interest). The payments began in January 1998. Your gross profit percentage is 40%. You reported the sale on the installment method on your 1997 income tax return. After the fourth monthly payment, the buyer defaults on the contract (which has an unpaid balance of $800) and you are forced to foreclose on the piano. The FMV of the piano on the date of repossession is $1,400. The legal costs of foreclosure and the expense of moving the piano back to your home total $75. You figure your gain on the repossession as follows:

1) FMV of property repossessed		$1,400
2) Unpaid balance of installment obligation	$800	
3) Unrealized profit (line 2 × gross profit %)	320	
4) Basis of obligation (line 2 – line 3)	480	
5) Plus: Repossession costs	75	555
6) Gain on repossession (line 1 – line 5)		$845

Basis in repossessed property. Your basis in repossessed personal property is its FMV at the time of the repossession.

Fair market value (FMV). The FMV of repossessed property is a question of fact to be established in each case. If you bid for the property at a lawful public auction or judicial sale, its FMV is presumed to be the price it sells for, unless there is clear and convincing evidence to the contrary.

Real Property

The rules for the repossession of real property allow you to keep essentially the same adjusted basis in the repossessed property as you had before the original sale. You can recover this entire adjusted basis when you resell the property. This, in effect, cancels out the tax treatment that applied to you on the original sale and puts you in the same tax position you were in before that sale.

Therefore, you must regard as income to you the total payments you have received from the buyer on the original sale. You report, as gain on the repossession, any part of the payments you have not yet included in income. These payments are amounts you previously treated as a return of your adjusted basis and excluded from income. However, the total gain you report is limited, as discussed later.

Conditions. The following rules are ***mandatory.*** You must use them to figure your basis in the repossessed real property and your gain on the repossession. They apply whether or not you reported the sale on the installment method. However, they apply only if all of the following conditions are met.

1) The repossession must be to protect your security rights in the property.
2) The installment obligation satisfied by the repossession must have been received in the original sale.
3) You cannot pay any additional consideration to the buyer to get your property back, unless either of the situations listed below apply.
    a) The reacquisition and payment of the additional consideration were provided for in the original contract of sale.
    b) The buyer has defaulted, or default is imminent.

"Additional consideration" includes money and other property you pay or transfer to the buyer. For example, additional consideration is paid if you reacquire the property subject to a debt that arose after the original sale.

Conditions not met. If any one of these three conditions is not met, use the rules discussed under *Personal Property,* earlier, as if the property you repossess were personal rather than real property. Do not use the rules for real property.

Figuring gain on repossession. Your gain on repossession is the difference between the following amounts.

1) The total payments received, or considered received, on the sale.
2) The total gain already reported as income.

See the earlier discussions under *Payments Received* for items considered payment on the sale.

Limit on taxable gain. Taxable gain is limited to your gross profit on the original sale minus the sum of the following amounts.

1) The gain on the sale you reported as income before the repossession.
2) Your repossession costs.

This method of figuring taxable gain, in essence, treats all payments received on the sale as income, but limits your total taxable gain to the gross profit you originally expected on the sale.

Indefinite selling price. The limit on taxable gain does not apply if the selling price is indefinite and cannot be determined at the time of repossession. For example, a selling price stated as a percentage of the profits to be realized from the buyer's development of the property is an indefinite selling price.

Character of gain. The taxable gain on repossession is ordinary income or capital gain, the same as the gain on the original sale. However, if you did not report the sale on the installment method, the gain is ordinary income.

Repossession costs. Your repossession costs include money or property you pay to reacquire the real property. This includes amounts paid to the buyer of the property, as well as amounts paid to others for such items as those listed below.

1) Court costs.
2) Legal fees.
3) Publishing, acquiring, filing, or recording of title.
4) Lien clearance.

Repossession costs do not include the FMV of the buyer's obligations to you that are secured by the real property.

Use the following worksheet to determine the taxable gain on a repossession of real property reported on the installment method.

1) Payments received before repossession		____
2) Minus: Gain reported		____
3) Gain on repossession		____
4) Gross profit on sale		____
5) Gain reported (line 2)	____	
6) Plus: Repossession costs	____	____
7) Subtract line 6 from line 4		____
8) Taxable gain (lesser of line 3 or 7)		____

Example. You sold a tract of land in January 1996 for $25,000. You accepted from the buyer a $5,000 down payment, plus a $20,000 mortgage secured by the property and payable at the rate of $4,000 annually plus interest (9.5%). The payments began on January 1, 1997. Your adjusted basis in the property was $19,000 and you reported the transaction as an installment sale. Your selling expenses were $1,000. You figured your gross profit as follows:

Selling price		$25,000
Minus:		
Adjusted basis	$19,000	
Selling expenses	1,000	20,000
Gross profit		$5,000

For this sale, the contract price equals the selling price. The gross profit percentage is 20% ($5,000 gross profit ÷ $25,000 contract price).

In 1996, you included $1,000 in income (20% × $5,000 down payment). In 1997, you reported a profit of $800 (20% × $4,000 annual installment). In 1998, the buyer defaulted and you repossessed the property. You paid $500 in legal fees to get your property back. Your taxable gain on the repossession is figured as follows:

1) Payments received before repossession		$9,000
2) Minus: Gain reported		1,800
3) Gain on repossession		$7,200
4) Gross profit on sale		$5,000
5) Gain reported (line 2)	$1,800	
6) Plus: Repossession costs	500	2,300
7) Subtract line 6 from line 4		$2,700
8) Taxable gain (lesser of line 3 or 7)		$2,700

Basis. Your basis in the repossessed property is determined as of the date of repossession. It is the sum of the following amounts.

1) Your adjusted basis in the installment obligation.
2) Your repossession costs.
3) Your taxable gain on the repossession.

To figure your adjusted basis in the installment obligation at the time of repossession, multiply the unpaid balance by the gross profit percentage. Subtract that amount from the unpaid balance.

Use the following worksheet to determine the basis of real property repossessed.

1) Unpaid balance of obligation		____
2) Minus: Unrealized profit (line 1 × gross profit %)		____
3) Adjusted basis (date of repossession)		____
4) Plus: Taxable gain on repossession	____	
Repossession costs	____	____
5) Basis of repossessed real property		____

Example. Assume the same facts as the preceding example. The unpaid balance of the installment obligation (the $20,000 note) is $16,000 at the time of repossession because the buyer made a $4,000 payment. The gross profit percentage on the original sale was 20%. Therefore, $3,200 (20% × $16,000 still due on the note) is unrealized profit. You figure your basis in the repossessed property as follows:

Unpaid balance of obligation		$16,000
Minus: Unrealized profit		3,200
Adjusted basis (date of repossession)		$12,800
Plus: Taxable gain on repossession	$2,700	
Repossession costs	500	3,200
Basis of repossessed real property		$16,000

Holding period for resales. If you resell the repossessed property, the resale may result in a capital gain or loss. To figure whether the gain or loss is long-term or short-term, your holding period includes the period you owned the property before the original sale plus the period after the repossession. It does not include the period the buyer owned the property.

If the buyer made improvements to the reacquired property, the holding period for these improvements begins on the day after the date of repossession.

Bad debt. If you repossess real property under these rules, you cannot take a bad debt deduction for any part of the buyer's installment obligation. This is true even if the obligation is not fully satisfied by the repossession.

If you took a bad debt deduction before the tax year of repossession, you are considered to have recovered the bad debt when you repossess the property. You must report the bad debt deduction you took in the earlier year as income in the year of repossession. However, if any part of the earlier deduction did not reduce your tax, you do not have to report that part as income. Your adjusted basis in the installment obligation is increased by the amount you report as income from recovering the bad debt.

Reporting an Installment Sale

Form 6252. Use Form 6252 to report a sale of property on the installment method. The form is used to report the sale in the year it takes place and to report payments received in later years. Also, if you sold property to a related person, you may have to file the form each year until the installment debt is paid off, whether or not you receive a payment in that year.

Related person. If you sell marketable securities to a related person, complete Part III, Form 6252, for each year of the installment agreement, even if you do not receive a payment in that year.

If you sell property other than marketable securities to a related person, complete Part III for the year of sale and the 2 years following the year of sale, even if you do not receive a payment. After this 2-year period, you do not have to fill out Part III.

If the related person to whom you sold your property disposes of it, you may have to immediately report the rest of your gain in Part III. See *Rule 2—Sale and Resale* under *Sale to Related Person,* earlier, for more information.

Several assets. If you sell two or more assets in one installment sale, you may have to separately report the sale of each asset. The same is true if you sell all the assets of your business in one installment sale. See *Single Sale of Several Assets* and *Sale of a Business,* earlier.

If you have only a few sales to separately report, you can use a separate Form 6252 for each one. However, if you have to separately report the sales of many assets that you sold together, do not prepare a separate Form 6252 for each one. Instead, prepare one Form 6252 and attach a schedule with all the information for each asset that is required by Form 6252. Complete Form 6252 by following the steps listed below.

1) Answer the questions at the top of the form.
2) In the year of sale, do not complete Part I. Instead, write "See attached schedule" in the margin.
3) For Part II, enter the total for all the assets on lines 24, 25, and 26.
4) For Part III, answer all the questions that apply. If none of the exceptions under question 29 apply, enter the totals on lines 35, 36, and 37 for the disposed assets.

Special situations. If you are reporting payments from an installment sale as income in respect of a decedent or as a beneficiary of a trust, including a partial interest in such a sale, you may not be able to provide all the information asked for on Form 6252. To the extent possible, follow the instructions given above and provide as many details as possible in a statement attached to Form 6252.

For more information on how to complete Form 6252, see the form instructions.

Other forms. The gain from Form 6252 is carried over and entered on Schedule D (Form 1040), *Capital Gains and Losses,* Form 4797, *Sales of Business Property,* or both.

Schedule D (Form 1040). Enter the gain figured on Form 6252 for personal-use property (capital assets) on Schedule D (Form 1040). If your gain from the installment sale qualifies for long-term capital gain treatment in the year of sale, it will continue to qualify in later tax years. Your gain is long-term if you owned the property for more than one year when you sold it.

Although the references in this publication are to the Schedule D for Form 1040, the rules discussed also apply to Schedule D for Forms 1041 (estates and trusts), 1065 (partnerships), 1120 or 1120–A (corporations), or 1120S (S corporations).

Form 4797. An installment sale of property used in your business or property that earns rent or royalty income may result in a capital gain, an ordinary gain, or both. All or part of any gain from its disposition may be ordinary gain from depreciation recapture. Use Form 4797 to report these transactions and to determine the ordinary or capital gain or loss.

Form 4797 is used with estate and trust, partnership, corporation, and S corporation returns, as well as individual returns.

Payments past due. If you use the cash method of accounting, do not report payments of principal you have not yet received, even if they are past due. However, if you use an accrual method of accounting, you accrue any payment due, even if you have not received it.

Examples

The following examples illustrate how to fill out Form 6252. Sample filled-in forms follow.

Example 1

On November 1, 1998, Mark Moore sold a lot that he bought on February 17, 1991, for $2,650. He borrowed more on the lot than he had paid for it. At the time of the sale, $6,500 remained outstanding on these loans. In the sales contract, the buyer agreed to assume these loans and pay Mark $200 a month (plus 7% interest) for 3 years. In addition, the buyer made a down payment of $1,000 on the sale.

Mark fills out his 1998 Form 6252 as follows:

Question 1. Mark writes in a description of the lot he sold.

Questions 2a and 2b. Mark enters the date he acquired the lot and the date he sold it.

Question 3. Because Mark sold the lot to Acme Design, a partnership of which he is a member, he checks the "Yes" box.

Question 4. The property Mark sold was not a marketable security (such as stock or a bond). He answers "No" to this question. Because he sold the lot to a related person, he must complete Part III for 1998 and the next 2 years.

Part I. Mark uses this part of the form to figure the contract price and his gross profit on the sale.

Line 5. Mark enters the selling price, $14,700. This includes the $1,000 down payment, the $7,200 (36 × $200) in monthly payments he is to receive, and the $6,500 in loans the buyer assumes.

Line 6. Mark enters the $6,500 in outstanding loans that the buyer assumes.

Line 7. Mark subtracts line 6 from line 5 and enters the difference, $8,200.

Line 8. Because he did not make any improvements to the lot, Mark's basis at the time of the sale was the lot's cost of $2,650.

Lines 9 and 10. Mark did not take depreciation deductions on the lot (land is never depreciable). The amount on line 8 carries over to line 10.

Line 11. Mark's only selling expenses were $150 in legal fees. If he had advertised the lot for sale or paid commission on the sale, he would have included those amounts also.

Line 12. Since no depreciation was claimed on the land, Mark has no recapture of income.

Line 13. Mark's installment sale basis is $2,800, the total of his adjusted basis in the property plus his selling expenses.

Line 14. Mark subtracts line 13 from line 5 and enters the result, $11,900.

Lines 15 and 16. The property Mark sold was not his home. He carries the amount on line 14 to line 16. This is his gross profit on the sale.

Line 17. Mark subtracts line 13, $2,800, from line 6, $6,500. The result, $3,700, is the amount by which the assumed loans are more than his installment sale basis in the property. This amount is treated as a payment in the year of sale on line 20.

Line 18. The contract price is the sum of all payments Mark will receive on the sale. This includes the down payment and all installment payments he will receive (line 7). It also includes the "payment"figured on line 17.

Part II. In this part, Mark figures the gain from the sale he must report for 1998.

Line 19. Mark's gross profit percentage for the sale is 100%. This is the gross profit on line 16, $11,900, divided by the contract price on line 18, also $11,900.

Line 20. Mark carries the amount he treats as a payment on line 17 to this line and it is added to the other payments he received in the year of sale.

Line 21. At the time of the sale, Mark received a down payment of $1,000. In December 1998, he received his first monthly installment payment. The total payment was $242, consisting of $42 interest (one month's interest on $7,200 figured at 7% a year) and $200 principal. This is the only installment payment he received in 1998. He enters the total received during 1998, $1,200 ($1,000 + $200), on this line. He reports the $42 interest on Form 1040.

Line 22. Mark enters $4,900, the sum of line 20 plus line 21. This is the total of all payments he is considered to have received in 1998.

Line 23. Since 1998 is the year of sale, Mark makes no entry here.

Line 24. The gross profit percentage (line 19) is 100%. Therefore, the entire amount on line 22, $4,900, is taxable gain. Mark enters this amount on line 24.

Lines 25 and 26. Because the lot Mark sold was not depreciable property, he does not have to recapture any depreciation deductions as ordinary gain. All his gain on the sale is long-term capital gain. He carries the amount on line 26 to Schedule D (Form 1040) where it is included with other long-term capital gains.

Part III. Because Mark sold the lot to his partnership, a "related person," he must fill out this part. The property he sold was not a marketable security and he completes this part for 1998, 1999, and 2000.

Line 27. Mark enters the name, address, and employer identification number of the partnership that bought the lot.

Line 28. The partnership did not sell the lot in 1998. Mark checks the "No" box and he does not have to fill out the rest of Part III.

Example 2

In December 1997, Cora Blue sold a painting she inherited. The buyer paid her $700 down and gave her an installment note for $3,800. The note calls for quarterly payments of $530 until the $3,800 debt is paid off, in about 2 years. Each $530 payment includes interest figured at 10% a year on the outstanding debt. She received her first 4 payments on the note in 1998. The principal and interest she received in each payment is given in the table below:

Payment	Interest	Principal
First	$95.00	$435.00
Second	84.13	445.87
Third	72.98	457.02
Fourth	61.55	468.45
	$313.66	$1,806.34

Cora rounds off cents on her tax return. She reports $314 interest as ordinary income on Form 1040. She completes Form 6252 as follows:

Question 1. Cora states the property she sold was an oil painting.

Questions 2a and 2b. She enters the date she acquired the painting and the date she sold it.

Question 3. The buyer was not related to Cora. She checks the "No" box.

Question 4. Because she checked "No" to question 3, Cora does not have to answer this question or fill out Part III of the form.

Part I. Cora completed Part I of her Form 6252 for the year of sale, 1997. She does not fill it out for the remaining years of the installment sale.

Part II. This is the only part of Form 6252 that Cora fills out.

Line 19. Cora figured a gross profit percentage of 22.7% on her 1997 Form 6252. She uses the same percentage on her 1998 Form 6252.

Line 20. Since this is not the year of sale, Cora enters zero on this line.

Line 21. Cora enters the total amount (minus interest) that she received on the sale in 1998, $1,806.

Line 22. The amount on line 21 carries over to line 22.

Line 23. Before 1998, Cora received only the $700 down payment.

Line 24. Cora multiplies the gross profit percentage of 22.7% (line 19), by the amount she was paid in 1998 (line 22), $1,806. The result, $410, is the gain she had on the sale in 1998.

Lines 25 and 26. Cora did not use the painting in a business. It was not depreciable and the recapture rules do not apply. The amount on line 24 carries over to line 26. Her gain is long-term capital gain. She carries the amount on line 26 to Schedule D (Form 1040), where it is included with other long-term capital gains.

Form **6252** — Department of the Treasury, Internal Revenue Service

Installment Sale Income

▶ See separate instructions. ▶ Attach to your tax return.
▶ Use a separate form for each sale or other disposition of property on the installment method.

OMB No. 1545-0228 — **1998** — Attachment Sequence No. **79**

Name(s) shown on return: Mark Moore — Identifying number: 222-00-3333

1 Description of property ▶ Undeveloped land

2a Date acquired (month, day, year) ▶ 2 / 17 / 91 **b** Date sold (month, day, year) ▶ 11 / 1 / 98

3 Was the property sold to a related party after May 14, 1980? See instructions. If "No," skip line 4. ☑ Yes ☐ No

4 Was the property you sold to a related party a marketable security? If "Yes," complete Part III. If "No," complete Part III for the year of sale and the 2 years after the year of sale ☐ Yes ☑ No

Part I Gross Profit and Contract Price. Complete this part for the year of sale only.

Line	Description		Amount
5	Selling price including mortgages and other debts. **Do not** include interest whether stated or unstated	5	14,700
6	Mortgages and other debts the buyer assumed or took the property subject to, but not new mortgages the buyer got from a bank or other source	6	6,500
7	Subtract line 6 from line 5	7	8,200
8	Cost or other basis of property sold	8	2,650
9	Depreciation allowed or allowable	9	-0-
10	Adjusted basis. Subtract line 9 from line 8	10	2,650
11	Commissions and other expenses of sale	11	150
12	Income recapture from Form 4797, Part III. See instructions	12	-0-
13	Add lines 10, 11, and 12	13	2,800
14	Subtract line 13 from line 5. If zero or less, **stop here. Do not** complete the rest of this form	14	11,900
15	If the property described on line 1 above was your main home, enter the amount of your excluded gain. Otherwise, enter -0-. See instructions	15	-0-
16	**Gross profit.** Subtract line 15 from line 14	16	11,900
17	Subtract line 13 from line 6. If zero or less, enter -0-	17	3,700
18	**Contract price.** Add line 7 and line 17	18	11,900

Part II Installment Sale Income. Complete this part for the year of sale **and** any year you receive a payment or have certain debts you must treat as a payment on installment obligations.

Line	Description		Amount
19	Gross profit percentage. Divide line 16 by line 18. For years after the year of sale, see instructions	19	100%
20	**For year of sale only:** Enter amount from line 17 above; otherwise, enter -0-	20	3,700
21	Payments received during year. See instructions. **Do not** include interest whether stated or unstated	21	1,200
22	Add lines 20 and 21	22	4,900
23	Payments received in prior years. See instructions. **Do not** include interest whether stated or unstated	23	
24	**Installment sale income.** Multiply line 22 by line 19	24	4,900
25	Part of line 24 that is ordinary income under recapture rules. See instructions	25	-0-
26	Subtract line 25 from line 24. Enter here and on Schedule D or Form 4797. See instructions	26	4,900

Part III Related Party Installment Sale Income. Do not complete if you received the final payment this tax year.

27 Name, address, and taxpayer identifying number of related party: Acme Design, W. Main Street, Small Town, NY 12899, 10-7654321

28 Did the related party, during this tax year, resell or dispose of the property ("second disposition")? ☐ Yes ☑ No

29 **If the answer to question 28 is "Yes," complete lines 30 through 37 below unless one of the following conditions is met. Check only the box that applies.**

a ☐ The second disposition was more than 2 years after the first disposition (other than dispositions of marketable securities). If this box is checked, enter the date of disposition (month, day, year) ▶ / /

b ☐ The first disposition was a sale or exchange of stock to the issuing corporation.

c ☐ The second disposition was an involuntary conversion where the threat of conversion occurred after the first disposition.

d ☐ The second disposition occurred after the death of the original seller or buyer.

e ☐ It can be established to the satisfaction of the Internal Revenue Service that tax avoidance was not a principal purpose for either of the dispositions. If this box is checked, attach an explanation. See instructions.

Line	Description		Amount
30	Selling price of property sold by related party	30	
31	Enter contract price from line 18 for year of first sale	31	
32	Enter the **smaller** of line 30 or line 31	32	
33	Total payments received by the end of your 1998 tax year. See instructions	33	
34	Subtract line 33 from line 32. If zero or less, enter -0-	34	
35	Multiply line 34 by the gross profit percentage on line 19 for year of first sale	35	
36	Part of line 35 that is ordinary income under recapture rules. See instructions	36	
37	Subtract line 36 from line 35. Enter here and on Schedule D or Form 4797. See instructions	37	

For Paperwork Reduction Act Notice, see separate instructions. Cat. No. 13601R Form **6252** (1998)

Form **6252**

Department of the Treasury
Internal Revenue Service

Installment Sale Income

► See separate instructions. ► Attach to your tax return.
► Use a separate form for each sale or other disposition of property on the installment method.

OMB No. 1545-0228
1998
Attachment Sequence No. 79

Name(s) shown on return: Cora Blue

Identifying number: 095-00-0000

1 Description of property ► Oil painting -- Inheritance

2a Date acquired (month, day, year) ► 7 / 3 / 89 **b** Date sold (month, day, year) ► 12 / 11 / 97

3 Was the property sold to a related party after May 14, 1980? See instructions. If "No," skip line 4 . . . ☐ Yes ☑ No

4 Was the property you sold to a related party a marketable security? If "Yes," complete Part III. If "No," complete Part III for the year of sale and the 2 years after the year of sale . . . ☐ Yes ☐ No

Part I Gross Profit and Contract Price. Complete this part for the year of sale only.

Line	Description	Inner line	Inner amount	Line	Amount
5	Selling price including mortgages and other debts. **Do not** include interest whether stated or unstated			5	
6	Mortgages and other debts the buyer assumed or took the property subject to, but not new mortgages the buyer got from a bank or other source	6			
7	Subtract line 6 from line 5	7			
8	Cost or other basis of property sold	8			
9	Depreciation allowed or allowable	9			
10	Adjusted basis. Subtract line 9 from line 8	10			
11	Commissions and other expenses of sale	11			
12	Income recapture from Form 4797, Part III. See instructions	12			
13	Add lines 10, 11, and 12			13	
14	Subtract line 13 from line 5. If zero or less, **stop here. Do not** complete the rest of this form			14	
15	If the property described on line 1 above was your main home, enter the amount of your excluded gain. Otherwise, enter -0-. See instructions			15	
16	**Gross profit.** Subtract line 15 from line 14			16	
17	Subtract line 13 from line 6. If zero or less, enter -0-			17	
18	**Contract price.** Add line 7 and line 17			18	

Part II Installment Sale Income. Complete this part for the year of sale **and** any year you receive a payment or have certain debts you must treat as a payment on installment obligations.

Line	Description	Inner line	Inner amount	Line	Amount
19	Gross profit percentage. Divide line 16 by line 18. For years after the year of sale, see instructions			19	22.7%
20	**For year of sale only:** Enter amount from line 17 above; otherwise, enter -0-			20	-0-
21	Payments received during year. See instructions. **Do not** include interest whether stated or unstated			21	1,806
22	Add lines 20 and 21			22	1,806
23	Payments received in prior years. See instructions. **Do not** include interest whether stated or unstated	23	700		
24	**Installment sale income.** Multiply line 22 by line 19			24	410
25	Part of line 24 that is ordinary income under recapture rules. See instructions			25	-0-
26	Subtract line 25 from line 24. Enter here and on Schedule D or Form 4797. See instructions			26	410

Part III Related Party Installment Sale Income. Do not complete if you received the final payment this tax year.

27 Name, address, and taxpayer identifying number of related party

28 Did the related party, during this tax year, resell or dispose of the property ("second disposition")? . . . ☐ Yes ☐ No

29 **If the answer to question 28 is "Yes," complete lines 30 through 37 below unless one of the following conditions is met. Check only the box that applies.**

- **a** ☐ The second disposition was more than 2 years after the first disposition (other than dispositions of marketable securities). If this box is checked, enter the date of disposition (month, day, year) ► / /
- **b** ☐ The first disposition was a sale or exchange of stock to the issuing corporation.
- **c** ☐ The second disposition was an involuntary conversion where the threat of conversion occurred after the first disposition.
- **d** ☐ The second disposition occurred after the death of the original seller or buyer.
- **e** ☐ It can be established to the satisfaction of the Internal Revenue Service that tax avoidance was not a principal purpose for either of the dispositions. If this box is checked, attach an explanation. See instructions.

Line	Description	Line	Amount
30	Selling price of property sold by related party	30	
31	Enter contract price from line 18 for year of first sale	31	
32	Enter the **smaller** of line 30 or line 31	32	
33	Total payments received by the end of your 1998 tax year. See instructions	33	
34	Subtract line 33 from line 32. If zero or less, enter -0-	34	
35	Multiply line 34 by the gross profit percentage on line 19 for year of first sale	35	
36	Part of line 35 that is ordinary income under recapture rules. See instructions	36	
37	Subtract line 36 from line 35. Enter here and on Schedule D or Form 4797. See instructions	37	

For Paperwork Reduction Act Notice, see separate instructions. Cat. No. 13601R Form **6252** (1998)

How To Get More Information

You can order free publications and forms, ask tax questions, and get more information from the IRS in several ways. By selecting the method that is best for you, you will have quick and easy access to tax help.

Free tax services. To find out what services are available, get Publication 910, *Guide to Free Tax Services.* It contains a list of free tax publications and an index of tax topics. It also describes other free tax information services, including tax education and assistance programs and a list of TeleTax topics.

Personal computer. With your personal computer and modem, you can access the IRS on the Internet at **www.irs.ustreas.gov**. While visiting our Web Site, you can select:

- *Frequently Asked Tax Questions* to find answers to questions you may have.
- *Fill-in Forms* to complete tax forms on-line.
- *Forms and Publications* to download forms and publications or search publications by topic or keyword.
- *Comments & Help* to e-mail us with comments about the site or with tax questions.
- *Digital Dispatch* and *IRS Local News Net* to receive our electronic newsletters on hot tax issues and news.

You can also reach us with your computer using any of the following.

- Telnet at **iris.irs.ustreas.gov**
- File Transfer Protocol at **ftp.irs.ustreas.gov**
- Direct dial (by modem) **703–321–8020**

TaxFax Service. Using the phone attached to your fax machine, you can receive forms, instructions, and tax information by calling **703–368–9694.** Follow the directions from the prompts. When you order forms, enter the catalog number for the form you need. The items you request will be faxed to you.

Phone. Many services are available by phone.

- *Ordering forms, instructions, and publications.* Call **1–800–829–3676** to order current and prior year forms, instructions, and publications.
- *Asking tax questions.* Call the IRS with your tax questions at **1–800–829–1040**.
- *TTY/TDD equipment.* If you have access to TTY/TDD equipment, call **1–800–829–4059** to ask tax questions or to order forms and publications.
- *TeleTax topics.* Call **1–800–829–4477** to listen to pre-recorded messages covering various tax topics.

Evaluating the quality of our telephone services. To ensure that IRS representatives give accurate, courteous, and professional answers, we evaluate the quality of our telephone services in several ways.

- A second IRS representative sometimes monitors live telephone calls. That person only evaluates the IRS assistor and does not keep a record of any taxpayer's name or tax identification number.
- We sometimes record telephone calls to evaluate IRS assistors objectively. We hold these recordings no longer than one week and use them only to measure the quality of assistance.
- We value our customers' opinions. Throughout this year, we will be surveying our customers for their opinions on our service.

Walk-in. You can pick up certain forms, instructions, and publications at many post offices, libraries, and IRS offices. Some libraries and IRS offices have an extensive collection of products available to print from a CD-ROM or photocopy from reproducible proofs.

Mail. You can send your order for forms, instructions, and publications to the Distribution Center nearest to you and receive a response 7 to 15 workdays after your request is received. Find the address that applies to your part of the country.

- **Western part of U.S.:**
  Western Area Distribution Center
  Rancho Cordova, CA 95743–0001
- **Central part of U.S.:**
  Central Area Distribution Center
  P.O. Box 8903
  Bloomington, IL 61702–8903
- **Eastern part of U.S. and foreign addresses:**
  Eastern Area Distribution Center
  P.O. Box 85074
  Richmond, VA 23261–5074

CD-ROM. You can order IRS Publication 1796, *Federal Tax Products on CD-ROM,* and obtain:

- Current tax forms, instructions, and publications.
- Prior-year tax forms, instructions, and publications.
- Popular tax forms which may be filled in electronically, printed out for submission, and saved for recordkeeping.
- Internal Revenue Bulletins.

The CD-ROM can be purchased from National Technical Information Service (NTIS) for $25.00 by calling 1–877–233–6767 or for $18.00 on the Internet at **www.irs.ustreas.gov/cdorders.** The first release is available in mid-December and the final release is available in late January.

Index

■

Tax Publications for Individual Taxpayers

See *How To Get More Information* for a variety of ways to get publications, including by computer, phone, and mail.

General Guides

- **1** Your Rights as a Taxpayer
- **17** Your Federal Income Tax (For Individuals)
- **225** Farmer's Tax Guide
- **334** Tax Guide for Small Business
- **509** Tax Calendars for 1999
- **553** Highlights of 1998 Tax Changes
- **595** Tax Highlights for Commercial Fishermen
- **910** Guide to Free Tax Services

Specialized Publications

- **3** Armed Forces' Tax Guide
- **378** Fuel Tax Credits and Refunds
- **463** Travel, Entertainment, Gift, and Car Expenses
- **501** Exemptions, Standard Deduction, and Filing Information
- **502** Medical and Dental Expenses
- **503** Child and Dependent Care Expenses
- **504** Divorced or Separated Individuals
- **505** Tax Withholding and Estimated Tax
- **508** Educational Expenses
- **514** Foreign Tax Credit for Individuals
- **516** U.S. Government Civilian Employees Stationed Abroad
- **517** Social Security and Other Information for Members of the Clergy and Religious Workers
- **519** U.S. Tax Guide for Aliens
- **520** Scholarships and Fellowships
- **521** Moving Expenses
- **523** Selling Your Home
- **524** Credit for the Elderly or the Disabled
- **525** Taxable and Nontaxable Income
- **526** Charitable Contributions
- **527** Residential Rental Property
- **529** Miscellaneous Deductions
- **530** Tax Information for First-Time Homeowners
- **531** Reporting Tip Income
- **533** Self-Employment Tax
- **534** Depreciating Property Placed in Service Before 1987
- **537** Installment Sales
- **541** Partnerships
- **544** Sales and Other Dispositions of Assets
- **547** Casualties, Disasters, and Thefts (Business and Nonbusiness)
- **550** Investment Income and Expenses
- **551** Basis of Assets
- **552** Recordkeeping for Individuals
- **554** Older Americans' Tax Guide
- **555** Community Property
- **556** Examination of Returns, Appeal Rights, and Claims for Refund
- **559** Survivors, Executors, and Administrators
- **561** Determining the Value of Donated Property
- **564** Mutual Fund Distributions
- **570** Tax Guide for Individuals With Income From U.S. Possessions
- **575** Pension and Annuity Income
- **584** Nonbusiness Disaster, Casualty, and Theft Loss Workbook
- **587** Business Use of Your Home (Including Use by Day-Care Providers)
- **590** Individual Retirement Arrangements (IRAs) (Including Roth IRAs and Education IRAs)
- **593** Tax Highlights for U.S. Citizens and Residents Going Abroad
- **594** Understanding the Collection Process
- **596** Earned Income Credit
- **721** Tax Guide to U.S. Civil Service Retirement Benefits
- **901** U.S. Tax Treaties
- **907** Tax Highlights for Persons with Disabilities
- **908** Bankruptcy Tax Guide
- **911** Direct Sellers
- **915** Social Security and Equivalent Railroad Retirement Benefits
- **919** Is My Withholding Correct for 1999?
- **925** Passive Activity and At-Risk Rules
- **926** Household Employer's Tax Guide
- **929** Tax Rules for Children and Dependents
- **936** Home Mortgage Interest Deduction
- **946** How To Depreciate Property
- **947** Practice Before the IRS and Power of Attorney
- **950** Introduction to Estate and Gift Taxes
- **967** IRS Will Figure Your Tax
- **968** Tax Benefits for Adoption
- **970** Tax Benefits for Higher Education
- **971** Innocent Spouse Relief
- **1542** Per Diem Rates
- **1544** Reporting Cash Payments of Over $10,000
- **1546** The Problem Resolution Program of the Internal Revenue Service

Spanish Language Publications

- **1SP** Derechos del Contribuyente
- **579SP** Cómo Preparar la Declaración de Impuesto Federal
- **594SP** Comprendiendo el Proceso de Cobro
- **596SP** Crédito por Ingreso del Trabajo
- **850** English-Spanish Glossary of Words and Phrases Used in Publications Issued by the Internal Revenue Service
- **1544SP** Informe de Pagos en Efectivo en Exceso de $10,000 (Recibidos en una Ocupación o Negocio)

Commonly Used Tax Forms

See *How To Get More Information* for a variety of ways to get forms, including by computer, fax, phone, and mail. For fax orders only, use the catalog numbers when ordering.

Form Number and Title	Catalog Number
1040 U.S. Individual Income Tax Return	11320
Sch A & B Itemized Deductions & Interest and Ordinary Dividends	11330
Sch C Profit or Loss From Business	11334
Sch C-EZ Net Profit From Business	14374
Sch D Capital Gains and Losses	11338
Sch E Supplemental Income and Loss	11344
Sch EIC Earned Income Credit	11339
Sch F Profit or Loss From Farming	11346
Sch H Household Employment Taxes	12187
Sch J Farm Income Averaging	25513
Sch R Credit for the Elderly or the Disabled	11359
Sch SE Self-Employment Tax	11358
1040A U.S. Individual Income Tax Return	11327
Sch 1 Interest and Ordinary Dividends for Form 1040A Filers	12075
Sch 2 Child and Dependent Care Expenses for Form 1040A Filers	10749
Sch 3 Credit for the Elderly or the Disabled for Form 1040A Filers	12064
1040EZ Income Tax Return for Single and Joint Filers With No Dependents	11329
1040-ES Estimated Tax for Individuals	11340
1040X Amended U.S. Individual Income Tax Return	11360

Form Number and Title	Catalog Number
2106 Employee Business Expenses	11700
2106-EZ Unreimbursed Employee Business Expenses	20604
2210 Underpayment of Estimated Tax by Individuals, Estates and Trusts	11744
2441 Child and Dependent Care Expenses	11862
2848 Power of Attorney and Declaration of Representative	11980
3903 Moving Expenses	12490
4562 Depreciation and Amortization	12906
4868 Application for Automatic Extension of Time To File U.S. Individual Income Tax Return	13141
4952 Investment Interest Expense Deduction	13177
5329 Additional Taxes Attributable to IRAs, Other Qualified Retirement Plans, Annuities, Modified Endowment Contracts, and MSAs	13329
6251 Alternative Minimum Tax–Individuals	13600
8283 Noncash Charitable Contributions	62294
8582 Passive Activity Loss Limitations	63704
8606 Nondeductible IRAs	63966
8812 Additional Child Tax Credit	10644
8822 Change of Address	12081
8829 Expenses for Business Use of Your Home	13232
8863 Education Credits	25379

Tax Publications for Business Taxpayers

See *How To Get More Information* for a variety of ways to get publications, including by computer, phone, and mail.

General Guides

- **1** Your Rights as a Taxpayer
- **17** Your Federal Income Tax (For Individuals)
- **225** Farmer's Tax Guide
- **334** Tax Guide for Small Business
- **509** Tax Calendars for 1999
- **553** Highlights of 1998 Tax Changes
- **595** Tax Highlights for Commercial Fishermen
- **910** Guide to Free Tax Services

Employer's Guides

- **15** Employer's Tax Guide (Circular E)
- **15-A** Employer's Supplemental Tax Guide
- **51** Agricultural Employer's Tax Guide (Circular A)
- **80** Federal Tax Guide For Employers in the U.S. Virgin Islands, Guam, American Samoa, and the Commonwealth of the Northern Mariana Islands (Circular SS)
- **179** Guía Contributiva Federal Para Patronos Puertorriqueños (Circular PR)
- **926** Household Employer's Tax Guide

Specialized Publications

- **378** Fuel Tax Credits and Refunds
- **463** Travel, Entertainment, Gift, and Car Expenses
- **505** Tax Withholding and Estimated Tax
- **510** Excise Taxes for 1999
- **515** Withholding of Tax on Nonresident Aliens and Foreign Corporations
- **517** Social Security and Other Information for Members of the Clergy and Religious Workers
- **527** Residential Rental Property
- **533** Self-Employment Tax
- **534** Depreciating Property Placed in Service Before 1987
- **535** Business Expenses
- **536** Net Operating Losses
- **537** Installment Sales
- **538** Accounting Periods and Methods
- **541** Partnerships
- **542** Corporations
- **544** Sales and Other Dispositions of Assets
- **551** Basis of Assets
- **556** Examination of Returns, Appeal Rights, and Claims for Refund
- **560** Retirement Plans for Small Business (SEP, SIMPLE, and Keogh Plans)
- **561** Determining the Value of Donated Property
- **583** Starting a Business and Keeping Records
- **587** Business Use of Your Home (Including Use by Day-Care Providers)
- **594** Understanding the Collection Process
- **597** Information on the United States-Canada Income Tax Treaty
- **598** Tax on Unrelated Business Income of Exempt Organizations
- **686** Certification for Reduced Tax Rates in Tax Treaty Countries
- **901** U.S. Tax Treaties
- **908** Bankruptcy Tax Guide
- **911** Direct Sellers
- **925** Passive Activity and At-Risk Rules
- **946** How To Depreciate Property
- **947** Practice Before the IRS and Power of Attorney
- **953** International Tax Information for Businesses
- **1544** Reporting Cash Payments of Over $10,000
- **1546** The Problem Resolution Program of the Internal Revenue Service

Spanish Language Publications

- **1SP** Derechos del Contribuyente
- **579SP** Cómo Preparar la Declaración de Impuesto Federal
- **594SP** Comprendiendo el Proceso de Cobro
- **850** English-Spanish Glossary of Words and Phrases Used in Publications Issued by the Internal Revenue Service
- **1544SP** Informe de Pagos en Efectivo en Exceso de $10,000 (Recibidos en una Ocupación o Negocio)

Commonly Used Tax Forms

See *How To Get More Information* for a variety of ways to get forms, including by computer, fax, phone, and mail. Items with an asterisk are available by fax. For these orders only, use the catalog numbers when ordering.

Form Number and Title	Catalog Number
W-2 Wage and Tax Statement	10134
W-4 Employee's Withholding Allowance Certificate*	10220
940 Employer's Annual Federal Unemployment (FUTA) Tax Return*	11234
940EZ Employer's Annual Federal Unemployment (FUTA) Tax Return*	10983
941 Employer's Quarterly Federal Tax Return	17001
1040 U.S. Individual Income Tax Return*	11320
Sch A & B Itemized Deductions & Interest and Ordinary Dividends*	11330
Sch C Profit or Loss From Business*	11334
Sch C-EZ Net Profit From Business*	14374
Sch D Capital Gains and Losses*	11338
Sch E Supplemental Income and Loss*	11344
Sch F Profit or Loss From Farming*	11346
Sch H Household Employment Taxes*	12187
Sch J Farm Income Averaging*	25513
Sch R Credit for the Elderly or the Disabled*	11359
Sch SE Self-Employment Tax*	11358
1040-ES Estimated Tax for Individuals*	11340
1040X Amended U.S. Individual Income Tax Return*	11360
1065 U.S. Partnership Return of Income	11390
Sch D Capital Gains and Losses	11393
Sch K-1 Partner's Share of Income, Credits, Deductions, etc.	11394
1120 U.S. Corporation Income Tax Return	11450
1120-A U.S. Corporation Short-Form Income Tax Return	11456
1120S U.S. Income Tax Return for an S Corporation	11510
Sch D Capital Gains and Losses and Built-In Gains	11516
Sch K-1 Shareholder's Share of Income, Credits, Deductions, etc.	11520
2106 Employee Business Expenses*	11700
2106-EZ Unreimbursed Employee Business Expenses*	20604
2210 Underpayment of Estimated Tax by Individuals, Estates, and Trusts*	11744
2441 Child and Dependent Care Expenses*	11862
2848 Power of Attorney and Declaration of Representative*	11980
3800 General Business Credit	12392
3903 Moving Expenses*	12490
4562 Depreciation and Amortization*	12906
4797 Sales of Business Property*	13086
4868 Application for Automatic Extension of Time To File U.S. Individual Income Tax Return*	13141
5329 Additional Taxes Attributable to IRAs, Other Qualified Retirement Plans, Annuities, Modified Endowment Contracts, and MSAs*	13329
6252 Installment Sale Income*	13601
8283 Noncash Charitable Contributions*	62299
8300 Report of Cash Payments Over $10,000 Received in a Trade or Business*	62133
8582 Passive Activity Loss Limitations*	63704
8606 Nondeductible IRAs*	63966
8822 Change of Address*	12081
8829 Expenses for Business Use of Your Home*	13232

APPENDIX 11: Glossary

abstract of title—A compilation of the recorded documents relating to a parcel of land, from which an attorney may give an opinion as to the condition of title. Also known in some states as a *preliminary title report*.

acceleration—A condition in a financing instrument giving the lender the power to declare all sums owed to the lender immediately due and payable upon an event such as sale of the property.

acknowledgment—A declaration made by a person signing a document before a notary public or other officer.

adverse possession—Most states have laws that permit someone to claim ownership of property that is occupied for a number of years. This is common where a fence is erected over a boundary line (called an *encroachment*) without the objection of the rightful owner. After a number of years, the person who erected the fence may be able to commence a court proceeding to claim ownership of the property.

agency—A relationship in which the agent is given the authority to act on behalf of another person.

all-inclusive deed of trust—See *wraparound mortgage*.

ALTA—American Land Title Association

amortize—To reduce a debt by regular payments of both principal and interest.

appraised value—The value of a property at a given time, based on facts regarding the location, improvements, and so on, of the property and surroundings.

appreciation—An increase in the net value of real estate.

appurtenance—Anything attached to the land or used with it, passing to the new owner upon its sale.

ARM—An adjustable-rate mortgage; that is, a loan with an interest rate that may adjust over time depending on certain factors or a predetermined formula.

arrears—A payment made after it's due is in arrears. Interest is said to be paid in arrears because it's paid to the date of payment rather than in advance.

assignment of contract—A process by which a person sells, transfers, and/or assigns rights under an agreement. Often used in the context of the assignment of a purchase contract by a buyer or the assignment of a lease by a tenant.

assumable loan—A loan secured by a mortgage or deed of trust containing no due-on-sale provision. Most pre-1989 FHA loans and pre-1988 VA loans are assumable without qualification. Some newer loans may be assumed with the express permission of the note holder.

assumption of mortgage—Agreement by a buyer to assume the liability under an existing note secured by a mortgage or deed of trust.

attorney-in-fact—An agency relationship in which a person holds a power of attorney allowing him or her to execute legal documents on behalf of another.

balloon mortgage—A note calling for periodic payments that are insufficient to fully amortize the face amount of a note prior to maturity so that a principal sum known as a balloon is due at maturity.

bankruptcy—A provision of federal law whereby a debtor surrenders assets to the bankruptcy court and is relieved of the obligation to repay unsecured debts. After bankruptcy, the debtor is discharged and unsecured creditors may not pursue further collection efforts against him or her. Secured creditors continue to be secured by property but may not take other action to collect.

basis—The financial interest one has in a property for tax purposes. Basis is adjusted down by depreciation and up by capital improvements.

beneficiary—One for whose benefit trust property is held. Also known as the *lender* under a deed of trust.

binder—A report issued by a title insurance company setting forth the condition of title and setting forth conditions that, if satisfied, will cause a policy of title insurance to be issued. Also known as a *title commitment*.

building restriction line—A required setback a certain distance from the road within which no building may take place. This restriction may appear in the original subdivision plat, in restrictive covenants, or by building codes and zoning ordinances.

buyer's agent—A real estate broker or agent who represents the buyer's interests, though typically the fee is a split of the listing broker's commission. Also known as the *selling agent*.

capital gain—Profit from the sale of a capital asset such as real property. A long-term capital gain is a gain derived from property held more than 12 months. Long-term gains can be taxed at lower rates than short-term gains.

caveat emptor—"Buyer beware." A seller is under no obligation to disclose defects but may not actively conceal a known defect or lie if asked.

certificate of occupancy—A certificate issued by a local governmental body stating that a building may be occupied.

chain of title—The chronological order of conveyance of a parcel of land from the original owner to the present owner.

closing—The passing of a deed or mortgage, signifying the end of a sale or mortgage of real property. Also known in some areas as *passing papers* or *closing of escrow*.

closing costs—Expenses incurred in the closing of a real estate or mortgage transaction. Most fees are associated with the buyer or borrower's loan. Closing costs typically include an origination fee, discount points, appraisal fee, title search and insurance, survey, taxes, deed recording fee, credit report, and notary fees.

cloud on title—An uncertainty, doubt, or claim against the rights of the owner of a property such as a recorded purchase contract or option.

collateral—Property that is pledged to secure a loan.

commitment—A written promise to make or insure a loan for a specified amount and on specified items. Also used in the context of title insurance (title commitment).

community property—In community property states (Arizona, California, Idaho, Louisiana, Nevada, New Mexico, Texas, Washington, Wisconsin) all property of husband and wife acquired after the marriage is presumed to belong to both, regardless of how it's titled.

comparables—Properties used as comparisons to determine the value of a specified property.

condemnation—A judicial proceeding through which a governmental body takes ownership of a private property for a public use.

condominium—A structure of two or more units, the interior spaces of which are individually owned. The common areas are owned as tenants in common by the condominium owners and ownership is restricted by an association.

contingency—The dependence on a stated event that must occur before a contract is binding. Used both in the context of a loan and a contract of sale.

contract—A legally enforceable agreement between two or more parties.

contract of sale—A bilateral (two-way) agreement wherein the seller agrees to sell and the buyer agrees to buy a certain parcel of land, usually with improvements. Also used to reference an installment land contract.

contract for deed—See *installment land contract.*

conventional mortgage—A loan neither insured by the FHA nor guaranteed by the VA.

cooperative apartment—A cooperative is a corporation that holds title to the land and building. Each co-op owner has shares of stock in the corporation that corresponds to an equivalent proprietary lease of an apartment space. Co-ops were popular in New York City at one time but are less common because of their lack of marketability due to high association fees.

counteroffer—A rejection of a seller's offer, usually with an amended agreement to sell the property to the potential buyer on different terms from the original offer.

credit report—A report documenting the credit history and current status of a person's credit.

deficiency—The difference between the amount owed to a note holder and the proceeds received from a foreclosure sale. The lender may, in some states, obtain a deficiency judgment against the borrower for the difference.

delivery—The transfer of a deed to the grantee so that the grantor may not revoke it. A deed that is signed but held by the grantor doesn't pass title.

depreciation—A decrease in value to real property improvements caused by deterioration or obsolescence.

documentary tax stamps—Stamps affixed to a deed showing the amount of transfer tax. Some states simply charge the transfer tax without affixing stamps. Also known as *doc stamps*.

double closing—A closing wherein a property is bought and then sold simultaneously. Also called *double escrow* and *flipping*.

due-on-sale clause—A provision in a mortgage or deed of trust that gives the lender the option to require payment in full of the indebtedness on transfer of title to the property (or any interest therein).

earnest money—A good faith deposit or down payment.

easement—An interest that one has in the land of another. May be created by grant, reservation, agreement, prescription, or necessary implication.

eminent domain—A constitutional right for a governmental authority to acquire private property for public use by condemnation and the payment of just compensation.

encroachment—Construction or imposition of a structure onto the property of another.

encumbrance—A claim, lien, or charge against real property.

equitable title—The interest of the purchase under an installment land contract.

equity—The difference between the market value of the property and the homeowner's mortgage debt.

escrow—Delivery of a deed by a grantor to a third party for delivery to the grantee on the happening of a contingent event.

escrow agent, escrow company—Individual or company that performs closing services for real estate loans and sales transactions.

escrow payment—That portion of a borrower's monthly payment held in trust by the lender to pay for taxes, mortgage insurance, hazard insurance, lease payments, and other items as they become due. Also know as *impounds*.

estate—From the English feudal system, this defines the extent of one's ownership in a property.

estate for years—An estate limited to a term of years. An estate for years is commonly called a lease. On the expiration of the estate for years, the property reverts back to the former owner.

Federal Housing Administration (FHA) —A federal agency that insures first mortgages, enabling lenders to lend a high percentage of the sale price.

fee simple—The highest form of ownership. An estate under which the owner is entitled to unrestricted powers to dispose of the property and that can be left by will or inherited. Also known as *fee* or *fee simple absolute*.

fixture—An item of personal property attached to real property.

Freddie Mac (Federal Home Loan Mortgage Corporation, FHLMC)—A federal agency purchasing first mortgages, both conventional and federally insured, from members of the Federal Reserve System and the Federal Home Loan Bank System.

foreclosure—A proceeding to extinguish all rights, title, and interests of the owner(s) of property in order to sell the property to satisfy a lien against it. About half of the states use a mortgage foreclosure, which is a lawsuit in court. About half use a power of sale proceeding, which is dictated by a deed of trust and is usually less time-consuming than a foreclosure.

Ginnie Mae (Government National Mortgage Association, GNMA)—A federal association working with FHA that offers special assistance to obtain mortgages and purchases mortgages in a secondary capacity.

good-faith estimate—A lender's estimate of closing costs and monthly payment required by RESPA.

grant deed—A deed commonly used in California to convey title. By law, a grant deed gives certain warranties of title.

grantee—A person receiving an interest in a property.

grantor—A person granting or giving up an interest in a property.

grantor/grantee index—The most common document recording indexing system is by grantor (the person conveying an interest, usually the seller or mortgagor) and grantee (the person receiving an interest, usually the buyer or mortgagee). All documents conveying property or an interest therein (deed, mortgage, lease, easement, etc.) are recorded by the grantor's last name in the grantor index. The same transaction is cross-indexed by the grantee's last name in the grantee index.

heirs and assigns—Words usually found in a contract or deed that indicate that the obligations assumed or interest granted or binding upon or insure to benefit of the heirs or assigns of the party.

homeowners association—An association of people who own homes in a given area for the purpose of improving or maintaining the quality of the area. Also used in the context of a condominium association.

impound account—Account held by a lender for payment of taxes, insurance, or other payments. Also known as an *escrow account*.

installment land contract (ILC)—The ILC is an agreement wherein the buyer makes payments in a manner similar to a mortgage. The buyer has equitable title. However, the seller holds legal title to the property until the contract is paid off. The buyer has equitable title, and, for all intents and purposes, is the owner of the property. Also known as a *contract for deed* or *contract of sale*.

installment sale—A sale that involves the seller receiving payments over time. The Internal Revenue Code contains specific definitions and promulgates specific rules concerning installment sales and tax treatment of them. Also known as an *owner-carry sale*.

insured mortgage—A mortgage insured against loss to the mortgagee in the event of default and failure of the mortgaged property to satisfy the balance owing plus costs of foreclosure.

intestate—When a person dies without a will.

interest rate—The percentage of an amount of money that is paid for its use for a specified time.

joint and several liability—A liability that allows a creditor to collect against any one of the debtors for the entire amount of the debt, regardless of fault or culpability. Most mortgage notes that are signed by husband and wife create joint and several liability.

joint tenancy—An undivided interest in property, taken by two or more joint tenants. The interests must be equal, accruing under the same conveyance, and beginning at the same time. On death of a joint tenant, the interest passes to the surviving joint tenants rather than to the heirs of the deceased.

judgment—The decision of a court of law. Money judgments, when recorded, become a lien on real property of the defendant.

junior mortgage—Mortgage of lesser priority than the previously recorded mortgage.

land lease—Owners of property will sometimes give long-term leases of land up to 99 years. A lease of more than 99 years is considered a transfer of fee simple. Land leases are commonly used to build banks, car lots, and shopping malls.

land trust—A revocable, living trust primarily used to hold title to real estate for privacy and anonymity. Also known as an *Illinois land trust* or *nominee trust*. The land trustee is a nominal titleholder, with the beneficiaries having the exclusive right to direct and control the actions of the trustee.

lease/option—An agreement by which the lessee (tenant) has the unilateral option to purchase the leased premises from the lessor (landlord). Some lease/option agreements provide for a portion of the rent to be applied toward the purchase price. The price may be fixed at the beginning of the agreement or be determined by another formula, such as an appraisal at a later time. Also referred to as a *lease/purchase*.

lease/purchase—Often used interchangeably with the expression *lease/option* but technically means a lease in conjunction with a bilateral purchase agreement. Often used by real estate agents to mean a purchase agreement whereby the tenant takes possession prior to the close of escrow.

license—An authority to do a particular act or series of acts upon the land of another without possessing any estate or interest therein (for example, a ski lift ticket). A license is similar to an easement in that it gives someone permission to cross property for a specific purpose. An easement is a property interest, whereas a license is a contractual right.

lien—An encumbrance against property for money, either voluntary (for example, mortgage), involuntary (for example, judgment), or by operation of law (for example, property tax lien).

life estate—An estate in real property for the life of a living person. The estate then reverts back to the grantor or to a third party.

lis pendens—A legal notice recorded to show pending litigation relating to real property and giving notice that anyone acquiring an interest in said property subsequent to the date of the notice may be bound by the outcome of the litigation. Often filed prior to a mortgage foreclosure proceeding.

liquidated damages—A contract clause that limits a party to a certain sum in lieu of actual damages. In the case of a real estate purchase and sale contract, the seller's legal remedy is limited to the buyer's earnest money deposit.

loan-to-purchase value—The relation between the purchase price of a property and the amount of the acquisition loan.

loan-to-value ratio—The ratio of the mortgage loan amount to the property's appraised value (or the selling price, whichever is less).

marketable title—Title that can be readily marketed to a reasonably prudent purchaser aware of the facts and their legal meaning concerning liens and encumbrances.

market analysis—A report estimating the resale value of a property, usually prepared by a real estate agent showing comparable sales of properties in the vicinity based on tax records and information from the Multiple Listing Service.

mechanic's lien—A lien created by state law for the purpose of securing priority of payment for the price of value of work performed and materials furnished in construction or repair of improvements to land and which attach to the land as well as the improvements.

metes and bounds—A method of describing land by directions and distances rather than reference to a lot number.

mortgage—A security instrument given by a borrower to secure performance of payment under a note. The document is recorded in county land records, creating a lien (encumbrance) on the property. Also known as a *deed of trust* in some states. The borrower is also called a *mortgagor*.

mortgage broker—One who, for a fee, brings together a borrower and lender and handles the necessary applications for the borrower to obtain a loan against real property by giving a mortgage or deed of trust as security.

mortgagee—A lender.

Mortgage Guaranty Insurance Corporation (MGIC)—A private corporation that, for a fee, insures mortgage loans similar to FHA and VA insurance, although not insuring as great a percentage of the loan.

mortgage insurance—Insurance required for loans with a loan-to-value ratio above 80 percent. Also called *PMI* or *MIP*.

mortgagor—A borrower.

Multiple Listing Service (MLS)—A service performed by the Local Board of REALTORS® that provides information to aid in the sale of properties to a wide market base.

nominal value—Numerical value without consideration to factors such as inflation.

notary public—One authorized by law to acknowledge and certify documents and signatures as valid.

note—A written promise to repay a certain sum of money under specified terms. Also known as a *promissory note*.

offer—A proposal to buy.

option—The unilateral right to do something, for example, the right to renew a lease or purchase a property. The optionee is the holder of the option. The optionor is the grantor of the option. The optionor is bound by the option, but the optionee isn't.

origination fee—A fee or charge for work involved in the evaluation, preparation, and submission of a proposed mortgage loan. Usually about 1 percent of the loan amount.

payoff amount—A total amount of money needed to satisfy full payment on an existing loan or lien.

performance mortgage—A mortgage or deed of trust given to secure performance of an obligation other than a promissory note.

periodic tenancy—An estate from week-to-week, month-to-month, and so on. In the absence of a written agreement (or on the expiration of a lease once payments are accepted), a periodic tenancy is created. Either party can terminate this type of arrangement by giving notice, usually equal to the amount of the period or as prescribed by state law.

PITI—Principal, interest, taxes, and insurance.

plat—A map showing the division of a piece of land.

points—A fee paid by a borrower to obtain a loan. A point is 1 percent of the principal amount of the loan. The borrower may pay more points to reduce the interest rate of the loan.

power of attorney—A written document authorizing another to act on one's behalf as an attorney in fact.

prepayment penalty—An additional charge imposed by the lender for paying off a loan before its due date.

probate—A court process to prove a will is valid.

promissory note—A written, unsecured note promising to pay a specified amount of money on demand, often transferable to a third party.

prorate—To divide in proportionate shares. Used in the context of a closing, at which time such things as property taxes, interest, rents, and other items are adjusted in favor of the seller, buyer, or lender.

purchase agreement—A binding agreement between parties for the purchase of real estate.

purchase money mortgage—A loan obtained in conjunction with the purchase of real estate.

quiet title proceeding—A court action to establish or clear up uncertainty as to ownership of real property. Often required if a lien or cloud appears on a title that can't be resolved.

quit claim deed—A deed by which the grantor gives up any claim he or she may have in the property. Often used to clear up a cloud on a title.

real estate—Land and anything permanently affixed to the land and those things attached to the buildings.

real property—Land and whatever by nature or artificial annexation is attached to it.

REALTOR®—Any member of the National Association of REALTORS®.

recording—The act of publicly filing a document such as a deed or mortgage.

recourse note—A note under which the holder can look personally to the borrower's personal assets for payment.

redemption—The right, in some states, for an owner of lien holder to satisfy the indebtedness due on a mortgage in foreclosure after sale.

refinancing—The repayment of a loan from the proceeds of a new loan using the same property as collateral.

reissue rate—A discounted charge for a title insurance policy if a previous policy on the same property was issued within a specified period (usually three to five years).

release—An instrument releasing a lien or encumbrance (such as a mortgage) from a property.

RESPA (Real Estate Settlement Procedures Act)—A federal law requiring disclosure of certain costs in the sale of residential property that is to be financed by a federally insured lender. Also requires that the lender provide a good-faith estimate of closing costs prior to closing of the loan.

secondary mortgage market—The buying and selling of first mortgages and deeds of trust by banks, insurance companies, government agencies, and other mortgagees.

second mortgage—A loan secured by a mortgage or trust deed, of which lien is junior to a first mortgage or deed of trust.

security instrument—A document under which collateral is pledged (such as a mortgage).

settlement statement—A statement prepared by a closing agent (usually a title or escrow company) giving a complete breakdown of costs and charges involved in a real estate transaction. Required by RESPA on a form HUD-1.

special assessment—Tax imposed by the local government for public improvements such as new streets.

special warranty deed—A seller warrants he or she has done nothing to impair title but makes no warranty prior to his or her ownership.

specific performance—An action to compel the performance of a contract.

subdivision—Dividing land into lots and streets, typically under strict requirements of the state and county.

sublet—To let or lease part of one's estate in a lease. A subtenant isn't in privity of contract with the landlord and neither can look to each other for performance of a lease agreement.

subject to—When transferring title to a property encumbered by a mortgage lien without paying off the debt or assuming the note, the buyer is taking title "subject to."

subordination—The process by which a lien holder agrees to permit a lien to become junior or subordinate to another lien.

tenancy by the entirety—A form of ownership recognized in some states by which husband and wife each owns the entire property. As with joint tenancy, in the event of the death of one, the survivor owns the property without probate. In some states, tenancy by the entirety protects the property from obligations of one spouse.

tenancy in common—With tenancy in common, each owner (called a tenant) has an undivided interest in the possession of the property. Each tenant's interest is salable and transferable. Each tenant can convey that interest by deed, mortgage, or will. Joint ownership is presumed to be in common if nothing further is stated on the deed.

testate—When a person dies with a will.

title—Title is the evidence of ownership. In essence, title is more important than ownership because having proper title is proof of ownership. If you have a problem with your title, you'll have trouble proving your ownership and thus selling or mortgaging your property.

title insurance—An insurance policy that protects the insured (purchaser and/or lender) against loss arising from defects in title. A policy protecting the lender is called a loan policy, whereas a policy protecting the purchaser is called an *owner's policy*. Virtually all transactions involving a loan require title insurance.

title search—An examination of the public records to disclose facts concerning the ownership of real estate.

truth in lending—Federal law requiring, among other things, a disclosure of interest rate charges and other information about a loan.

trust—A right to or in property held for the benefit of another, which may be written or implied.

trustee—One who holds property in trust for another party.

trustor—One who creates a trust by granting property to a trustee. Also known as the *borrower* on a deed of trust.

VA loan—A long-term, low down-payment or no down-payment loan guaranteed by the Department of Veterans Affairs, which is offered to individuals qualified by military service or other entitlements.

warranty deed—A deed under which the seller makes a guarantee or warranty that title is marketable and will defend all claims against it.

wraparound mortgage—A mortgage that is subordinate to and incorporates the terms of an underlying mortgage. The mortgagor (borrower) makes payments to the mortgagee (lender), who then makes payments on an underlying mortgage. Also referred to as an *all-inclusive deed of trust* in some states.

yield spread premium—A kickback from the lender to the mortgage broker for the additional profit made from marking up the interest rate on a loan.

zoning—Regulation of private land use and development by a local government.

Index

Y-Z